STUDIES IN
AMERICAN JEWISH
HISTORY

STUDIES IN AMERICAN JEWISH HISTORY

STUDIES AND ADDRESSES

BY

JACOB R. MARCUS

HEBREW UNION COLLEGE PRESS

CINCINNATI

1969

TO
THE ALUMNI OF THE HEBREW UNION COLLEGE-
JEWISH INSTITUTE OF RELIGION

*My Colleagues, My Students, and, Above All,
My Friends*

FOREWORD

In 1966, on the occasion of my seventieth birthday, friends and colleagues in the Alumni Association of the Hebrew Union College-Jewish Institute of Religion decided to honor me with the publication of a volume of my collected essays and studies. I am deeply grateful to them and thank them from the bottom of my heart, not only for their act of generosity, but for the constant and unfailing kindness they have accorded me in the many years that we have worked together.

Most thankfully, also, do I acknowledge the courtesy of the following publishers and institutions for their gracious permission to reprint materials under their copyright: the Jewish Publication Society of America, the American Jewish Historical Society, the Hebrew Union College Press, the American Jewish Archives, the *Jewish Exponent*, the Abba Hillel Silver Charitable and Educational Foundation, and the *American Israelite*.

There remains only the pleasant duty of singling out two of my good friends who were most helpful in the preparation of this volume. My associate, Dr. Stanley F. Chyet, reread these studies and made a number of helpful suggestions. My classmate and friend of many years, Dr. Abraham I. Shinedling, also reread them and, with his usual meticulosity, prepared the Index. To both of them, my heartfelt gratitude.

JACOB R. MARCUS

Hebrew Union College
Cincinnati, Ohio
January, 1968

CONTENTS

STUDIES IN
AMERICAN JEWISH
HISTORY

THE PERIODIZATION OF AMERICAN
JEWISH HISTORY

❧

The time has come, I believe, to periodize American Jewish history. Though Jews, as a community, have lived here for over three hundred years, it was not until the year 1800 that a young graduate of Columbia College, in a Hebrew commencement oration, attempted a brief survey of American Jewry. As far as we know, that was the first sketch of American Jewish history by an American. Since then, individual Jews, conscious of the growth and possible significance of the American Jewish community, have written on the history of their people in this land. As early as the pre-Civil War period, Jacques Judah Lyons, the hazzan of Congregation Shearith Israel in New York, began to collect materials for a history which he hoped to write. His published notes do not indicate that he had any scheme of periodization. His approach to the subject—and that is true of most writers in the mid-nineteenth century—was purely annalistic.

By the third quarter of the last century, students of American Jewish life were fully aware that there had been three "waves" of migration to this country: the Spanish-Portuguese, the German, and the East European. What is more, they were conscious of the fact that these "waves" represented different cultures. Consequently, three different periods in American Jewish life came to be commonly accepted, and when Peter Wiernik published his *History of the Jews in America* in 1912, he employed the obvious device of dividing all of American Jewish history according to the

Address of the president, delivered at the fifty-sixth annual meeting of the American Jewish Historical Society, held at the Coolidge Auditorium, The Library of Congress, Washington, D. C., February 15, 1958. Published originally in *Publications of the American Jewish Historical Society* [*PAJHS*], XLVII, 125–33.

three "successive strata of immigration." In my opinion, this division of the material of American Jewish history is natural and correct, and should be definitively adopted.

My purpose in this study is to reexamine and reappraise this now traditional form of periodization in order, if possible, to fix the limits of the various periods of Jewish history in this land.

As we know, periodization is the parcelling of time into separate and distinct periods. It is chronological division. In its simplest form, it becomes annals. Obviously, periodization is largely a convenience, a contrivance to ease the study of history. It is a skeleton on which to hang flesh, a frame on which to build. But in truth, it is more than a convenience, more than a mechanical arrangement determined by an arbitrary snip of the shears.

It has long been known to us that in all history there are different epochs and eras. They extend over fixed periods of time and are determined by stages in culture. They have characteristics of their own, a style and a tempo and manifestations that are typical and distinctive. They reflect differences in ethnic composition, in political, economic, social, cultural, and religious life. Aspects of culture often die or wither away in one era, only to rise again modified in a later period. New ages bring minor or radical changes. The differences, the new stresses, are significant.

Cannot the periodization adopted by historians for general American history apply also to American Jewish history? I do not think so. The Revolution, the establishment of the Republic, Jacksonian Democracy, Manifest Destiny, slavery, the Civil War and Reconstruction, to be sure, affected individual Jews and, ultimately, all of Jewry here. The Revolution, for instance, gave the Jew his first taste of full political freedom and opportunity. But a history of American Jewry built on the scheme of general American life would be merely a pale reflection and repetition of American history. It would tell us little or nothing about the history of the Jew *as Jew.* The periodization of American Jewish life is determined by factors that are characteristic in large part of the Jews alone, by elements that are inherent in, and relevant to, the Jewish group alone over a period of time. The epochs of American Jewish history may well be fixed by incidents and circumstances almost completely independent of general American history. On the whole, the complex of events and culture that go to make an era for the Jew in America is unique with the Jew.

If periodization of a people's or a nation's history has been based on a careful and thorough epochal analysis, then a brief exposition of the reasons for defining the termini will in effect constitute a précis of that history.

After this brief introduction, we may proceed to the actual periodization, beginning, of course, not with the coming of individuals, but with the first establishment of communities here on the North American mainland.

American Jewish history may well be divided into four great periods. Very roughly, we may call them the Sephardic, the German, the East European, and the American periods.

The Sephardic period is so named because the pattern set up by Spanish-Portuguese émigrés in the seventeenth and eighteenth centuries predominated in this country until the superimposition of another pattern no later than the year 1840. I call this the era of The Rise and Decline of Sephardic Jewry, 1654–1840.

Actually, this epoch is itself divisible into two main parts: the Colonial Period (1654–1776) and the early National Period (1776–1840). The Colonial Period is further to be divided into two parts: the Dutch Period (1654–1664) and the English Period (1664–1776).

The decade from 1654 to 1664 is called the Dutch Period because the only Jewish community on the North American mainland was then in New Amsterdam. Initiated with the coming of Jewish refugees from Dutch Brazil after its reconquest by the Portuguese, this period extended to the occupation of New Amsterdam by the forces of the Duke of York in 1664.

Under the Dutch, the Spanish and Portuguese Jews controlled Jewish life in the community. Their Sephardic ritual became traditional in synagogal American life and was to be accepted, apparently without appreciable protest, by the Central and East Europeans who were to outnumber the Spanish and Portuguese Jews by the second decade of the eighteenth century.

The Dutch era in America was, in its essence, medieval—in the worst sense of the term. This was due to the bigotry and the unbusinesslike attitude of Governor Peter Stuyvesant and his adherents. In a frontier country, where the skills and crafts of every individual might well be exploited, the Stuyvesant "party" attempted to ignore the directives of the profit-minded West India Company and to force the Jews out by denying them elementary religious and economic rights. It is obvious why the first Jewish community on the North American mainland did not thrive.

The succeeding era, the English phase, began, as we know, with the British conquest (1664) and ended with the Declaration of Independence (1776). The English language had, almost from the outset of the British occupation, become the vernacular of American Jewry. The British mercantilists, eager to further their Atlantic colonies, especially those on the American mainland, had seen to it that the Jewish settlers here were granted economic opportunities, adequate civil and religious rights, and ample scope for cultural advancement. Political liberties, however, were still circumscribed. Although the ethnic composition of Jewry had changed by the 1720's from Spanish and Portuguese to German and Polish, the Spanish rite was retained. Power in the Jewish community was exercised by the synagogue officers who coordinated and controlled all phases of religious, educational and social-welfare activity. In general, membership in this unitary type of synagogue-community was compulsory, and discipline was maintained through effective religious and social sanctions.

The Early National Period of the Sephardic era extended from the Declaration of Independence through the year 1840. Under the auspices of the new government of the United States, the Jews, for the first time, began to receive full political rights. Privileges and immunities of citizenship came first on the Federal level through the new Federal Constitution. Rights under the states came much more slowly. New York led the way in 1777, but it required a full one hundred years before the last of the original thirteen states, New Hampshire, emancipated its non-Protestants (1877).

Sephardic Jewry continued to exert cultural domination over the older seaboard Jewish communities all through this period. Its minhag, its ritual, persisted in those older synagogues, although by the late eighteenth century Ashkenazic (German and Polish) rituals were already being employed by more recent European immigrants. With the exception of Richmond, all new congregations established during this epoch adopted Ashkenazic rituals.

There was a sharp change in the economic life. Jews continued to be shopkeepers and merchants, but the vast majority of them confined themselves to urban domestic supply. Only a negligible few continued as merchant-shippers. Jews began to make their appearance in the professions, a few became brokers, and some began to nibble at industry.

The Sephardic age had atrophied by 1840. The Sephardic unitary synagogue-community died as German Jewish conventicles, formed in Philadelphia and New York, remained outside the Sephardic orbit.

Although the tightly governed Sephardic synagogue-community lost its power with the rise of voluntaristic, independent synagogues in the metropolitan centers and in the transallegheny towns as far west as St. Louis, national unity among Jews became more intense. A feeling of fellowship, of kinship, among American Jews was undoubtedly stimulated by the ritual-murder accusation directed against the Jews of

Damascus in 1840. In that crucial year, as the medieval-like charge was once more voiced abroad, American Jewry lifted its united voice against the Syrian libel. Though the leaders in denouncing this lie were very often the old-line Sephardim, Shearith Israel of New York, the mother synagogue of Sephardic American Jewry, refused to open its doors for a protest meeting. That act may well be designated the moral abdication of Sephardic hegemony. It was tantamount to a symbolic renunciation.

Ever since the middle 1830's, German Jews had been coming into the ports of the East Coast in substantial numbers. Fifteen of the twenty-one congregations in the country were, in fact, Germanic. In that same fateful year of 1840, Sephardic Beth Elohim of Charleston deserted Sephardic Orthodoxy and joined the ranks of the Germanic Reformers. When in 1841 the Sephardic-oriented Isaac Leeser called for a countrywide American Jewish organization, he was joined by a German colleague, and the call to action was published both in German and in English. The German Period had begun.

I call this second period in American Jewish history The Age of the Rise and Dominance of the German Jew and the Challenge to His Leadership, 1841–1920. Actually, as we have already said, the Germans and the related East Europeans had been in the numerical majority ever since the 1720's. They came into their own and determined the destinies of American Jewry after 1840. Their Ashkenazic rituals, the German and the Polish, were almost universally adopted, and German culture prevailed in practically all American Jewish communities. Religious institutionalism was characterized by independency and voluntarism. By the post-Civil War period, German Reform Judaism had set the tone in American Jewish religious and social life, though it never achieved the distinction of being a majority movement.

It was but a short step from voluntarism—the right to belong or not to belong—to secularism in Jewish organizational life. About the third decade of the nineteenth century, the social-welfare, educational, and socio-leisure agencies began to cut the umbilical cord that tied them to the synagogal matrix. By 1860, those Germans and their sons had created all the basic Jewish institutions or their prototypes, which now minister to the needs of some five and three-quarter million Jews in twentieth-century America.

As the industrial age moved into high gear in the days after the Civil War, Jews turned in ever increasing numbers to manufacturing. Their presence was most evident in the apparel industry. Some of the children of the German immigrants went to the better colleges and universities and entered the fields of law and medicine and science. As the last of the original states cancelled its disabilities against non-Christians, and as the immigrants and their children became acculturated, more and more of them went into politics and sought office. During the occupation of the West and the conquest of the frontier, Jews, from 1841 on, kept moving west from the Mississippi and, from 1849 on, east from California. During this German era there was a Jewish storekeeper, in one decade or another, in almost every town and hamlet between the Alleghenies and the Rockies. The increasing visibility of the Jew, his rise to relative prosperity and wealth, the incidence of frequent economic dislocations and the need for a scapegoat, the inflow of immigrant-borne European concepts of Judeophobia and anti-Semitism—all this led to a growing prejudice against the Jew. (But let it not be forgotten that there never was a period of American-Jewish history in which anti-Jewish prejudice was absent.)

By 1920, the "German" Jews, now largely native-born citizens who had absorbed the minuscule Sephardic group socially, ruled an empire of almost four million Jews, most of whom were of East European provenance. From 1914 on, however, the East Europeans, sensing the power of their numbers and of their improved economic status, essayed to challenge the leadership of the "natives." The East Europeans hoped not only to overthrow the hegemony of the older German Jewish stock, but, even more, to control completely the institutions and destinies of American Jewry. The instrument which they forged for that purpose was the American Jewish Congress, reorganized "provisionally" in 1920. The unquestioned leadership of the "German" Jew had now come to an end; his philosophy of the American Jewish way of life had been sharply challenged.

The third epoch in American Jewish life is The Age of the Advent and the Rise of the East European Jew and His Bid for Hegemony, 1852–1920. As the chronological termini indicate, this epoch ran concurrently with the German. Thus, there were two disparate, yet parallel, Jewish cultures in this country from 1852 on, when the first Russian Orthodox synagogue was established. By the late 1870's, there were dozens of such East European shuls and they increased into the hundreds and, finally, into the thousands after the Russian pogroms of the 1880's.

The East Europeans differed notably from their coreligionists already established here. When the Russians and Poles and Roumanians came to these shores, the westward movement had almost ground to a stop. It would not be long before the homesteader, the peddler, and the horse-drawn vehicle would become part of a romantic past. The machines of industry were humming at full force, the factories were spawning huge sprawling cities, and the incoming East European immigrants, keenly alive to the future trend of industry, poured into the metropolitan slums to work in the needle trades. For the first time in its history, America sheltered a substantial body of Jewish proletarians. It is worth bearing in mind, however, that, to a marked degree, this group was unique. Its members were not the sons of proletarians, nor were they destined to remain the fathers of proletarians.

In a religio-cultural sense, the "Russian" Jew *was* different. He had never had the advantages of the secular education which had nearly always been available to the German Jews in the tiniest of villages in the Fatherland. Perforce, the East European had found his outlet for cultural expression in Hebraic and rabbinic studies. He had, therefore, considerably more knowledge of Jewish tradition than his American coreligionists.

The typical East European here was Orthodox, observant, and determined to maintain his traditional Hebrew school system. Though his vernacular, Yiddish, was frowned upon as a "jargon" by native American Jews and the East European intelligentsia, he loved it and persisted in cultivating it. If not actively interested in latter-day Palestinian nationalism or Zionism, he was at least sympathetic to the ideal of a restored Jewish commonwealth in the ancient homeland. To the native American Jew, on the other hand, Zionism represented nothing so much as a return to the ghetto, a betrayal of the imminent messianic advent of complete social and cultural equality. A substantial minority of the East European immigrants were antireligious, radical in their political views, and disdainful of the Hebraic heritage and hope. Like the natives, they, too, were anti-Zionist, believing that Socialism would bring political salvation to all peoples and thus obviate the need for a specific Jewish haven of refuge.

With the beginning of World War I, the "Russians" felt strong enough to emancipate themselves from the natives, who were generally identified with the national civic defense organization known as the American Jewish Committee. As we have seen, the rival body established by the East Europeans to overthrow the power of the "Germans" was the "democratically" elected American Jewish Congress. That organ of the newcomers enunciated the goals which the masses here were determined to reach: an autonomous Jewish homeland in Palestine and minority rights for the oppressed Jews in the East European states created or strengthened by the Versailles Treaty of 1919. The power of an aroused American Jewish public opinion was so irresistible that the natives and their leaders thought it wise to subscribe to that program. Yet, conscious of their wealth, culture, and status, they refused to surrender their rule and to subject themselves to the dominance of the "Russian" or new immigration. By 1920, the two groups had apparently determined to continue on their own separate ways.

Though it seemed at first glance in 1920 that American Jewry was to be split into two hostile groups, forces were at work which were to compel a fusion of the two elements. That continuing unification is the outstanding characteristic of the fourth period, the one in which we now live. This is the period of The Emerging American Jewish Community, The Age of Fusion, The Epoch of the Rise of the *American Jew*. It began in 1921.

In that year the first immigrant quota law was passed, a law that was to restrict Jewish immigration and to serve as a forerunner for similar and more drastic acts. The quota laws, which, in effect, cut off immigration to these shores, meant that within a generation most Jews in this land would be natives. Cultural and social levelling and intramarriage and fusion were, therefore, inevitable. The "Spanish," the "German," the "Russian" Jews were doomed. There would be only "Americans," Jews with but little knowledge of their European origins and with a growing disregard for traditional "ethnic" differences.

In the last forty years, more or less, there have been pronounced economic changes. The Jews have concentrated themselves in the larger metropolises. The children of the East Europeans have moved upward in the economic and social scale into the white-collar class. They are largely in commerce and trade. An unusually large percentage of them have acquired a college education and are heavily represented in the professions.

In its social, religious, and communal life since 1921, Jewry has been subject to four forces that have profoundly affected its development: American cultural and economic opportunity, anti-Jewish prejudice in Europe and in the United States, an effective Jewish education, and Zionism. In consequence of the impact of these four factors, American Jewry has developed apparently along antipodal, if not ambivalent, lines.

Under the lure and attraction of the prevailing economic opportunity and the chance to participate in all phases of American cultural life, most Jews have entered completely and wholeheartedly into the world of business, culture, and science. Their acculturation has been remarkably rapid. On the other hand the anti-Semitism of the 1920's, the trauma of Hitlerism, the beneficial effects of an improved Jewish education, the fascination and inspiring appeal of Zionism, have all acted to intensify Jewish loyalties. There has been a remarkable growth of interest in all phases of "Jewishness," an interest that is manifested more strikingly in the postprandial life of the Jew in the metropolitan suburbs to which he has moved. It is no exaggeration to maintain that there has been a renascence of Jewish sympathies and Jewish culture—although, of course, its characteristics are not those of the Jewries of ancient Palestine, Babylonia, Spain, or Poland.

The American Jews of this generation are a middle-class group who have much in common socially, culturally, and economically. As they move into the suburbs and are touched by the prevailing Gentile concept of respectability, many of them, hitherto unaffiliated, have joined religious organizations. Some have entered the synagogue, if for no other reason than to provide their children with a Jewish education.

As the result of a historical development, now centuries old on this continent, the American Jew finds himself surrounded by a series of interlocking institutions which literally mount guard over him from a prenatal to a postmortem stage. In effect, he lives in a closely integrated, highly organized Jewish "community" which guarantees him civic defense, vocational guidance, medical and social-welfare care, religious and cultural edification, and opportunities for leisure in a most attractive environment. Sensitive—if not hypersensitive—to rejection, present-day American Jewry has tended to withdraw into itself. This new "community," most often held together by the device of a Jewish Community Council, has in effect reconstituted the all-providing kehillah

of Eastern Europe and the eighteenth-century American
Jewish Sephardic compulsory unitary community. There is
this difference: the early American Jewish form of living-
together was shot through with religious motifs; the present-
day community has strong secular overtones.

It is in this age of fusion that there has begun to emerge a
homo novus, the American Jew. Because of numerous inter-
marriages and other environmental factors, the "Semitic"-
looking Jew—more native to caricature than to reality—has
all but vanished. Typical Jewish names have begun to disappear. The American Jew, in appearance, dress, and manners,
is indistinguishable from his fellow-citizens. He is an urban
white-collar worker who is, at the very least, literate and,
indeed, often well-educated; he is liberal in his politics, sympathetic to Judaism and to Jewish education, and imbued
with a strong sense of kinship for all Jews. Paradoxical as it
may sound, this emerging "American" Jew is more assimilated, culturally, than was his father, yet in many respects as
good, if not a better Jew.

2

THE THEME IN AMERICAN
JEWISH HISTORY

※

History is the subjective record of the past. That past may well consist of a perennial "underground" stream over which are discernible the more temporal and spatial changes which a people constantly experiences. For American Jews, the substrata of Jewish life in this land are the Jewish people and a constantly changing Judaism. But the superstrata, all the events that occur daily, do not in themselves constitute history. At best they constitute annals, and even if we recorded the totality of deeds and accomplishments, the annals, infinite in number, would be meaningless. And yet even here dominant themes would recur.

We have no choice but to accept the thesis that there are movement and direction in the affairs of men. Recording that flow is imperative for the writing of history, if it is to have any meaning. The theme can and should serve to guide the student and the writer. If the theme is dominant and authentic, much that happens in a given period can be tied to this spinal column of an epoch.

The identification of themes or the discovery of a suitable framework on which to drape major and significant happenings in American Jewish history is a complicated problem. The American Jew has no national head, no hierarchy, no federal congress, and until relatively recently he had few truly national institutions. Yet there are golden threads in American Jewish history.

There is no problem in determining the theme in American Jewish life from 1654 to 1776. There is but one institu-

Address of the president, delivered at the fifty-seventh annual meeting of the American Jewish Historical Society, held at the Stern College for Women, Yeshiva University, New York, N. Y., February 21, 1959. Published originally in *Publications of the American Jewish Historical Society*, XLVIII, 141–46.

tion, the synagogue, and the immigrants and their children cling to it as the symbol and as the means of survival in a strange new land. It would require no extraordinary skill to write the history of all colonial Jewry around New York's Shearith Israel, the mother synagogue on this continent. The substance and the superstructure of colonial Jewish history are united in one calm, unruffled stream of movement.

After the Revolution, there is a very gradual change in the direction of American Jewry. The synagogue remains the spinal column of American Jewry, but there is a diminishing interest in matters religious. With the advent of the nineteenth century come the confraternities, the religiously based *hebrot*, slowly moving beyond the synagogal orbit. There is an increasing number of Jews who are more interested in survival as a social group than in survival through religion. By the 1840's, the process is complete. The synagogue—that is to say, Judaism—has gone "underground," to persist till today as the subsistent principle, the continuum of American Jewish history.

By the fourth decade of the last century, nationalism and federalism—in the literal sense of a closer union on a national basis—have become most characteristic of the United States as a whole. The development of rapid transportation and communication tends to reduce drastically the disabilities of time and space and to bring people nearer to one another. It is at this juncture that Jews from Central Europe begin coming to this country in substantial numbers. Here in the United States these Central European Jews are readily caught up in the stream of American unifying forces. The growing federalism which they encounter here recalls the Germanic tradition of a federated Jewish community, and as Jews, with a strong sense of kinship, they wish to come closer to one another as they fan out southward and westward to occupy the plains and the prairies. In the age of railroads and telegraph, there are no reasons why they cannot be tied to one another. This urge to unity, to establish agencies that will hold them together by implementing their religious and social aspirations, is the theme of American Jewish history from 1840 to the present day. If this desire for unity expresses the Jewish people's interest in maintaining itself, then the surface manifestations of Jewish history appear to reflect the substrative movement of the will to survive.

In the final analysis, it may be, there is no duality of the constant and the ephemeral; there is a unity.

The federalistic aspirations of American Jewry find expression in the lives of two men, religious leaders, both of them. Through institutions which they attempted to create, they hoped to unite all American Jews. These men are Isaac Leeser and Isaac M. Wise. The story of their efforts and their achievements is the story of American Jewry from 1840 to about 1880. Leeser is the hypostasis, the unique essence of nineteenth-century American Jewry, although, in his dynamic urge for accomplishment, he was far ahead of the people he led. In his fertile imagination he envisioned— and, in large part, ultimately did create for American Jewry —a national school system, basic textbooks, a translation of the Bible into English, a Jewish publication society, a magazine, a college, an ecclesiastical court with licensing powers, and a congregational union that would function as a national civic defense organization.

Leeser was active till his death in 1868, but by that time Isaac M. Wise had already become his legatee. Their programs were essentially the same. Wise was more clever, more realistic, more aggressive—more Americanistic, if you will— and he was less concerned with the norms of traditional Judaism. This was the man who held the center of the stage from the close of the Civil War till 1878. As the tide of settlement moved westward, Wise in Cincinnati, the Queen City of the West, became the spearhead of the Western bid for hegemony. By 1878, he had created a permanent union of American synagogues, a college, a periodical of some importance, and had taken over a nationwide instrumentality for civic defense, the Board of Delegates on Civil and Religious Rights.

The Union of American Hebrew Congregations and its

affiliates included the most influential Jewish congregations in the United States. Had its accomplishments matched its intentions, the activities of Wise's Union would have become the dominant theme in American Jewish history. Its ambitious program went so far as to envisage far-reaching plans for assimilating the East Europeans who had already begun to come to these shores in large numbers during the 1870's. But even at the height of its power in the early 1880's, the Union failed to become the theme and the substance of American Jewish history. Wise, already aging, concentrated his energies on the College. The Union, on the other hand, suffered a lack of adequate lay leadership, and the attempt to assimilate the East European émigrés exhausted the funds and the energies of American Jewry. There was neither money nor energy for anything else. The need for coping with the ever-present problem of the impoverished immigrant made it almost impossible to build institutions that would unite American Jewry and produce an indigenous Jewish culture.

On the surface, the twenty-five years between 1878 and 1903, the year of the Kishinev massacre, are thematically chaotic. It is an age that saw the last of the frontier, the dominance of Reform Judaism, the "counter-reformation" of Conservative Judaism, the coming and the struggles of the East Europeans as they eagerly strove to sense the rhythm of American life. Actually, it is the period that marked the emerging leadership of East Coast Jewish businessmen, financiers, and lawyers. The industrial revolution in this country had produced a new Jewish aristocracy of wealth, and those of its members who remained loyal to Judaism moved into the power vacuum created by a Union of American Hebrew Congregations that proved ineffectual as an instrument of overall national unification. The Union never succeeded during those years in winning the East European immigrant. The compact that brought the Board of Delegates on Civil and Religious Rights into being in 1878 brought the powerful and wealthy East Coast congregations into the Union of

American Hebrew Congregations. This has always been represented as a victory for the West of Isaac M. Wise; it may more correctly be viewed as the beginning of the East Coast mastery over the West.

The year 1903 was decisive. The crisis of providing leadership to expedite the federation of American Jewry exposed the existent vacuum. The Union of American Hebrew Congregations and the B'nai B'rith were not adequate to this crisis. Something was needed to give direction to American Jewish life, to continue the work of unification carried on by Leeser and Wise and by their predecessors, the men who had called the Damascus meetings of 1840 and, long before them, Manuel Josephson, who, in 1790, had unsuccessfully tried to unite all American Jews in a common congratulatory message to George Washington.

That the aspirations of the East Coast leaders were marked and accompanied by a struggle for personal power in no wise affects the fact that all efforts toward organization, from the early days of the American Jewish Committee to the latter-day National Community Relations Advisory Council, are subordinate to the main theme of national unity. Even the many-faceted approach to the cultural and social assimilation of the East European Jews and their children into the older American Jewish community is but a subordinate phase of the larger effort to blend all American Jews and their national agencies. The theme of American Jewish history since 1903 is the unification of all Jews, natives and immigrants, through the accommodation of the Jew and of his religion to American life and culture.

Pacing themselves, albeit unwittingly, by the growing concentration of power in the Federal Government, the self-appointed lay leaders of the first four decades of the twentieth century labored to centralize in their own hands all authority in American Jewish life. (But let it never be forgotten that as loyal Jews they worked within the framework of Jewish survival.) Riding the crest of the waves, those waves of the Jewish masses, the leaders fancied that they themselves determined the direction of movement. Because of their belief that the salvation of the Jewish masses lay in an adjustment of their religion and way of life to the common American pattern, the leaders strove to hasten the acculturation of the newer immigrants. It is questionable whether those leaders understood that, in fact, they did *not* control and could *not* hinder the newcomers in their insistence on the realization of their own hopes, on the acceptance of their own agencies, and on a tolerance for, if not a recognition of, their own way of life. Whether the old-line leaders knew it or not, they were but the objects of history carried along by every major event on the American Jewish scene since the news of Kishinev. It took them but a scant thirteen years to compromise with Zionism, and that accommodation was only the prelude to a final acceptance of the mass movement Zionism had become. In reality, it is the East European immigrant masses—they and their descendants—who have called the tune of American Jewish unity since the turn of this century. These Jewish masses have been motivated by Zionism, by the reminiscence of their foreign oppression, by the nativistic prejudices and social rejection they have encountered in this land, by Jewish ethnicism, and a growing sense of historic self-consciousness.

To express the federalist and *America-oriented* nationalistic hopes and needs of the Jewish group, aggressive leaders, stemming from the older and newer stock, have in our day succeeded in creating a series of countrywide agencies covering the entire field of Jewish activity. Thus, as an expression of the will to unity of almost 6,000,000 American Jews, we now have a foreign news-collecting service, a national vocational-economic agency, institutions to direct the Jewish community centers and to provide for the needs of Jews in the armed forces, agencies in the fields of religion, social welfare both here and abroad, education, and civic defense. Some of these organizations are feeble or moribund; others are powerful and successful. All of them are necessary; all are potentially important; all have a function to perform for the Jewish people.

There are Jews in this land today who look askance at these national agencies. Many feel that they are not truly representative. Due to the spirit of conservatism, and even of reaction, that followed in the wake of World War I and prevails in part today, some of these national organizations were and still are autocratic, hierarchical, and bureaucratic. As these agencies blossomed in the last fifty years, in answer to the needs of an emerging Americanized Jewry, the grass-roots Jewish communities, reacting against a paternalistic New York control, a control imposed by individuals from above, began to fashion a more democratic instrumentality to achieve unity. This was the Jewish community council, the attempt, in theory at least, to federalize all institutional forces in the local community.

The part that science plays generally in contemporary American life will not fail to affect the position of the Jewish community councils. Modern technology has already made communication almost instantaneous, while rapid transportation has brought all America within a few hours' flying time. In the light of these developments, the community councils, though largely impotent today, will surely grow in power. National agencies are likely, therefore, to come under local and more democratic control. Some of them, like the Council of Jewish Federations and Welfare Funds, already respond strongly to the sensibilities of the local communities. It may be a matter of decades, but ultimately every American Jewish national agency will be closely geared to the demands of American Jewry as a whole. Thus, the direction of American Jewish life today is toward the development of a series of national Jewish agencies, each different and each competent in its own field, answering a need of the larger American Jewish group. Over a period of time, national Jewish sentiment will effect the elimination of rival agencies in the same field and will oblige the individual institutions to work together, if only consultatively. Ultimately, a permanent congress of representative Jewish organizations, or of deputies of community councils, will appear on the scene. This will be in response to the demands of the highly articulate literate Jew that an instrumentality be created enabling him to survive politically, culturally, religiously, and economically, *as a Jew*. The overall theme of today and tomorrow is unity.

3

LETTERS AS A SOURCE
OF BIOGRAPHY

I take it that in this assembly my topic has not to do with
the mechanics of historical research, for it can here be taken
for granted that we are all acquainted with basic techniques
of methodology. I assume, therefore, that my topic, "Letters
as a Source of Biography," seeks to bring before us not gen-
eralities but something of particular interest to us in American Jewish history. I propose to limit the theme even more
and to restrict my discussion to the eighteenth century. It is
my intention to list the principal collections of letters, to
characterize them in a sentence or two, and to mention some
random research experiences which underline the need for
caution, balance, and good judgment in historical research.

As for any other period or subject, so for eighteenth-
century American Jews, letters are merely one type of
source material available to the student interested in the history of the men and women of the past. Every written or
printed record, even physical possessions, may serve our purpose. The last will of a Judah Hays, who cut off one of his
children with five shillings; the marriage settlement of a
Sheftall; the beautiful Torah ornaments created by the silversmith Myer Myers; the ship *Jacob*, named by the Gomezes after a dearly beloved brother who had been cut to
pieces by Spanish pirates in 1722—all these throw light on
the lives of men and women. Letters, as we know, are just
one additional source for the student, and are not necessarily
the most important one at our disposal.

It is true, however, that there are some rich collections of

This address was delivered at a conference of historians convened by the
American Jewish Historical Society at Peekskill, New York, September 13–
14, 1954. It was published originally in Moshe Davis and Isidore S. Meyer
(eds.), *The Writing of American Jewish History* (New York, 1957), pp.
420–25.

letters written by and to Jews. The leading ones merit passing mention. There is much material on Newport and New York Jews among the Brown Papers in the John Carter Brown Library in Providence. There are hundreds of Lopez letters in the Newport Historical Society Library. This is one of the largest bodies of colonial materials and is invaluable for a study of the economic background of American Jewry. The Mordecai Letters in the Library of Congress, in the University of North Carolina Library, and in the Duke University Library are very useful. They are practically all of a personal nature and are thus almost unique. They throw light on the Jew in relation to his larger cultural environment and are important for a study of acculturation in the postrevolutionary decades. In the Girard College Library and in the American Jewish Archives, there are a large number of the letters of Isaac Moses, Samuel Myers, and Moses Myers. These are useful to the historian because they supplement our knowledge of merchant shipping in the generation after the Revolution. They complement the Lopez Papers, which come to an end in the early 1780's. There are literally thousands of Gratz letters in the libraries at New York, Philadelphia, Washington, Chapel Hill, N. C., and Cincinnati. The correspondence of the Gratz brothers and their children touches nearly every facet of Jewish life in this country for almost a century beginning with the decade of the 1750's.

Let me now turn to some random observations. The customary simple division of letters into personal and business is not a happy one. The eighteenth-century man or woman wrote personal letters with reluctance, for it was difficult for him to write, to spell. Paper cost money; postage was expensive, and men were thrifty because they had to be. To be sure, there are personal letters, but frequently the polite phrases and the verbose paragraphs betray little thought and offer less information.

There is preserved a thank-you note from the hazzan of Shearith Israel Congregation, Gershom Mendes Seixas, when he was still a bachelor. It is nowhere exceeded in its politeness or self-pity. It is addressed to the merchant-shipper Aaron Lopez, who had some marriageable daughters. Was Seixas' self-pity the result of a disappointment in his marriage hopes? I am reasonably sure that it was. But the circumlocution, the prolixity, and the mannered preciousness of the style prevent certainty. Indeed, throughout eighteenth-century letters, the inflated manner of writing frequently tends to conceal almost as much as it reveals.

A characteristic which startles those researchers who are convinced that eighteenth-century Jews were of Spanish or Portuguese descent is the rather frequent presence of Yiddish. The Gratzes, especially in the materials assembled in the new Henry Joseph Collection at the American Jewish Archives, frequently broke into Yiddish in the midst of an English letter. In those days the privacy of letters was not respected, but anyone who opened a letter which he was carrying for the Gratzes got little satisfaction out of the Yiddish sentences that studded dozens if not hundreds of their business communications. How the bearer's eye would have glistened had he been able to translate: Be nice to Mr. X, but don't give him any credit.

Every now and then the historian will pick up a batch of Yiddish letters such as the Lazarus-Joseph collection in the Public Archives of Canada. These are a series written by an elderly woman to her husband who had left her to join his children in a Canadian village. Sick, lonely, hungry, she pours out her heart to her mate thousands of miles away. From her replies, we know what he has written to her. We learn to sense in a most realistic fashion the difficulties of making a living, of survival, in early America. In writings such as these, men and women bare their souls in the language which the heart can speak most eloquently.

Business letters, ninety-five percent of all extant correspondence, have an impact all their own. Not all shopkeepers and merchants had clerks who wrote out fair copies for them. There are some men who could not write a line without misspelling half the words. They composed as they pronounced, and it is no light thing to understand the so-called English of an immigrant who spoke with an Alsatian accent and sought to express the English he had learned in an Anglo-French environment.

One learns not to judge a man merely by his spelling. One sees, of course, that the writer was probably an immigrant and that he had little or no formal schooling. But some of the worst spellers were the best merchants. Aaron Isaacs, of Easthampton, Long Island, could not write a proper English sentence, but he made enough money to help found an academy. Aaron Hart, of Three Rivers, Canada, butchered the king's English mercilessly, but he was one of the richest Jews on the North American continent when he died in 1800.

Letters chart a man's travels, and you can follow a Samson Mears through the Connecticut mud on a wintry day riding from village to village, or you can travel with him from Boston to St. Eustatius in the West Indies. The story of the mobility of the colonial businessman is frequently reflected in the letters he wrote to the merchant-shipper who employed him.

From the correspondence of Aaron Isaacs, one discovers not only that he had no schooling, but, from his threats, that he was direct, tough, and crude. On the other hand, in the hundreds of Lopez letters which are extant, we notice that Aaron Lopez never forgot that he was a Portuguese gentleman. He never nodded. There is as much stark drama in one of his sailing orders as there is in the crack of a swivel gun pouring shot into a hostile privateer. No one can read Lopez' orders to a whaling fleet about to sail south thousands of miles to the Falkland Islands without being thrilled. The man who dictated that letter in the spring of 1775, as war was breaking out with England, and who hazarded a large part of his fortune on a single throw, must have possessed nerves of steel. Here was a merchant adventurer in the grand style.

The difference in men in similar or comparable situations is revealed in their letters. There exists the calm, almost cold letter from the Loyalist David Franks to Major John André, adjutant general of the British Army. In an almost impersonal fashion Franks asked payment of a bill for over £4,000 sterling which the British owed him for feeding English and Tory prisoners in American hands. Franks had vouchers for 500,000 rations which he had issued, but the English refused to pay. He was left "holding the bag." The way a man handles adversity is a prime index to an understanding of him. By contrast, Jonas Phillips and his business colleagues in Philadelphia were not quite so calm when the quartermaster general and the clothier general requisitioned the stocks which they had just run through the British blockade. Such goods could not be easily replaced. They had already advanced in price considerably since their seizure by Congress; insurance alone amounted to fifty percent of the original cost; prices continued going up, and they indignantly spluttered that they were entitled to a profit.

When Jews wrote letters to one another they rarely failed to add the personal note. That is why no business letter is all business; and there are practically no personal letters that do not touch on commercial matters. A son, writing to his father, might warn him against trusting an old neighbor who was up to some trick. And when a nephew wrote to Lopez at a time when the uncle was trying to save a cargo unjustly seized by Connecticut privateers, his comforter referred to them as a pack of *ganabim* ["thieves"]. Jealousies, squabbles, intolerance, hatreds—all these are likely to creep out in the words written by embittered, frustrated men trying to eke out a living in a pioneer economy where almost every decade brought war, tragedy, and misfortune. Different men reacted differently. And the recognition of these differences is essential if we seek biographical and psychological insight.

One word is almost sufficient to tell a man's life-story. James Lucena, a Portuguese émigré, was naturalized in Rhode Island, "on the true faith of a Christian." Yet in some of his letters to Aaron Lopez he addresses the latter as "Cousin." That one word "Cousin" tells us that here was a Jew who had fled the Inquisition merely to escape its rapac-

ity, but not because of any religious conviction. The two
men were friends and kin, but they trod different paths.
Cousin James ran away from Portugal and became an Angli-
can; Cousin Aaron fled from the same country and became
the president of a synagogue.

In a letter of March, 1772, we are informed that Barnard
Gratz sent a slave of his to be sold on the auction block at
Reading, Pennsylvania. The Negro had to be handcuffed because of his threats to do violence to anyone who would buy
him. Is this incident of any significance when evaluating the
character of the owner?

Letters from both Gentiles and Jews appealing for financial aid and charity are found in the Lopez correspondence.
All of them refer to Lopez' generosity and breathe an expectation of help. The Brown letters in Providence contain
notes from Jews asking those shippers to provide passage for
unfortunates returning to their families in the West Indies or
in Surinam. There are references in eighteenth-century letters touching on the messengers who had come from Palestine to collect money for the ancient homeland or for themselves. It is important to note the respect usually accorded
these men and the generosity shown to almost all suppliants.

Correspondence of the Revolutionary period shows a man
of over ninety, Joseph Simson, going into exile rather than
remain in British-occupied New York. Another exile, Daniel
Gomez, a scion of a great family, tired, sick, impoverished,
appealed to the Supreme Executive Council of Pennsylvania
for permission to send a young grandson to New York to
collect some rents in order to keep himself alive. Within a
year, the seventy-nine-year-old émigré was dead.

One of the richest sources for biographical data and in-
sights is in the occasional sentence interwoven in a business
letter or tacked on as a postscript: Congratulations upon the
arrival of your brother who has just escaped from the Inquisition. Here is a pair of phylacteries for him. Let me give you
some hints about the circumcision. Or: Would you mind
sending me out a *Sefer Torah* ["Scroll of the Law"] from

London? Or: Have you a big *yorzeit* ("memorial") candle in stock? Would you care for a pot of kosher fat? Thank you for your order, and may I present you with some geese, apples, and a turkey. The oranges you sent me from Charleston arrived in good shape. Or: Please excuse me for not writing any more; the Sabbath is approaching and I must close.

Joseph Simon, writing from his frontier town of Lancaster to a kinsman in Philadelphia, made inquiry about a sale of raccoon and beaver. But the postscript tells the story: "Send me up two rockfish." Frontier or no frontier, *Shabbat* ["Sabbath"] was coming!

Reading a man's letters teaches you to be wary in making hasty judgments. In twenty letters you find him rough, tough, and uncouth in word and thought, but, in the twenty-first, you find that he plays the violin and reads the latest book of plays sent over from England. (It is the hope—and the fear—of finding the twenty-first letter that makes you hedge in summing up any man's life.) You know Samuel Jacobs, the Canadian sutler and shopkeeper, lived with a Catholic girl and reared a brood of Christian children and sent his girls to the convent to be educated. You know he was not a member of the Montreal synagogue, but he belligerently documented his Jewishness in almost every note that he wrote. In hundreds of his letters, he signed himself with the word *Shemuel* in Hebrew in the final flourish of the "l" of Samuel, his first name.

Biography is more than the skeletal facts of birth and death, progeny, business, wealth, and poverty. This information can be dug out of the religious and civil records, out of the synagogue books and the courthouse files. But letters cover the skeleton with flesh and blood. They turn names into live, vibrant, pulsating human beings. No man can read the correspondence of Aaron Lopez, Samuel Jacobs, Jacob Mordecai, and Moses Myers, for example, without seeing those men and knowing them almost as intimately as one does one's own father or brother. Letters give one insight into the emotions, the hopes, the meanness, and the nobility of the men and women whom we seek to understand.

A biography is not history, but the sum total of scores of biographies can give us an understanding of an age and its people—a penetration into depth that is rarely attained by even the most important declarations, proclamations, and constitutional documents. In the final analysis, the core of a people's history is the determination of that which is typical in the lives of the men and women who constitute that people. And for us their lives are often their letters.

4

MAJOR TRENDS IN AMERICAN JEWISH HISTORICAL RESEARCH

❧

Victorian Filiopietism

For many Americans—particularly those of the upper classes—the 1890's may have been a "gilded age." For American Jews, however—even Jews of wealth and position—it was an age of insecurity. Generally foreign-born, the community's leaders, however well Americanized, could not forget that they had come from European lands where it was de rigueur to impose political disabilities on Jews. They were equally conscious of America's emergent anti-Semitism, of the racialism that had spread through France and Germany in the 1880's and was not long in penetrating American life.

The recognition that anti-Jewish prejudice was not to be confined to the European past colored the American Jew's view of his history in this country. It made for an essentially apologetic tendency in American Jewish historical research —when it was first undertaken in the 1890's—and led the historian of American Jewry to emphasize the Jewish contribution to early America. "As American Jews," said Oscar S. Straus in 1896, "we feel it our duty to cast every light it is possible to bring to bear upon early colonization and development of civilization upon this great continent of ours."

The fin-de-siècle American Jew wanted nothing so much as to prove his pioneering credentials. The money used to outfit Christopher Columbus' caravels, Oscar Straus proudly proclaimed, had been "furnished by no other person than the Treasurer General of Aragon, who was born of a Jewish mother and a Jewish father." Luis de Santangel and Gabriel Sanchez, both of Jewish ancestry, were "really the patrons

---

This essay appeared originally in the June 21, 1963, issue of the Philadelphia *Jewish Exponent*. With the permission of the editors of that newspaper, it was reprinted in *American Jewish Archives*, XVI, 9–21.

of Columbus," and "the reports made by Columbus and sent home were addressed to the first two American Jews, as I think I must call them." Straus also took much pride in the fact that there were "undoubtedly five Jews" among the men who sailed with Columbus. This desire—to celebrate the pioneer origins of American Jewry—had a great deal to do with the formation of the American Jewish Historical Society in 1892, just 400 years after Columbus' discovery of the New World.

The Victorians who founded the American Jewish Historical Society were, in many instances, devoted and gifted amateurs, capable of producing thoroughly scientific studies. But it was not science so much as filiopietism that motivated their efforts, and they were at pains to exclude anything that might cast discredit on their spiritual—and, for some at least, physical—ancestors, the early Sephardim, Jews of Spanish-Portuguese background, who had established the foundations of American Jewry. These early American Jews had to be portrayed as victims of Inquisitional bigotry and as a cultured élite which contributed significantly to the nascent American economy. Nothing else was admissible, so that, when Barnett A. Elzas wrote his history of South Carolina Jewry, he stressed the fact that a Sephardi, Jacob Ramos, had landed at Charleston in 1773, but omitted all mention of Ramos' subsequent conviction for receiving stolen goods from a Negro slave. And when the early minutes of New York City's colonial congregation, Shearith Israel, were published by the American Jewish Historical Society in 1913, the editors took care to delete the names of all whose behavior at religious services was less than decorous. The name of a Jewish girl who bore a child out of wedlock was meticulously suppressed. For that turn-of-the-century generation, it was out of the question to publish anything that might project a negative image of the American Jew.

ARRIVAL IN ACADEME

By the 1930's and 1940's, great changes had taken place in American Jewish life. The gates of immigration had closed in 1924, and out of what had been a dual—and often enough mutually scornful—community of "Germans" and "Russians" there was beginning to emerge a homogeneous native-born American Jewish community. For this community, much less troubled by immigrant self-doubts, the trappings of Victorianism—including a defensive view of history—had scant appeal. These "new" American Jews had successfully coped with the dislocations of the Great Depression, the anti-Semitic agitation of the 1930's, the challenges of military service during the Second World War, and postwar attempts to cripple their Palestinian brethren. The self-esteem generated by this experience held much more meaning for them than a quest for colonial forebears, and they were fortified by another consideration as well: the War, with its destruction of European Jewry, had left America's Jewish community the greatest and most opulent that the world had ever seen. This community—some six million strong, generous, interested, proud—was catapulted into a position of hegemony over all other Jewish communities. Such responsibility demanded an increasing measure of self-understanding, and American Jewry began taking a serious—and realistic—look at its own American origins. The result was a developing trend towards American Jewish history as a scientific discipline.

This trend had actually begun even before the War's end. During the late 1930's, the Work Projects Administration (WPA), guided largely by non-Jewish scholars for whom facts took precedence over sentiment, had undertaken inventories of American synagogal archives. In 1943, three years after the WPA inventories began appearing, a required course in American Jewish history was initiated at the Hebrew Union College in Cincinnati. The first of its kind ever

to be offered at an institution of higher learning, it testified to
the critical methodology which American Jewish historical
research had absorbed and also to the hitherto unprecedented
academic respectability that American Jewish history had
achieved. After 289 years, American Jewish history had
finally "arrived"—in Academe.

There were other evidences of widespread interest in
American Jewish history. The tendency manifested itself
during the 1940's, when the National Jewish Welfare Board
inaugurated an annual "Jewish History Week," the Yiddish
Scientific Institute (YIVO) issued the first volume of the
Yivo Annual of Jewish Social Science which included material on American Jewish life, the Hebrew Union College established the American Jewish Archives on its Cincinnati
campus, and the American Jewish Committee-sponsored
Commentary magazine called a conference to study the
problems of recording and interpreting American Jewish history. Toward the end of the decade, the American Jewish
Archives began publishing a semiannual journal, and the annual publication of the American Jewish Historical Society
was expanded into a quarterly. In the early 1950's, the American Jewish History Center was founded at the Jewish Theological Seminary of America in New York City, and plans
were formulated at the Hebrew Union College to add an
American Jewish periodical center to its campus.

No Longer a Fable

By 1953, amateurs as well as professional historians from
one end of the country to the other were digging through
records in search of material to commemorate the American
Jewish community's tercentenary—for 1954 would mark
300 years since a fugitive company of twenty-three Jews dis-
embarked at the tiny Dutch village of New Amsterdam on
the Hudson River to establish the first Jewish community on
North American shores. Before long, a special committee
was formed to prepare for publication an ambitious ten-

volume documentary source book, dealing with Jewish life in the United States. The boom in American Jewish historical studies achieved further dimensions when local American Jewish historical societies made their appearance in Los Angeles, Richmond, Baltimore, Washington, Detroit, and other communities. All this was additional testimony to the security which Jews had by now found in America. The mass of American Jews had long since abandoned its anxious quest for acceptance and had begun to develop a natural and healthy interest in its past on these shores. This in itself was a trend of no small significance.

As the 1960's dawned, it became evident that the study of American Jewish history was gaining a thoroughly scientific base, and that the field had drawn far away from the Napoleonic approach to history as "a fable agreed upon." More and more Jews were emerging from the universities with indoctrination in the critical method; some of them had become professional historians and were devoting themselves to various problems related to the American Jewish scene. Today, increasing numbers of researchers in the field, whether they work as students or as professionals, turn to documentary sources and newspapers in an attempt to determine the facts as they actually happened—without partisanship or prejudice. Not all these historical craftsmen are Jews, for many non-Jews, aware that the American people is a congeries of many backgrounds and creeds, have come to see—and to study—the American Jew as an important component of the American nation. Historians recognize that, though Jews constitute only three percent of America's population, their strategic massing in urban centers, their achievements in nuclear physics, medicine, law, music, and literature, and their influence on trade have led them to play central roles in American life and culture.

BASIC DOCUMENTS

The professionalization of American Jewish historical research has been responsible for numerous changes in the portrait of the American Jew. Oliver Cromwell urged Peter Lely to paint him "warts and everything, as you see me," and increasingly that is how historians are now rendering the American Jewish experience. For the professionally trained historian, there are no sacrosanct personalities. Isaac Markens, writing seventy-five years ago, might rhapsodize over Rebecca Gratz's "elegant and winning manners," her "instinctive refinement and innate purity," her "wonderful beauty" and "loveliness of character," but the mid-twentieth-century historian sees in her a woman "outstanding . . . in a limited area," a woman "charming in some ways, . . . prosaic in others . . . a rather strait-laced individual," who "had few, if any, original thoughts, but . . . was sensitive to the needs of others and . . . knew how to care for them." The historian dealing with Jewish life during the American Revolution is no longer anxious to forget that Jews, too, were found in Loyalist (Tory) ranks, nor does he find it difficult to attempt a dispassionate assessment of Haym Salomon's services to the Revolutionary cause. He has uncovered ample evidence to support the view that Salomon was an energetic fighter for civil liberties, a generous philanthropist, an earnest patriot, a devoted Jew, and an efficient aid to Robert Morris, the Superintendent of Finance, but our latter-day chronicler does not balk at disposing of the myth—for myth it is—that Salomon ever lent vast sums to the Continental Congress. He knows, and does not hesitate to say, that Salomon was most certainly not a vital factor in financing the Revolution!

Reasons abound why American Jewish historical research lacked a scientific and systematic approach before the Second World War, but among the most important of these reasons is that the field was virtually devoid of the auxiliary reference works without which no worthwhile history can be written. It was only after the War that bibliographies— books about the important books—were systematically assembled, or that efforts were made to reconstruct the skeletal outline—the chronology and periodization—of American Jewish history. It is only in very recent years that a vast genealogical compendium of the early families was published at the Hebrew Union College and that a beginning was made in preparing reliable biographical dictionaries of notable American Jews.

The colonial origins of the American Jewish community are now being reexamined—this time without recourse to apologetics. Recognition of the fact that the early history of American Jewry is incomprehensible without an understanding of the seventeenth-century milieu out of which the community came has stimulated the production of works on the Jewish community of Dutch Brazil during the mid-1600's and the equally important community of Curaçao. Today, there are scholars delving into the history of early Mexico in an effort to determine to what extent, if any, the Marranos of colonial New Spain had a group religious life of their own. The study of the Jewish experience on the North American mainland has been impressively advanced by the publication of source books containing basic documents and memoirs. About ten volumes are thus far available or in preparation, all of them with introductory material and notes and most of them scientifically conceived. All this work signifies a major trend, for in this way the field is acquiring an effective historiographic apparatus indispensable for comprehensive and accurate research.

The time is not yet for attempting general overall histories of enduring scientific calibre. Historians of American Jewry recognize that no adequate presentation of the American Jewish experience can precede the preparation of reliable city and state histories, based on careful and critical analyses of available sources. Although the tercentenary celebrations of the mid-1950's called forth at least a dozen local—town and state—histories, not all, unfortunately, were of lasting value or professional calibre. Still, a beginning has been made, and today historians have recourse to recently published works throwing light on Jewish life in, among other places, New York City, Philadelphia, Newport (Rhode Island), Chicago, St. Paul, Milwaukee, Rochester, Buffalo, Utica, Portland (Oregon), Charleston (South Carolina), Des Moines, and Petersburg (Virginia). When enough accurate local histories have seen the light of day, they will serve as the monographic tools which well-trained and literate historians will be able to use in writing the history of the American Jew.

"GERMANS" AND "RUSSIANS"

What are the trends in American Jewish historical writing in this seventh decade of the twentieth century? That is not easy to say. Perhaps 100 good essays in the field appear annually in various scientific and scholarly publications, each writer following his own bent and working in the area that appeals to him most. Still, certain trends are to be discerned.

The pre-"Russian" period—the period prior to mass immigration from Eastern Europe—continues to command the attention of professional historians. Some are working primarily in the colonial period, covering the years between 1649 and 1776. Other researchers, realizing that the nineteenth-century Philadelphia "rabbi," Isaac Leeser, was probably the leading American Jewish historical figure before the Civil War, have been undertaking detailed studies of Leeser's life and career. The centennial anniversary of the Civil War stimulated a series of studies on the American Jewish attitude to slavery and abolitionism, and it is now clearer that most antebellum Jews, those in the North as well as in the South, cared little about the moral issues of human bondage. The Civil War itself, in its effect on the Jews, found its prime authority in the Philadelphia scholar, Bertram W. Korn, whose book on the subject went into a second printing and is

now available as a paperback. There are certain gaps in research on the pre-Russian period, for—excepting three volumes of memoirs, dealing mostly with German Jewish immigrants—recent years have seen few adequate attempts to
describe in detail the life of the "German" Jews who dominated American Jewry through much of the nineteenth century. The German Jewish peddler has caught the imagination of some historians, but the value of his economic services
and of his cultural contributions remains to be objectively
assessed.

One of the most interesting and promising of current
trends is the increasing attention given to the "Russian" Jew
—the Jew of East European background who began coming
to America in huge numbers during the 1880's and whose
children and grandchildren now constitute an overwhelming
majority in the American Jewish community. As an object
of historical research, he is a newcomer on the historiographic scene, and the novelty of subjecting his life to study
is thrown into relief only when one considers the sparsity of
articles about him in the *Publications of the American Jewish
Historical Society* during the first half-century of the Society's existence. Up to the Second World War, where the
"Russian" was concerned, historians suffered a prodigious
lapsus memoriae. He was ignored despite the fact that, by
1940, there were in this land nearly five million Jews of
"Russian" stock. In part, this neglect was due to the lingering
influence of the anti-immigrant, Nordic racial views held by
nineteenth- and early twentieth-century historians and sociologists; in part, it was due to the "Russian" 's own remote-
ness from communal leadership and authority and to his desire to Americanize himself by dismissing his immigrant
beginnings. But when Jews of "Russian" stock, along with
other Americans of immigrant origin—Italians, Slavs, etc.—
began to achieve power on the American scene, American
historical research generally deserted its traditional emphasis
on "Anglo-Saxonism" and notable historians in the general
American field—some of them Jews—realized that the

"Anglo-Saxons" were not alone in determining the course of American life. As a result, Nordic historiography and sociology have been rapidly falling into disfavor as well as disuse, a great deal of effort, research, and writing has been going into studies of America's various immigrant groups, and a sympathetic view of the Jewish immigrants from beyond the Vistula River is now gaining ground.

An important facet of the growing trend towards immigrant history is the fact that scholars are now turning seriously to a study of the "Jewish" labor movement, which produced personalities like Sidney Hillman, David Dubinsky, and Jacob Potofsky. That, where the apparel industry is concerned, Jews, both as employers and as employees, have been a significant force in the American economy is well understood today, and quite a number of works on this subject have appeared in recent years. The subject is, however, a highly complex one, requiring a thorough knowledge of Yiddish, a familiarity with the workers' Russian-Jewish background, and an understanding of their involvement in a host of European socio-economic and political ideologies. To write the history of these Jewish one-generation proletarians —who, in most cases, were neither the sons nor the fathers of manual laborers—the scholar needs also an acquaintance with the Yiddish-speaking Socialist movement of a generation ago. It is not surprising, therefore, that truly definitive studies of the so-called Jewish unions remain to be written. Economic and labor history has been closely associated with the struggle for social justice, and, although some efforts are being made to determine the extent, large or small, to which Jews have pioneered in this area, here, too, definitive studies have yet to appear.

Another, and salient, aspect of the "Russian"'s life and the life of his descendants in the United States is Zionism, that curious mixture of, on the one hand, religious universalism and messianism and, on the other, political nationalism and secular idealism. To what degree it is possible today to speak of Zionism in terms of historiographic trends is problematic.

It is true enough that veritable hosts of essays and books proliferate in the area of Zionism and the Hebraic literature which the movement has fostered in America, but, unfortunately, much of this activity is propagandistic rather than scholarly, and to date no one has presented the story of American Zionism historically and critically. Nevertheless, Zionism is declining today owing to the attainment of its prime objective with the creation of the Israeli republic in 1948, and its decline as a movement may make it possible before long to view the development of this incalculably important and influential phenomenon on the American Jewish scene with historical objectivity and dispassion.

AN ADEQUATE HISTORY

Historians now display a growing interest in the acculturation of the Jew to American life and mores. This process of acculturation has been, of course, remarkable for its speed; in most cases, immigrant Jews in America have become well acculturated in less than a generation. What intrigues scholars most about the process is its communal expression—the way it has been reflected in the rise of a vast network of social-welfare agencies and the way it has affected pedagogical standards in Jewish elementary and secondary schools. Acculturation is a prime instance of the interaction between Jewish community life and the American environment, for, on the one hand, Jewish social-welfare activities have become exemplary for their general American counterparts and, on the other, American educational practices have vastly influenced Jewish education. Both areas—social welfare and education—have been widespread objects of research, but as yet very few of the studies and monographs in print may be said to meet the needs of the scholar or to represent the best canons of historical writing.

One area, both here and abroad, which suffers no dearth of study is anti-Semitism. Its manifestations in American life have aroused the interest of both Jewish and non-Jewish scholars, and a few good essays and useful books on the subject have already appeared. Still, much more remains to be done, and a definitive work on the subject has yet to appear. The interest in anti-Semitism has, however, been stimulating a great deal of research in the related field of civil liberties. Since problems involving anti-Semitism and civil liberties perennially are and will be a Jewish concern, historians, constitutional lawyers, and civic-defense technicians work almost feverishly in this field. Much that has appeared, however, is pragmatically and propagandistically motivated, and the subject still lacks a good one-volume book.

Jewish life in suburbia is another subject beginning to attract scholarly attention. The subject, a very complicated one, involves a grasp of social, economic, and political data. For example, the Jews who have trekked to the suburbs during the last two decades have had to cope with problems of civil liberties and civil rights in the public schools where they feel themselves threatened by the constant efforts to breach the wall of separation between church and state. This is, of course, but one of a host of suburban problems. To understand the growth of the Jewish community in the sprawling suburbs, numerous surveys have been made by sociologists, demographers, and social workers, but no effort of enduring value has yet been undertaken in this generation to collate the vast amount of very important data already available. Works on Jewish suburbia have, however, already begun to appear and will no doubt increasingly engage the attention of historians.

All these trends, all this activity, will ultimately lead to a comprehensive understanding of American Jewish life. It will take time, but there is every reason to hope that, within this very decade, new overall histories of the American Jewish experience will appear, based on the studies which are constantly coming off the presses. An adequate history of American Jewry must be accurate and unbiased, but it can also be extremely interesting and exciting. It will tell the story of a community which began in 1654 with twenty-three Jews and has now grown to nearly six million people who, though in the main a middle-class, white-collar group of city dwellers, are involved in virtually every aspect of American life and in the last decade have produced a large number of America's Nobel Prize winners.

5

THE OLDEST KNOWN SYNAGOGUE RECORD BOOK OF CONTINENTAL NORTH AMERICA, 1720–1721

The first Jewish religious service in North America was held probably during the High Holy Days in September, 1654, in the Dutch town of New Amsterdam. A congregation was speedily organized—certainly no later than 1655—but with the decline of the Jewish community in the 1660's the congregation faded away. Within a decade or less, however, a reorganization was effected, although it was not, in all probability, until the 1690's that the new synagogal group had rented quarters of its own. By the turn of the century this Spanish and Portuguese congregation was securely established.[1]

In 1706, a new constitution was prepared—there certainly had been older ones, for colonial Jewish congregations were constantly rising and falling and writing or modifying their organic statutes.[2] The name of the congregation in 1706—if it had one—was probably Shearith Jacob, the Remnant of Jacob. The phrase is biblical, of course, and is taken from Micah 5:6–7:

> And the remnant of Jacob shall be in the midst of many peoples,
> As dew from the Lord, as showers upon the grass. . . .
> And the remnant of Jacob shall be among the nations,
> in the midst of many peoples,
> As a lion among the beasts of the forest.

This essay appeared originally in Daniel Jeremy Silver (ed.), *In the Time of Harvest: Essays in Honor of Abba Hillel Silver on the Occasion of His 70th Birthday* (New York, 1963), pp. 227–34.

1. David de Sola Pool, *An Old Faith in the New World* (New York, 1955), pp. 8 ff., 34 ff.; *American Jewish Archives (AJA)*, VII, 56; *Publications of the American Jewish Historical Society (PAJHS)*, XVIII, 1 ff.
2. *PAJHS*, XXI, 1 ff.

Certainly, no later than 1720–1721, the congregation was known as the Remnant of Jacob (*shearith yaakob*).[3] By 1728, however, when a new constitution was promulgated, the congregation referred to itself also as the Remnant of Israel (*shearith yisrael*), as it looked forward to the messianic promise of Micah 2:12: "I will surely gather the remnant of Israel." [4] Unfortunately, the constitution of 1706 has not survived; prior to the discovery of the Simson ledger, the earliest known congregational records were the minute books beginning with the year 1728. The initial entry in these minute books is the 1728 constitution, a revision of that of 1706.[5]

Among the members of the community in the first decade of the century was a man who might well have participated in preparing the lost constitution of 1706.[6] This was Nathan Simson, a German-born merchant-shipper. In 1720, he was probably the parnas, or president, and had as such the duty of keeping the synagogue's financial accounts. Normally the *gabbai* ("collector"), or treasurer, was responsible for the finances of a congregation, but it is very likely that in a small Jewish group, such as the one in New York, the financial records, too, were the province of the all-powerful parnas. Although the word *gabbai* does occur in the Shearith Israel minutes, there is no evidence that a *gabbai* functioned as such until after the Revolution of 1775–1783.[7] Within a year after his term of office had expired, Simson returned to England (1722), whence he had originally emigrated and where

---

3. J. M. Corcos, *A Synopsis of the History of the Jews of Curaçao* (Curaçao, 1897), p. 21. Data cited but not documented are taken from the unpaged Simson synagogal account book to be described below. Simson, in 1720–1721, called the congregation the Remnant of Jacob, *shearith yaakob*.

4. *PAJHS*, XXI, 3. Apparently, in 1728–1729, the congregation sometimes referred to itself as Shearith Israel and sometimes called itself Shearith Jacob. Were there two congregations then? This is very improbable.

5. These, the oldest records of the congregation hitherto known, were published in *PAJHS*, XXI, 1–171.

6. Simson was in New York by 1703, probably even earlier. Public Record Office, London, 258, C. 104/13, p. 68a. All page numbers in C. 104/13–14 are those inserted in the copy in the American Jewish Archives.

7. The term *gabbai* in *PAJHS*, XXI, 30, seems to be a synonym for parnas. See also *PAJHS*, XXI, 142.

no doubt he had anglicized his Hebrew name of *shimshon*
("Samson") to Simson or Simpson. When he sailed back to
London, he took his papers with him and inadvertently included the congregational financial records for 1720–1721
(5481). Long after his death in 1725, the papers of this child-
less man were deposited in the Public Record Office in London, where they are found in category 258, C. 104/13–14.
Through the good offices of Daniel J. Cohen, Director of
Jerusalem's Jewish Historical General Archives, the commercial papers were brought to the attention of the American Jewish Archives and were carefully examined by me.
There I came across the congregational record and recognized immediately that Simson, like many of his predecessors
and successors, had retained them instead of surrendering
them to the new parnas. And we are indeed very thankful
that he did, for otherwise the account book, too, would
probably have gone the way of all its precursors in Shearith
Israel. None of them are extant—as far as is now known.
The Simson record book enables us to push back the history
of the congregation in some detail for at least eight years.[8]

This Simson ledger covers approximately the Jewish year
5481. Actually it includes the preceding month, for it began
September 4, 1720, and went to September 10, 1721, stop-
ping about twelve days before the New Year of 5482 (1721–
1722). When finally posted, it was presumably to have been
submitted by Simson to his successor, Jacob Franks.

Simson was very systematic in all that he did—he was a
successful merchant—and his methodical approach is evident
in this sixteen-page record. He identified the book by affixing
to its cover a Yiddish superscription which, unfortunately,
has been worn away by time. Enough has been left, however, to indicate that he was describing his ledger as the annual record of the congregational accounts. He followed the

---

8. Joseph R. Rosenbloom, *A Biographical Dictionary of Early American
Jews* (Lexington, Ky., 1960) [*BDEAJ*], under "Simson, Nathan"; *Anglo-
Jewish Notabilities* (London, 1949), p. 217; *PAJHS*, XXV, 87 ff. The ac-
count book is in C. 104/13, pp. 261–76.

Yiddish statement with the English: "New York, September the 10, 1721." Then came, in beautifully printed Hebrew square characters, the proud legend: "I, Nathan ben Moses Samson, of blessed memory, of Bonn in the Rhine River Country." Thus he started off with three languages! All Jewish merchants of that day were at least bilingual; many were polylingual. Simson was a German who had lived in Holland and England for years; he was consequently at home in German, Yiddish, Dutch, English, and, very probably, Hebrew. His nephew, Joseph Simson, whom he had already brought to America on a trip back from London in 1718, was reputed to be a Hebraist of unusual capacity.[9]

Following the title or cover page, Simson proceeded to post the financial record of every member of the congregation—men, of course—with the debits entered on the left side and the credits on the right side. The entries of debts still owed to the congregation from the administration of the preceding president were noted in Portuguese, and all the offerings of those called to the reading of the Torah were also indicated by the usual Portuguese phrases. The Ashkenazi-born Simson, in his religious life, was an assimilated Sephardi and quite possibly understood the Spanish-Portuguese language of the Sephardic Jews with whom he associated and did business in Holland, England, and the Americas, even though his Sephardic correspondents in the West Indies seem always to have addressed him in English. On the last three pages of the ledger, the parnas summarized all disbursements and receipts, with ample explanatory comments, and for that, too, we are deeply grateful. His accounts balance to the penny.

Undoubtedly, Simson, as the president, had a board of ajuntos to consult with him, but the actual congregational religious work was carried on, in 1720, by three paid officials: the hazzan or cantor, Moses Lopez Da Fonseca; the

---

9. *PAJHS*, XXV, 89–90; *BDEAJ*, under "Simson, Joseph"; F. B. Dexter (ed.), *The Literary Diary of Ezra Stiles* (New York, 1901), II, 553; III, 3, 32.

shohet and teacher, Benjamin Wolf (Benjamin Elias, Rebbe
Wolf); and the sexton, Vallentine Compenall (Campanall).[10]
These three men were still living in 1728, although Wolf-
Elias was then on pension. The other two were still active in
their posts.[11]

The congregation then occupied a rented house on Mill
Street, now South William Street; the house was owned by
Jan Harpendingh.[12] They also rented from a Mr. Cooper a
house which was probably used as a school or turned over to
one of the congregational employees. All these expenses had
to be met out of congregational funds. Their chief source in
1720–1721 was the offerings made by the generous members
who were called to the reading of the Torah. In addition,
freewill gifts of money were made on the Day of Atonement
and on the "Pilgrimage Festivals" of Passover, Pentecost, and
Tabernacles. On the eve of the New Year, a number of the
members—primarily the wealthy—made substantial contributions to Shearith Jacob, and those New Year gifts probably served as the core of the budget for the ensuing year.
There were no fixed dues.

In addition to the rentals for the *snoga* (synagogue) and
the other building, the congregation had to pay the hazzan
£50 a year (New York currency, not sterling), the shohet
£15, and the *smass* (shammash-sexton) £2.20 a year. The
latter certainly secured extras in the form of wood, rent, and,
possibly, cash grants. Although all three were professionals,
there can be no question that they also engaged in business
ventures on the side to augment their incomes.[13] The salaries

10. Moses Lopez Da Fonseca appears in the Simson Papers no later than
1714 (C. 104/13B, p. 894); Vallentine Compenall, no later than 1718
(C. 104/13C, p. 68).
11. *PAJHS*, XXI, 4.
12. David de Sola Pool, *The Mill Street Synagogue, 1730–1817* (New
York, 1930), pp. 16 ff.
13. The commercial transactions of Hazzan Lopez Da Fonseca and of
Vallentine Compenall are documented frequently in the Simson Papers.
For the former as a businessman, see also Isaac S. Emmanuel, *Precious
Stones of the Jews of Curaçao* (New York, 1957), pp. 315 ff. Benjamin
Wolf, the shohet, was also in business (cf. C. 104/13B, p. 840; C. 104/13, p.
348).

alone amounted to about £67, while the rent—£9 for the synagogue and £6 for the congregation's house—brought the total to a fixed expenditure of at least £82. Additional requirements were the sums needed for pensioners and the local poor, of whom there were at least three individuals or families. They received cash, beef, wood, and rent money or housing. In 1720–1721, when Simson was parnas, Benjamin Jacobs was a beneficiary of the congregation, receiving a grant; in 1725, Simson, back in London, was shipping goods to Jacobs! By 1728, Jacobs had so improved his lot that he was able to make a modest contribution to the reorganized Jewish community of that year when it purchased additional cemetery ground.[14] Rapid social mobility was a characteristic of colonial America. The charity petitioner of yesterday might well become a self-sustaining householder or even a substantial citizen a decade later.

Modest sums were required also to purchase beeswax and oil for the candles and lamps, for servants to clean the synagogue and the street fronting the house of worship, for replacing window glass, for carpentry, for repairing with red silk the frayed Torah mantle or the Torah band, and for haroset, a Passover "salad" which was supplied gratis to every member and client of the congregation. The bill for spades was mute testimony to the fact that Shearith Jacob buried its own dead. There was at that time probably no *hebrah*, or confraternity, to perform this last act of "loving kindness" for those who had died.

Payments of sums vowed or promised were usually in the form of cash, casually and informally handed over to the parnas, the hazzan, or the teacher, who may have served as the collector. Collection, however, was traditionally the job of the sexton. On occasion, a debtor paid his offering to one of the pillars of the synagogue—a man like the famous merchant, Rodrigo Pacheco[15]—who would meet him and dun him. The debtor, needing credit from the merchant who sold

---

14. Simson Papers, C. 104/13, p. 17; *PAJHS*, XXI, 8.
15. For Pacheco, see *BDEAJ*, under "Pacheco, Benjamin Mendez."

him goods wholesale, would not dare to refuse payment of what he owed. Having no ready cash, some of the debtors, including even the wealthy merchants, paid by note, and it is not improbable that such notes circulated as a form of currency. Others paid in kind or services, giving beeswax for the Yom Kippur candles or sending in a Negro domestic to clean the synagogue.

According to Simson's records—and we may be sure that they were accurate—there were thirty-seven paying or active members. Of these, fifteen were of Sephardic origin and twenty-two were Ashkenazic. Other Jews in town were beneficiaries of the community's generosity and were not included as members. The fifteen Sephardim were Abraham (Haim) de Lucena, Abraham Pinto, Abraham Burgos—formerly of Barbados and Rhode Island—Jacob Louzada, Abraham Gomez Caseres, Benjamin (Rodrigo) Pacheco—the first of the Seixas clan in town—Daniel Nunes (Da Costa)—who may already have moved to New Jersey[16]—David Angell, Isaac De Medina, (Luis, Lewis) Moses Gomez, Mordecai Gomez, Moses Lopez Da Fonseca, Abraham Gutieres, Moses Cohen Peixotto, and Samuel Coronell.

The twenty-two Ashkenazim were Abraham bar Isaac (Abraham Isaacs), Asher Myer(s), Baruch Judah, Benjamin Wolf (Elias), Nathan Simson, Eliezer bar Judah, Jacob bar Higuell (Ezekiel), Isaac Cohen,[17] Jacob Franks, Isaac Jacobs —who may already have moved to Branford, Connecticut, where he was a shopkeeper and whaler[18]—Joseph Simson, Moses Levy, Moses Michell, Moses Seby (Hart), Nehemiah Marks, Solomoh Michaell, Simon Moses, Solomon ben Mehir (Myers), Baruch Levy, Michael Asher—who was probably then living in Boston—Isaac Polack—later of Rhode Island—and Joseph bar Isgak (Isaacs).

There was one woman listed not only as having promised a

---

16. *PAJHS*, XXXIII, 253.
17. If this was Isaac Cohen de Lara (Larah), then he was a Sephardi (*PAJHS*, II, 85).
18. Jacob R. Marcus, *American Jewry-Documents-Eighteenth Century* (Cincinnati, 1959), pp. 317–20.

contribution, but also as having paid it, thus setting an example which some of the men might well have followed. She was Rachele Levy, very probably the widow of Samuel Levy, a distinguished merchant and Jewish communal leader.[19]

Aron Levy and Isaac Emanil (Emanuel) are mentioned in the records as donors. They were probably visitors from another town or village. Emanuel was then living in Freehold, New Jersey.[20] Among the residents of New York who were charity clients of Shearith Jacob were a Mr. Silva, one of the Campanalls, and Benjamin Jacobs. Sabee (Tzebi) Barr Ahron, who was also on the social-welfare rolls, may have been an itinerant.[21]

Of the above active members, the following were not on the rolls of the congregation in 1728 when the next extant record begins: Abraham Gutieres, Samuel Coronell, Baruch Levy, Solomoh Michaell, Isaac Cohen, David Angell, Jacob bar Ezekiel, Abraham Gomez Caseres, Simon Moses, Nehemiah Marks, Isaac Jacobs, and Moses Cohen Peixotto. The last-named died in 1721.[22] Solomoh Michaell (Michaels), who may have been a brother of Moses Michell, is documented in the Simson Papers no later than 1714.[23] David Angell appears in the Simson Papers no later than 1718.[24] Gomez Caseres, Moses, Marks, Jacobs, and Peixotto are documented in other sources and thus were already known to have been in the colonies. As far as I know, there is as yet no record of the others in the North American provinces except in this Simson ledger. The fact that eleven of the above twelve—or at least most of them—were probably still alive in 1728, but were not members of Shearith Israel, is further proof of the

19. David de Sola Pool, *Portraits Etched in Stone* (New York, 1952), pp. 459–60.
20. *PAJHS*, XXXV, 173.
21. For the biographies of most of the thirty-seven members listed above, see *BDEAJ*.
22. Pool, *Portraits*, p. 455.
23. C. 104/13B, pp. 646, 990; C. 104/14, p. 156.
24. C. 104/13C, p. 68.

physical mobility of the Jewish businessmen of the eighteenth century. They hastened to leave for other, presumably greener, pastures. Some may have fled after failing in business. It is difficult for us today to appreciate the terror that the fear of imprisonment for debt struck in the hearts of bankrupt shopkeepers or merchants.

The prevailing ritual was Sephardic (Spanish-Portuguese), and the Ashkenazim or "German" Jews, although already in the majority, accepted that ritual because by 1720 it had been the only one in use in North America for over sixty years. It was traditional and common practice in Jewish life for the newcomers to accept the liturgy of the host community.[25]

On the basis of about forty male "householders" in town —not all of whom, to be sure, were married—it is safe to assume that there were anywhere from 175 to 200 Jews in the synagogal community.[26]

The total of expenditures for the year amounted to over £128, leaving a balance of almost £4, which Simson dutifully turned over to the new parnas. About 30 percent of the members, eleven men, made no payment on their accounts during the entire year. Either they were poor, had moved away, had died, or were indifferent to the needs of the community. One of them, Nehemiah Marks, was later to become a convert, as was his brother Mordecai.[27] Of the thirty-seven active members, twenty-four were in arrears in their payments when the accounts were closed. All told, a sum of about £88 was due the congregation in present and remote

---

25. Mishnah, *Pesahim*, IV, 1.

26. This estimate is based on the assumption that about thirty of the forty "householders," or members, in town were married and that there were about six to a family, inclusive of men, women, children, and Jewish servants. The estimate of six to a family is derived from Evarts B. Greene and Virginia D. Harrington, *American Population Before the Federal Census of 1790* (New York, 1932), p. xxiii.

27. *BDEAJ*, under "Marks, Mordecai." See the Index under "Marks, Mordecai," and "Marks, Nehemiah," in Jacob R. Marcus' forthcoming *Colonial American Jew*. This Nehemiah is not to be confused with Nehemiah, the son of Mordecai, who was born and baptized a Christian.

debts.[28] One man, Joseph Isaacs, a butcher who was a militia-man in 1691 during King William's War, had apparently not paid anything on his debts since 1718. Abraham (Haim) da Lucena owed over £24. This former "minister of the Jewish nation"(1710), who was also a merchant-shipper, must have fallen on evil days. By 1723 he was already bankrupt and may have been in a debtors' prison.[29]

Six men contributed about £79 of the total budget of £132. They were Benjamin Pacheco, Moses Gomez, Mordecai Gomez—who was parnas in 1718—Moses Levy, Jacob Franks, and Nathan Simson. The first three were Sephardim; the latter three, Ashkenazim. Moses and Mordecai Gomez were father and son; Levy and Franks were father-in-law and son-in-law, and Simson was a kinsman of the Levys—although not always friendly![30] The Simson records show that the three Ashkenazim contributed approximately as much as the three Sephardim for the support of the congregation; and one is not venturing far in suggesting that these six men constituted the "power" group, that the Levy-Franks-Simson constellation, together with the Gomezes and Pacheco, ran the congregation. If one may judge by their contributions, six of the thirty-seven members were wealthy, or at least in the upper middle class; the remaining thirty-one were in the middle or lower middle class. As has been pointed out, there were three individuals or families on the charity lists, unless —and this is a possibility—the Silvas and one of the Campanall families were retired communal servants living on their pensions.

On the whole, there were no radical differences between the community of 1720 and that of 1728, but it is a step forward (or backward!) in uncovering the past to be able to make this statement with assurance.

28. If Simson's ambiguous note that £87.18.6 was due the congregation refers only to old and remote debts, then the amount due Shearith Jacob altogether was substantially larger than the total given above.

29. Simson Papers, C. 104/14, p. 674; Jacob R. Marcus, *Early American Jewry* (Philadelphia, 1951), I, 45–50.

30. *Abstracts of Wills* ("Collections of the New-York Historical Society for the Year 1893"), II, 189; *PAJHS*, XXV, 87–89.

6

LIGHT ON EARLY CONNECTICUT
JEWRY

Although the first permanent Jewish congregation was not established in Connecticut till 1843, there were Jewish families in the scattered towns and even an occasional religious service long before that time. Individual Jews had peddled, traded in horses, and done business in the Connecticut river towns and seaports ever since 1659, but they were hardly welcomed in that colony which so strongly reflected the spiritual influence of neighboring intolerant Massachusetts.

As early as 1670 Jacob Lucena, a New York and Hartford peddler and merchant, had been fined severely by the Connecticut magistrates. This man, a son or a brother in all probability of one of the first Jewish immigrants to New Amsterdam, made a living trading with the settlers and the Indians. In 1670 he ran into a great deal of trouble across the New York border, in Connecticut, where he was tried and found guilty of having been "notorious in his lascivious daliance and wanton carriage and profers to severall women." The Court of Assistants fined him £20 and threatened him with a severe flogging if he failed to pay. We are quite safe in assuming that the fine and the threat contributed mightily to the cooling of his ardour. Twenty pounds was a huge fine and he immediately appealed his case. Two days later the General Court abated half of the sum imposed . . . because he was a Jew! Is it possible that they did not expect a Jew to maintain the same high moral standards as a Christian? They were hardly that naive, for they were certainly conscious of the fact that the colony's standards were anything but high. The last three decades of the century, we know, witnessed a decline in colonial morals due, in part, to the immigration of

This study appeared originally in *American Jewish Archives*, I, No. 2, pp. 3–52.

foreigners with non-Puritan standards, and, in part, to the natural reaction of the settlers themselves to the prurient censorship of the magistrates and ministers. Drunkenness and sexual vice were altogether too common in Connecticut and New England at this time. It is far more probable that Lucena's Connecticut judges cut his fine in half because he was one of God's Chosen People . . . but ten pounds was still too much to pay. Consequently our amorous hero appealed to Asser Levy, the New York butcher and amateur attorney, who had sufficient influence to have the penalty again halved. No doubt Lucena paid the five pounds.

By the first quarter of the next century, a few Jewish merchants had established themselves in Hartford, Stratford, and other towns. Their activities are documented primarily in court records which reveal them as litigants along with some of their coreligionists from neighboring New York. Among the more notable merchants whom we find enmeshed in the court proceedings during the first half of the eighteenth century were men like Moses Levy, Jacob Franks, and Judah Hays, all of New York City.

One of the more venturesome of these New York families, the Pintos, moved eastward from the border county of Fairfield and settled in New Haven in the 1750's; by the time of the Revolution they were a well-known clan, active Whigs and patriots, fighting as soldiers and officers in the ranks of the Continental troops. The so-called Jewish families resident in the state—most of whom, as we shall see, had deserted their original faith and had joined their neighbors religiously—received additional recruits, with the outbreak of war, from the Jewish émigrés of Newport and New York who sought safety in nearby Connecticut. Isaac Seixas, for instance, fled Newport, which was occupied by the British in December, 1776, and took refuge in Stratford. Quite a number of Jews had assembled in this Connecticut village on the Boston Post Road. As far as we know, most of the refugees who fled to this town and county hailed from New York and neighboring Long Island. They brought their rabbi with them, the Reverend Gershom Mendes Seixas, the son of Isaac of Newport.

These exiles, some of them competent and successful businessmen, merchants, were drawn into the life of the larger community in which they lived, and when the Tories and British raiders on Long Island Sound threatened the villages in which they were now settled, they joined with their Gentile neighbors in appealing to the Council of Safety to provide them with armed vessels to cruise and patrol the endangered shore. Most of these newcomers, who had fled to escape the British, remained in the state to the end of the war, and it was no doubt during this period of exile that the first Jewish religious service was held in Connecticut. Although the Scrolls of the Law of nearby Congregation Shearith Israel of New York had been carried off to this state, there was no attempt, as far as we know, to create a permanent synagogal organization in this temporary asylum. Here in their new Connecticut homes they married, begot children, died . . . and carried on their traffic as best they could, in spite of the severe state embargo laws, waiting impatiently until the conflict was over and they could return to their homes, to their synagogues, and to more familiar surroundings.[1]

---

1. This brief sketch summarizes the present state of our knowledge of the Jewish element in Connecticut to the end of the Revolution. The literature is as follows: *The Jewish Encyclopedia*, "Connecticut," IV, 227 ff. The most inclusive article on early Connecticut Jewry was written by Leon Hühner, "The Jews of New England (Other than Rhode Island) Prior to 1800," in *Publications of the American Jewish Historical Society* [*PAJHS*], XI, 86–95. Hühner has exploited the interesting and essential material in *The Public Records of the Colony of Connecticut (1636–1776)*, compiled by J. H. Trumbull and C. J. Hoadly, 15 vols. (Hartford, 1850–1890). He did not use *The Public Records of the State of Connecticut (1776–1784)*, 5 vols., ed. by Charles J. Hoadly and L. W. Labaree (Hartford, 1894–1943), except insofar as some of the state material was published in Royal R. Hinman, *A Historical Collection from Official Records . . . of the Part Sustained by Connecticut during the War of the Revolution* (Hartford, 1842). The Hühner article is a good survey and makes use of most of the material published as of 1903. Scattered references to colonial and early Connecticut Jewry were published in ensuing volumes of *PAJHS*. These can be secured by consulting the index at the end of each volume. For example, *PAJHS*, XXVII, 171 ff. and 367, deal with the Seixases in Stratford and the engagement of Benjamin Seixas to Zipporah Levy. Lee M. Friedman wrote a note on "Early Hartford" (*PAJHS*, XXXV, 293) in which he made use of an

Further investigation will unquestionably demonstrate that individual Jews had been moving into various Connecticut towns ever since the seventeenth century, coming to do business and to remain as settlers if permitted to do so. A case in point is the story of John Carsen. In March, 1685/6, Carsen, who had chartered the brigantine *Prosperous*, landed a load of goods at New London. On the fifteenth of the

item in *The Public Records of the State of Connecticut*, Vol. III. Under the title, "Aaron Lopez' Long Deferred 'Hope'" (*PAJHS*, XXXVII, 103–13), Friedman described the attempt of Aaron Lopez to recover his schooner *Hope*, which had been seized by Connecticut privateers. Stanley F. Chyet, in his forthcoming biography of Aaron Lopez, treats the *Hope* case in even greater detail than Friedman did. No attempt has yet been made, however, to rework into one article all the material that has appeared since 1903. Abram Vossen Goodman, in *American Overture: Jewish Rights in Colonial Times* (Philadelphia, 1947), pp. 24–31, explored the Jacob Lucena case in the original sources. In brief, practically all that we know of colonial Connecticut Jewry derives from the Hühner article, which included only published materials and did not consider the manuscript records.

The following essay exploits or reinterprets, in part, materials in *The Public Records of the Colony of Connecticut*, and makes use of the new material in *The Public Records of the State of Connecticut*. The above represent published documents. In addition, the writer has used whatever manuscript material he could find in the archives of the Connecticut State Library, in the library of the American Jewish Historical Society, and in the archives of the Newport Historical Society. He has leaned heavily on the letters of Samson Mears to Aaron Lopez of Rhode Island which are found in the Lopez letter books in the collections of the Newport Historical Society. He gladly takes this opportunity to express his thanks to James Brewster, the Connecticut State Librarian, and to his staff for their many courtesies. Miss Marjorie E. Case was particularly gracious in aiding the writer in his search for manuscript materials. Rabbi Isidore S. Meyer, the Librarian of the American Jewish Historical Society, and Herbert O. Brigham, of the Newport Historical Society, were most helpful in making available the manuscript materials at their disposal. The writer desires also to thank Mr. Brewster, Rabbi Meyer, Mr. Brigham and their respective organizations for permission to publish from their collections the manuscripts which are appended to this article. Thanks are also due to Stephen T. Riley and to the Massachusetts Historical Society for permission to republish a letter of Samson Mears, Wilton, Connecticut, January 31, 1780, to Aaron Lopez, which had originally appeared in the *Commerce of Rhode Island* [M.H.S., Collections, Seventh Series, Vol. X] (Boston, 1915), II (1775–1800), 83–84. This Mears letter, published in Appendix I(N), includes a closing paragraph and a postscript omitted in the printed edition. There are other references to Mears in *Commerce of Rhode Island*.

There is no intention in these pages to attempt to write a definitive study of colonial and early Connecticut Jewry to about 1800. This essay does attempt to bring the early history of this colony and state up to date, on the basis of published and manuscript sources, insofar as they were known and available to the writer.

month, a warrant was issued, and his goods were seized and
impounded pending investigation and trial. The charge made
by William Dyre, the surveyor general of customs for all the
British American colonies, was that the goods were non-Eng-
lish and that their owner, John Carsen, was a Dutch Jew, an
alien, therefore, and not entitled to trade in the English plan-
tations, according to the terms of the Navigation Acts. It is
true that Dyre had had trouble in New York prior to this on
the charge that he was malicious in the imposition of customs, and it is reported that Daniel Wetherell, a deputy, who
was concerned in the seizure of Carsen's wares, was later
turned out on the ground that he was a "great rogue"; it is
also true that Dyre stood to share in a large part of the cargo
as an "informer" if it could be proved that Carsen had con-
travened the Navigation Acts. However, we need look for
no malice on the part of this officer. He had been appointed
in 1683 to bring order and system into the practices of the
revenue officers. It was part of his job to watch for violations
of the Navigation Acts. It is quite immaterial that he stood to
benefit personally by his delation. If Carsen was an alien, a
Hollander from Rotterdam, as alleged, and not an Englishman as he claimed, then Dyre was justified in the action he
took, even as he had been justified the previous year when he
arranged for the seizure of the property of the "alien" Jews
in Newport, Rhode Island. Although we have no record of
the decision of the Admiralty Court in this Connecticut case,
we may assume that Carsen saved his cargo on the contention
that he was a native-born Englishman—he did not deny, or
affirm either, that he was a Jew; he evaded that question.

The Carsen and the Newport affair are cut of the same
cloth. In 1685, two years after Roger Williams died, this
same Major William Dyre brought charges against the Newport Jews as "aliens" that resulted in the seizure of their
property. What was behind all this?

About this time similar charges had been brought against
foreign-born Jews in London. As endenized aliens they had
for years been exempt from special taxes, particularly those

envisaged in the first Navigation Act, and in matters economic they were practically on the same footing as native-born Christian merchants. Nevertheless, in London, in 1685, on the death of Charles II, the attempt was made to cancel their endenization patents, dub them "aliens," subject them to special onerous taxes, and thus squeeze them out of business. The London merchants thought this an excellent idea. Major William Dyre evidently heard of the London scheme —he had been in that city for a time—and attempted similar action in the Newport court. Had he won, the Jews would have been unable to compete economically and would have been forced out. The attempt failed in London; it failed in Newport, too. The Jews of Rhode Island, as a matter of fact, if not of law, had already been accepted as endenized aliens, for in the preceding year the General Assembly had for all practical purposes encouraged them to remain in the colony.

The Newport Jews, who appeared for trial on March 31, 1685, received back their goods, not because the charges of the Major against them were false, but because the Newport magistrates took advantage of a legal technicality. They wanted to keep the Jews as merchants in town and had already expressed their intention to this effect on June 24, 1684, when they permitted them to remain and to do business there in spite of the fact that they were "strangers," aliens. This decision of the Rhode Island authorities was really an evasion of the Navigation Acts . . . and that evasion certainly did not lie heavily on their consciences.

Whether the motivations behind the London, the Newport, and the New London coups were the desire to implement the Navigation Acts, to earn rewards as informers, or to drive the Jews out of business, the attempts all failed, because in both lands, in that age of mercantilism, the authorities believed that the Jew was an economic asset. If this was their hope, then future events in both London and the Americas fully vindicated them.[2]

2. The Carsen papers are in the Connecticut State Library, Ms. Archives, Trade and Maritime Affairs, 1668–1789, Series I, Vol. I, Doc. 15–33. See also

New London—where Carsen had his troubles—apparently did not encourage the settlement of Jews. It was one of the few large towns of Connecticut in the eighteenth century which did not shelter even a single Jewish family. The attitude toward Jews manifested in 1753 by a Mr. Andrew McKenzie, a merchant, may account in some degree for the absence of Jews from this port. Hearing that one of his correspondents, Miguel De St. Juan, was utilizing the services of a [Spanish?] Jew, he wrote St. Juan and reproached him for "being led by the nose by a faithless Jew whose nation sold their God for money and crucified him afterward. How cou'd you think that he [a Jew] cou'd be true to you [a Spaniard] who is of a place where none of their sect is tollerated?" [3]

Throughout this entire period, the people of Connecticut were governed by the charter of 1662, which was to remain substantially in effect till 1818; it declared significantly that the Christian faith "is the only and principal end of this plantation." It is not without its touch of irony that this famous charter, which left little room for religious tolerance of Jews, was decorated with a beautiful miniature portrait of Charles II drawn in all probability by the greatest miniature portraitist of Restoration England, Samuel Cooper, whose older brother, Alexander, was a convert to Judaism.[4]

The Public Records of the Colony of Connecticut, III, 344-45; C. M. Andrews, *The Colonial Period of American History* (New Haven, 1948), IV, 73–74. Check also "William Dyer" in the Index of Andrews' work. Dyre did not appear against the Rhode Island Jews in March, 1685, and he may not have appeared against Carsen in 1685/6 because his commission had expired in January, 1685 (Andrews, IV, 199). Andrews, however, still refers to Dyre as surveyor general in March, 1685 (IV, 196). For Wetherell, see Andrews, IV, 196–97. See also M. A. Gutstein, *The Story of the Jews in Newport* (New York, 1936), pp. 40 ff. See also Goodman, *American Overture*, pp. 40 ff. For the London attempt to cancel the endenization of the Jews, see Cecil Roth, *History of the Jews in England* (Oxford, 1941), pp. 179 ff.

3. *Collections of the Connecticut Historical Society*, XVI, 275. See also pp. 203, 289, 298, 304.

4. "Connecticut," in *Harper's Encyclopaedia of United States History* (New York, 1905), 328a; Franz Landsberger, *A History of Jewish Art* (Cincinnati, 1946), p. 228.

It was because of the typical religious exclusivism, of which this patent is but a minor evidence, that no organized Jewish life was possible in this colony, although, as we know, there were scattered Jewish families in various towns and villages. Some of these Jews had lived in Connecticut for decades; others, like Samuel DeLucena, for instance, were only birds of passage. Samuel was a native New Yorker, son of the merchant Abraham DeLucena who had been doing business in the city ever since 1708, and, incidentally, serving as rabbi of the congregation. Evidently, the father had given Samuel a sound training in the mercantile field, for years later the son boasted that he was "born and brought up a merchant in the city of New York." But apparently all his instruction and experience availed him little; he does not seem to have been very successful, if we may judge from his constant shifting to new ventures. Certainly no later than the 1750's, Samuel was in business for himself, but by the end of the French and Indian War he was quite ready to seek fresh pastures. Like other merchants, he had been buying goods from England but now found it difficult to balance his accounts—"of late years. . . . it is hard making returns to Europe."

It was time for him to try something new. Some of his friends and coreligionists were always flirting with new ideas and new products. This appealed to him, too, for he was a sanguine spirit, readily responsive to novelties. One of the Lucenas—not necessarily a relative—was given a special license in Newport, in 1761, to manufacture Castile soap, not improbably the first instance of the manufacture of this article in British North America. This enterprising Rhode Islander, James Lucena, maintained that his formula was genuine and that it came from no meaner source than the royal factory in Portugal. Several years before this, another of the Newport Sephardim, Moses Lopez, had been granted a license to manufacture potash, for he was one of the very few in the British Empire who had really made himself master of the true art and mystery of preparing this valuable staple

. . . so he said. Mayhap Samuel had learned the skill from Lopez. At any event, in May, 1765, he was already living in Norwalk and had petitioned the General Assembly of the Colony of Connecticut, now meeting in Hartford, for special privileges in the manufacture of this commodity. He wrote that he had already built a factory in the south end of the town, had already invested £200 in buildings and equipment, and confidently hoped that his new enterprise would prove of good advantage to the government . . . and to himself.

What he now wanted was some "incouragement," preferably a long-term monopoly in the manufacture of his product, to apply to the area for twenty miles around his factory. As the pioneer, the first to carry on such a business in the county, he asked for special consideration by the Assembly. Since monopolistic grants were common in the colonies and the states into the nineteenth century, his request was neither unreasonable nor unusual. Unfortunately, we do not know whether his factory ever went into production. One is inclined even to doubt his statement that he had already sunk £200 in the enterprise before seeking protection from the General Assembly. If he did begin operations he was probably unsuccessful, if we may judge from the fact that when the Revolution rolled around he was engaged in another economic adventure: the search for sulphur mines. Gunpowder was essential to the winning of any war. Here, too, he had no luck or ability. When he submitted a bill to the Continental Congress in 1779 for his expenses in the search for sulphur mines, the Board of War refused to acknowledge the justice of his claim and paid him nothing. Toward the end of the conflict—if not before—he was in Philadelphia, either as a refugee from the British in New York or to press his claims with Congress. At any rate, he joined the new émigré congregation Mikveh Israel and made a contribution . . . a very modest one. He was obviously without means. The last we hear of him is in 1787, a member of the New York congregation . . . slightly in arrears with his dues. He probably never returned to Norwalk.

Lucena, like other New York patriots, had moved to the capital city of Philadelphia, where the advantages of safety, opportunity, and the appeal of a large Jewish community were not to be denied. Many of the Philadelphia newcomers had traveled directly from New York; others, like Hazzan Gershom Mendes Seixas and his brother Ben, had stopped over in Connecticut before finally moving to the Pennsylvania metropolis. There were enough refugees in Stratford, Connecticut, and the immediate vicinity after 1776 to hold a religious service with the minimum number of ten adult males present. It was here in this town that Isaac Seixas sought in marriage the hand of Zipporah Levy for his thirty-year-old son, Benjamin. Zipporah was eighteen. Her father, Hayman Levy, the famous Indian trader and merchant, was now in Philadelphia, whither he had fled when the British occupied New York. Although Isaac Seixas wrote in a rather formal fashion to Levy, the two families knew each other well; Levy certainly knew Ben through their common synagogal activities in Shearith Israel. The patriarchal character of this Sephardic Jewish family is reflected in these lines sent November, 1778, by the elder Seixas to Levy: "It is at the request of my son Ben. Seixas that I presume to trouble you with this, to acquaint you that he had inform'd his mother and my self that he has a very great regard for y'r daughter, Miss Zipporah Levy, and shou'd think himself very happy if he cou'd obtain your consent and approbation, as well as your amiable spouse's, . . . in permitting him soon to be joined to her in the sacred bonds of matrimony. We have no manner of objection thereto, etc."

Ben married Zipporah the following January. It was a very successful marriage, certainly in one respect: they had seventeen children. Seixas stayed on in Philadelphia until the war was over, when he returned to New York about the same time that his brother Gershom came back. In later years he became one of New York's most distinguished Jewish citizens, a founder of the New York Stock Exchange and a president of the synagogue.[5]

The Seixases were but one of the many families that took refuge in nearby Connecticut. Most of the Jewish refugees—there were of course many Gentiles, too—who had fled from New York to the neighboring state settled in Fairfield County, just across the line, in the towns of Stamford, Norwalk, Wilton, Danbury, and Stratford, where they could keep an eye on their property and their interests in British-occupied New York. To their dismay, some of them found that they had gone from the frying pan into the fire, literally. The English and the Tory governor, General William Tryon, started a series of raids in 1777 that increased in violence until they reached their peak in July, 1779. All the harbor and river towns were now exposed to fire and plunder and the hazards of guerrilla warfare. Long Island and the Sound were completely in the hands of the enemy. Feeling themselves particularly exposed, the Norwalk citizens besought the Connecticut state authorities for an armed vessel to patrol the Sound. A number of the signers of this October, 1777, petition were Jewish émigrés, and among them were members and relatives of the widespread Mears family.

The name Mears was probably an anglicization of the German Meyers or a variation of the Prussian town name, Meurs. The fact that they were German in origin did not deter them from using Spanish or Portuguese phrases in their letters. This they picked up in the Sephardic synagogues or from their Spanish-Portuguese Jewish friends. By the same

5. Samuel DeLucena: biographical details in *PAJHS*, VI, 102; XXI, 38, 79; XXIII, 150; XXVII, 41, 248, 461–62; XXXI, 86. See also M. A. Gutstein, *The Story of the Jews of Newport* (New York, 1936), p. 55. The petition to the General Assembly, now in the archives of the Connecticut State Library, Industry, 1708–1789, Series I, Vol. II, Doc. 110, was reprinted in *Norwalk After Two Hundred And Fifty Years*, p. 361, and in Jacob Rader Marcus, *American Jewry: Documents, Eighteenth Century* (Cincinnati, 1959), p. 332. The petition of Lucena to Congress is in the *Journals of the Continental Congress*, IV, 396; XIV, 734, 844. See also *PAJHS*, I, 68–69.

The Seixas family: *PAJHS*, XXVII, 161 ff., 171–72. Zipporah Levy: *PAJHS*, IV, 210.

token, Gershom Mendes Seixas did not hesitate to use Judeo-German terms . . . especially for the foods which tickled his palate!

The Mearses—one branch at least—had come from England and had settled in New York some time during the first quarter of the eighteenth century. There was also a Mears family—probably a branch of the English group—in Jamaica as early as the late seventeenth century. Samson Mears, a New York merchant, was one of the numerous agents and clients of Aaron Lopez. Some years before the Revolution he was in St. Eustatius, one of the West India islands, but by the time the war broke out he was back in North America, where we meet him as a refugee in Norwalk, Connecticut. The Mearses and their "in-laws" sought safety in this town after they had fled before the British in New York. Gershom Seixas was here for awhile, too. Besides the Mearses, the Simsons and the Myerses were here. Solomon Simson, the New York merchant, Myer Myers, the silversmith, and his brother Asher, the coppersmith, had all married Mears girls, sisters of Samson.

Samson, the first-born and the only boy in the Mears family, carried on an active correspondence with Aaron Lopez throughout the year 1779. This well-known Newport merchant and shipper was then at Philadelphia trying to recover his schooner *Hope* and its valuable cargo from the hands of Connecticut privateers, who were frequently little better than pirates. But even though his hands were full fighting his case before the Continental Congress and the Connecticut courts, he was, at the same time, carrying on an extensive interstate trade by coastwise shipping and inland wagon transport. Overseas commerce was hazardous because of the British fleet.

Throughout the year 1779, and into 1780, Mears was trying to obtain velvets, woolens, worsted stockings, men's clothes, tobacco, snuff, spermaceti candles, iron wire, and salt from Lopez. But, unfortunately, goods were frequently late in arrival, and by the time the carts came lumbering into town prices had changed, the market was overstocked, and the paper money depreciated. Business was carried on under most trying circumstances. Textiles were at a premium because of the successful British blockade. Salt was an important item and Mears traded it for other stores, primarily for flaxseed which Lopez was eager to secure. In April, 1779, the rate of barter was thirteen or fourteen bushels of flaxseed for one of salt. The staples mentioned in the price-current list included sugar, West India rum and domestic "Continental" rum, Madeira wine, tea, domestic and foreign salt.

Lopez was in the market not only for flaxseed but also for flour, an important staple. However, the difficulty of securing this latter commodity in wartime was aggravated by the laws of the different sovereign states which forbade its export.

Mears was ready to do business with Lopez on a commission basis, as the latter's agent, or as a partner. Commerce was hampered, however, not only by the inflation which had already set in with a vengeance, but also by the difficulties of transport and travel. Mears was frequently on the road executing commissions for his chief, riding as far as Newport or pushing on to the "happy hills of Leicester" in a snowstorm, but recoiling from an extra seventy miles on a sick horse through winter mud to New London. On some occasions he was away for weeks, returning to his family to find them distraught because his letters had not come through and they had conjured up the worst.

The vicissitudes of a bonnet-box of plumes for the women of the Lopez clan are an eloquent commentary on the difficulties of transportation, if not on the vanity of woman. Lopez bought these plumes in Philadelphia early in 1779 while prosecuting his case before the Continental Congress for the recovery of his schooner. Employing a cumbersome overland cart, he sent them in a large box to Mears who, knowing that the Lopez women at Leicester set great store by this finery, examined them carefully on arrival to make sure that nothing was damaged. Hearing that a Norwalk neighbor was driving to Boston, he arranged to have the plumes taken along, knowing they would be turned over to one of Lopez' agents there and then forwarded to Leicester. But the box was too big to be fastened onto the sulky and was sent by fast ship to Providence and thence on to its final destination. To make sure it would be protected adequately this time, Mears sewed it up carefully in two of Lopez' sheepskins which he had for sale in his shop. The chances are that it arrived safely for we hear no more about it in the correspondence.

The difficulties of transportation were caused only in part by the bad roads. During the war there were hostile forces on all sides, regulars and guerrillas, to say nothing of the customs officers at the borders. Teamsters hesitated to leave home with their horses in those parlous days. Mears once scoured the countryside for twenty miles to find a man willing to take a load of goods to Philadelphia, and the man he finally found agreed to make the round trip for about $450 (paper money), exclusive of his expenses which amounted to $307.

Not the least of the hazards was the teamster himself: as a true son of New England he liked his rum, and if he carried a hogshead of "spirits," it was almost inevitable that he would drill "spoil-holes" and syphon off a few gallon to while away the tedium of a long slow journey. After one trip, Mears found a wantage of nine gallon!

Mr. Lopez' problem of preserving his spirits from thirsty teamsters was nothing new in the history of Jewish commercial activity. In the early sixteenth century, a visiting Jewish merchant had died while at the fair in Leipzig. Unfortunately, no Jewish cemetery or community was tolerated in that city at that time. The friends of the deceased were concerned about returning his body to his home community for burial, but feared that the Leipzig magistrates and the states across whose borders the body was to be carried would, as was their wont, utilize this golden opportunity to impose a crushing tax on the unfortunate family. To avoid this form of robbery, the body was put into a hogshead of brandy and dispatched home. The teamsters, not knowing the grim contents of the barrel, made "spoil-holes" and enjoyed a rousing good trip. "The drivers," says Luther, who tells this story in his *Table Talk*, "never knew they were drinking Jew-pickle."

The third anniversary of the creation of the new American republic on July 4, 1779, was no holiday for Samson Mears. Not that he was worried about the enemy. Norwalk, he had written as far back as April, was so small the English "have greater objects to attend to than this insignificant place." "I don't apprehend much danger here from the enemy, especially as it is near opening the campaign." He was feeling miserable, and in the July letter poured out his heart to Lopez who was always ready to listen to any man. Mears felt cooped up. The restrictions on trade enforced by the neighboring states had almost brought business to a standstill. Sick and tired of an idle life, and seeking something to do, he suggested to Lopez and his father-in-law, Rivera, that they join with him in a company to speculate in Continental currency. People were beginning to buy it abroad; it was being quoted on the markets. He was ready to establish a company in Amsterdam and in his old stamping ground of St. Eustatius. Little did he realize that beginning on the morrow he would have other problems that would so engross him that he would have no time to think of starting a new business in the West Indies, or anywhere else, for on the 5th the English began the most devastating of their raids on the Connecticut shore. Eager to divert Washington and to get at him, Sir Henry Clinton urged General Tryon to attack the towns along the Sound again. This Tory needed no second invitation and, starting on the 5th of July, he struck at New Haven, Fairfield, Norwalk, and other towns. It was on the 11th that he and his German mercenaries burnt the houses, barns, and churches of Norwalk, plundering where they could, exhibiting "cruel, barbarous, inhumane, and unmerciful conduct and behaviour," destroying even the "wheat in the sheaf," and the "grain in store." How wrong Mears was in his prognostication to Lopez that Norwalk at least was safe!

Wilton, a few miles to the north, up the Norwalk River, was the next refuge of this wandering Jew. He had found no real home since the July raid, in spite of the fact that he had been riding all over the countryside looking for a shelter. It was very difficult to find a suitable house not too close to the enemy or to the seacoast with its blasting winds. All this in a letter of Mears to Lopez on October 8th. The primary purpose of this letter, however, was to thank Lopez for his generous aid to Norwalk Jewry. The Newport shipper, who was truly a prince among men, had been quick to send money and supplies through Mears to the sufferers. Even though the Myers brothers—Samson's brothers-in-law—had been hard hit, they refused any help for themselves. Another brother-in-law, Solomon Simson, had suffered even greater losses, but he too sought nothing for himself from Lopez. Those who needed help most were Moses Isaacs, Michael Judah, and Samuel Israel.

The last named was an English immigrant who had come to New York some time before the year 1770. For a while he augmented his income by boarding one of the old women who had been granted a pension by the congregation. His brother Joseph had been more successful. After leaving New York, where he had spent some time, he went to Calcutta, got himself a native wife and family, and, judging by his will, also acquired a considerable fortune. Joseph called himself Joseph Israel Levy; his mother, who lived in Houndsditch, London, was known as Rosey Israel. By the time the Revolution had broken out, Rosey had come to America. Tryon's raid found her with her other son, Sam, in Norwalk.[6]

---

6. Mears: Most of the material on Mears is derived from his manuscript letters, all of which are in the Lopez letter books in the archives of the Newport Historical Society, except the letter from Wilton, January 31, 1780. This last was published in *Commerce of Rhode Island*, II, 83–84. All these Mears letters are printed in Appendix I. For further details on Mears see *PAJHS*, II, 66; XI, 92, 151; XXI, 79; XXXIII, 200 ff.; H. S. Morais, *Jews*

In response to a petition of the Norwalk sufferers, a committee of the General Assembly interviewed the inhabitants, estimated the losses, and recommended tax abatements which were later granted. Among the eight or more Norwalk Jews who were given relief in this fashion over a period of years was the well-known New York silversmith, Myer Myers. He was no permanent settler in Connecticut but had come in 1776, like most of the others, to avoid living under the English. The preceding year he had been visited by a Mr. Benjamin Henshaw, who had been dispatched by a committee of the State Assembly to find a refiner of lead ore who was competent to take charge of the smelting of the lead deposits in the village of Middletown, Connecticut. Stimulated by the desperate need of lead for bullets, the State of Connecticut was ready to spend considerable sums of money to attain its purpose. After considering a number of possible candidates for the post, Henshaw did not hesitate to recommend Myer Myers, not only as "honest and skillfull" in his profession as a gold- and silversmith, but also as an expert refiner. Myers agreed to come for £200 a year, New York currency, but although Mr. Henshaw recommended him,

---

of Philadelphia (Philadelphia, 1894), p. 22. The reference to Mears journeying to the "happy hills of Leicester," arriving in a snowstorm, is found in a ms. letter of David Lopez, Jr., Leicester, December 7, 1779, to his Uncle Aaron Lopez (Lopez letter book in the archives of the Newport Historical Society; also in *Commerce of Rhode Island*, II, 79). Mears returned to the island of St. Eustatius in 1780 (*Commerce of Rhode Island*, II, 99) and died there in 1786 or 1787. Letters of administration were granted in February, 1787, to Solomon Simson (*Collections of the New-York Historical Society*, XXXVIII [1906], 348). Asher Myers, a coppersmith: *ibid.*, p. 353.

Moses Isaacs: This Moses Isaacs presented a memorial in May, 1780, to the General Assembly for permission to transport some beef, flour, and grain from Connecticut to Rhode Island. He pleaded his dire need as a refugee with a number—eight—of small children to support. His petition was granted, the embargo notwithstanding (*The Public Records of the State of Connecticut*, III, 79; *PAJHS*, XXXV, 293). Isaacs, too, was a brother-in-law of Mears; Isaacs' wife was Mears's sister (*PAJHS*, XXXIII, 202).

The Israel or Levy family: *PAJHS*, XXI, 107. Will of Joseph Israel Levy, Calcutta, January 2, 1772; proved, April 27, 1786. Solomon Simson was one of the two witnesses. Samuel Israel, brother of Joseph, was made administrator on April 28, 1786 (*Collections of the New-York Historical Society*, XXXVII [1905], 331–32).

there is no record that he was offered or that he accepted the position.[7]

---

7. The following petitions and memorials from citizens of Norwalk to the Connecticut General Assembly include Jewish subscribers:

1777, October 14: petition for a well-fixed vessel of six or eight guns to cruise the Sound for the protection of the western shore against the British. Among the signatories were: Myer Myers, Asher Myers, Solomon Simson, and Benjamin Jacobs (Connecticut State Library, Ms. Archives, Revolutionary War, 1763–1789, Series I, Vol. VIII, Doc. 82, pp. a–b. See also *PAJHS*, XI, 92).

1779, October 18: petition for tax abatement because of the Tryon raid. Among the signers were: Samson Miers (Mears), Michael Judah, Myer Myers, Asher Myers, Solomon Simson (Connecticut State Library, Ms. Archives, Revolutionary War, 1763–1789, Series I, Vol. XV, Doc. 265, pp. a–d).

1780, March 16: report to the General Assembly of committee to investigate the hostile incursions of the British troops. Losses of the following citizens were included: Myer Myers, David Judah, Rose Israel, Samuel Israel, Solomon Simson (about the sixth largest loss), Moses Isaacs, Asher Myers. In the tax abatement list that follows, Rose Israel and David Judah received nothing (*ibid.*, Series III, Vol. I, Doc. 100, pp. a–h).

1780, May: tax abatements granted by the General Assembly included names of Asher Myers, Michael Judah, Samuel Israel, Myer Myers, Solomon Simson (*ibid.*, Series I, Vol. XVIII, Doc. 269, pp. a–b).

1780, October 10: committee's report of tax abatement included names of Michael Judah, Asher Myers, Myer Myers, Solomon Simson (*ibid.*, Series I, Vol. XIX, Doc. 76, pp. a–d).

1780, November: tax abatements granted by the General Assembly included names of Asher Myers, Myer Myers, Solomon Simson, Michael Judah (*ibid.*, Series I, Vol. XIX, Doc. 78, pp. a–c).

1780: another committee-recommended abatement list included names of David Judah and Michael Judah. The recommended abatement sums are resolved, in three parallel columns, into Continental currency, state currency, and hard coin (*ibid.*, Series I, Vol. XX, Doc. 379, pp. a–g).

1781, May: tax abatements granted by the General Assembly included names of David Judah and Michael Judah (*ibid.*, Series I, Vol. XX, Doc. 380, pp. a–h).

All the above tax abatements were designed to give relief to the suffering inhabitants of the town of Norwalk who had experienced losses during the Tryon raid. Benjamin Henshaw's report to a State Assembly committee, June 30, 1775: Connecticut State Library, Ms. Archives, Revolutionary War, 1763–1789, Series I, Vol. I, Doc. 246, pp. a–b. For details concerning the committee to secure the lead in Middletown, and the difficulties it experienced, see *The Public Records of the Colony of Connecticut*, XV, 37, 99, 130, 255, 368, 459, 507; also, *The Public Records of the State of Connecticut*, I, 129–30, 480; IV, 237.

Solomon Simson, who seems to have had an interest in the lead mine in Middletown—this is implied in the above Henshaw report—may have been the one who drew Benjamin Henshaw's attention to Myers' technical training. Simson might well have recommended his brother-in-law, Myers, to Nathaniel Wales and Pierpont Edwards, members of the General Assem-

Not all the émigrés from British-occupied New York left at the same time. Some waited till the English had entered this important port; others, like Myer Myers, left as early as September, after the defeat of the Colonials at the battle of Long Island when it was obvious that the foe would take the city itself. A patriot like Myers, who had given up his home and his business to avoid living under the enemy, and who had suffered for his political convictions, would have had little sympathy or patience for the mutterings or the bragging of a Tory. We can, therefore, well understand the reaction of this patriot when, while drinking a convivial glass with a neighbor in a Norwalk tavern, he heard the well-known New Haven merchant, Ralph Isaacs, speak disparagingly of the Continental troops. The Whigs, said this Tory, had suffered a severe defeat because they could not hold their lines under fire. As the British moved forward into the territory of the Continentals, he added, the people would readily submit and return to their former allegiance. This conversation was very discouraging with respect to the success of the Continental side. As far as Myers and his friend Peter Betts were concerned, this was treason, and they did not hesitate, therefore, on October 16, 1776, to fill out an affidavit and forward it to the secretary of the General Assembly at New Haven denouncing this notorious defeatist.[8]

---

bly, who had visited and studied the lead mines at Middletown in May, 1775. Wales and Edwards, as we shall see later, were both well known to Simson; Edwards was his lawyer. The Simsons and Myerses were not only related, but were also business partners no later than the decade before the Revolution. In 1765, Samson Simson, Solomon's older brother, Myer Myers, and George Trail, as partners, had purchased a tract of land in Woodbury, Litchfield County, Connecticut (*The Public Records of the State of Connecticut*, V, 222–23).

8. The Myer Myers and Peter Betts affidavit against Ralph Isaacs (Connecticut State Library, Ms. Archives, Revolutionary War, 1763–1789, Series I, Vol. V, Doc. 427) is printed in Appendix II.

Ralph Isaacs is said to have been of Jewish origin (*PAJHS*, VI, 151–53). Until some evidence to bolster this statement is adduced, he will have to be considered a non-Jew. As far as this writer knows there are no data to support this assertion. The name "Isaacs" is not necessarily a proof of Jewishness or of Jewish origin. As we know "Jewish" names mean very little, particularly in New England. Moses Simonson arrived at New Plymouth on the *Fortune* in November, 1621. See J. C. Hotten, *The Original Lists of*

That Myer Myers was motivated by patriotism in his affidavit against Ralph Isaacs is hardly to be doubted. A few years later another Connecticut Jew brought suit against a presumptive Tory, a fellow-Jew, and attempted to influence the court against his opponent by pointing out that the absent defendant was "now under the protection of the common enemy." The plaintiff was Hyman Jacob Boghragh (Bachrach!) of Salisbury, of whom we know nothing; the defendant was Naphtali Hart Myers, of whom we know a great deal.

Myers was a distinguished, successful, and philanthropic merchant who must have come to New York in the early 1740's, for by 1746 he was an officer in Shearith Israel. The following year he was the sixth largest taxpayer in the congregation, ranking with Isaac Seixas and Judah Hays, and by 1756 he was president of the congregation. Three years before this, however, he had gone to England, found himself a bride and brought her back to New York. This merchant— he dealt in European and East India goods, "very cheap for ready money"—was generous in his gifts to Jewish and Gentile institutions. To the Redwood Library in Newport, he donated some good books when it first opened; to the synagogue there, he gave a chandelier and in addition purchased the right, at a handsome sum, of laying one of its

Persons of Quality, etc. (New York, 1873 [?]), p. xxviii. Solomon Mears, a Connecticut contemporary of Samson Mears, was very probably a Gentile (Connecticut State Library, Ms. Archives, Supplementary Index to Revolutionary Mss). Gentile Hayses were not uncommon in Connecticut.

A letter of Ralph Isaacs to Aaron Lopez indicates that they were not acquainted (Letter from New Haven, December 4, 1774, in Lopez letter book, library of the Newport Historical Society). Possibly of significance is the fact that Isaacs was a friend and executor of the will of Andris Trube, a Fairfield Jew (Will of Andris Trube, Connecticut State Library, Fairfield district, 1759, No. 1949. See also *The Public Records of the Colony of Connecticut,* XI, 533).

Jacob and Abraham Pinto were among the New Haven Whigs who signed a petition, September 17, 1776, to Governor Jonathan Trumbull and the Council of Safety, voicing their suspicion of Tories who were believed to be agents of the British. Among the Tories listed was Ralph Isaacs (Connecticut State Library, Ms. Archives, Revolutionary War, 1763–1789, Series I, Vol. V, Doc. 425, pp. 2–4; also in Hinman, *Historical Collection,* pp. 566–67).

cornerstones. To the New York congregation, he gave five candelabra which gave light to synagogue worshippers for seventy years before they were taken down, carted and shipped across the mountains, to grace the new sanctuary just built in Cincinnati, the first Jewish house of worship west of the Alleghenies.

In May, 1780, Boghragh petitioned the General Assembly at Hartford to stay all proceedings directed against him by Myers who, in order to secure payment of certain debts, had taken possession of Boghragh's property on which he held a mortgage. The complainant was very careful to point out that Myers had returned to Great Britain. The implication, of course, was that he was a Tory. He probably was. Like other elderly and wealthy businessmen his first loyalty was to the mother country, England.[9]

When the Myerses, the Mearses, and the Simsons crossed the Connecticut border in the summer and fall of 1776 and sought safety in patriotic Norwalk, they were probably welcomed into town by Michael Judah, a permanent settler who had been living there for at least thirty years. He was one of those who was hard hit in 1779 by the Tryon raid and who availed himself of the generosity of Lopez and Rivera. As far back as 1746, Judah was already sending orders from Norwalk to the Gomezes of New York, financing his little business, possibly, on the £5 which the congregation had lent him on his note. Three years later he joined the other merchants in town in a petition to the Connecticut General Assembly. After the treaty of Aix-La-Chapelle, in 1748, which

---

9. Connecticut State Library, Ms. Archives, Revolutionary War, 1763–1789, Series I, Vol. XVIII, Doc. 357. This document was published also in *The Public Records of the State of Connecticut*, III, 97. I differ with the editor in the transcription of the name of the plaintiff. Mr. Hoadly reads: Bagraugh. For N. H. Myers, see *PAJHS*, II, 82; XII, 167; XXI, 53, 60, 88, 220; XXVII, 405, 408, 450. Personal details of his marriage, etc., are found in letters of N. H. Myers, London, November 16, 1753, to Aaron Lopez in Newport, and New York, August 18, 1754, to Lopez in Newport (Mss. in Lopez letter books in the archives of the Newport Historical Society). For litigation of N. H. Myers in Connecticut in 1753, see *The Public Records of the Colony of Connecticut*, X, 268–69.

brought King George's War with the French to an end, a provincial war tax of 5 percent on imports was removed. Unfortunately, many of the merchants who had not envisaged the end of the conflict had bought large stocks in advance at high prices, and when the treaty was signed and prices slumped, they found themselves saddled with heavy inventories which cost them more at wholesale than newer goods were now selling at retail. Their chagrin is very much reminiscent of the dolorous remark of a Jewish merchant of a later generation who had just been informed by Philip Hone, of New York, that the Treaty of Ghent had been signed: "Thank you, Mr. Hone, but I wish I hadn't bought them calicos." Needing relief badly in 1749, the merchants of the county—and of course Michael Judah among them—petitioned the Assembly for the return to them of the unexpended sums that had come into the treasury in the form of the 5 percent duty on imported merchandise. Among the other merchants who signed this petition were Isaac Pinto and Andris Trube. Like Michael Judah these two were also old settlers. At least three of the twenty-two merchants in the county at this time were Jews.[10]

In the adjoining county of New Haven, there was a London Jew by the name of Mordecai Marks, who had married a Derby girl to become the founder of an old Connecticut family. We may assume that he first came to New York, moved on to Stratford, and then went up the Housatonic River to the town of Derby. Since we know that the Boghraghs lived in Salisbury, that there were Solomonses during the French and Indian War in Middletown, and a family of Venetian Jews in New Haven in the 1770's, we may be sure that this does not exhaust the list of Jewish settlers and that

---

10. Memorial of the traders in the County of Fairfield to the General Assembly, April, 1749 (Connecticut State Library, Ms. Archives, Trade and Maritime Affairs, 1668–1789, Series I, Vol. I, Doc. 138, pp. a–b). There is a similar petition, dated September 29, 1752, which does not include the name of Michael Judah, but does include the names of Isaac Pinto and Andris Trube. The endorsement on this latter petition indicates that it was denied in both houses (*ibid.*, Series I, Vol. III, Doc. 25, pp. a–c).

there were other families scattered in the different villages throughout the colony.

What sort of "Jews" were the Pintos, of Stratford, the Trubes, of Fairfield, the Judahs, of Norwalk, and the Markses, of Derby, after two or three generations in a colonial Connecticut village? What happened to a Jew *qua* Jew who lived alone, religiously speaking, away from a Jewish community and Jewish family life, in a homogeneous Christian world?

Michael Judah did not have to consult his Bible to learn that it is not good that a man should be alone, and so he married Joshua Raymond's daughter, Martha, a Christian. Surely it was not easy for him to make this decision, for he was a loyal Jew, desirous of maintaining his affiliations with his fellow-Jews. When in the course of time Martha gave him a son, Michael turned to Abraham I. Abrahams, the ubiquitous mohel of New York, and asked him to circumcise the child. This was done on November 23, 1756. It is obvious that an observant Jew would want his son to be circumcised; it is not clear under what pretext Abrahams performed this rite for the child of an unconverted Gentile woman. It is doubtful if Martha Raymond ever became an adherent of the Jewish faith. At all events the child entered the world as David, the son of Meir, which proves also that Michael was only the civil, not the religious name of Mr. Judah. Twenty years later, in 1776, young David was a soldier in Captain Gregory's Company in the Connecticut line. Ultimately he made his home in neighboring Fairfield, married Constance Bennet, and became one of the town's leading citizens. He was, of course, lost to Judaism.[11]

In his description of the people of Fairfield, at the time of the Tryon raid, Bancroft, the American historian, wrote that they were "all of unmixed lineage, speaking the language of the English Bible." This statement was not quite accurate, for long before David Judah had settled there—during or

---

11. See below for references to Michael and David Judah in note No. 18.

after the war—another Jew had made his home and reared a family in this charming town on Long Island Sound.

About the year 1720, there came to New York a German- or Polish-Jewish settler named Asher Truby. By 1722, he was already engaged in business in Fairfield, Connecticut, and must have been a man of some means, for he was able— with a cosignatory—to underwrite a bond for £1,000 for John Gold, a non-Jew, who had been appointed Naval Officer of the Port of Fairfield. This immigrant could hardly have been less than thirty years of age then, in 1722. By 1729, he was an established member of Shearith Israel Congregation in New York. The fees he paid the Jewish community indicated that he was not wealthy, but was earning sufficient to carry his share of the load. This is the first and the last reference to him in the congregational accounts. He next appears in the Connecticut records—twenty years later —as one of the signatories of the 1749 petition of the Fairfield County storekeepers to the General Assembly. It is interesting to note that he subscribed his name twice: first in beautiful Hebrew characters: *Anshil Troib*, and then in Latin script, Andris Trube. There is no question, the Latin script signature is also his. The double form was employed by him on occasion as an "official" signature.[12]

His friends in town called him Andris Trube or Trubee or Truby. He, like Michael Judah, realized that he could not live alone, yet he hesitated to marry his sweeetheart, whether for religious scruples or not cannot now be determined. It should not be forgotten, however, that at least seven years after he had landed in this town—it may have been longer than that—he was still loyal to Judaism and was a contributor to the New York synagogue. It would certainly not have been easy to induce the Jews of New York to convert his bride, although it was not until 1763 that Shearith Israel issued a formal prohibition against the conversion of the Gentile wives of the Jewish settlers.[13] On the other hand, it is by

---

12. For a variation of this procedure, see below under Manuel Myers.
13. *PAJHS*, XXI, 217.

no means improbable that Anshil's girl was unwilling to become a proselyte, preferring to remain Christian and unmarried rather than become Jewish and married. Evidently he lived with Abigail Crane as her common-law husband until a few days before the birth of their second child, when he entered into a formal marriage. This child was a boy; the first had been a girl. The boy was given the good Jewish name of Samuel Cohen Trube, after his deceased paternal grandfather, we may be sure. The next child, a girl, was given the typical German-Jewish or East European name of Geetlow (Gitla), but when she sickened and was about to die her mother had her baptized. Ansel (Anshil!) was the name of the next to come along, and he grew up to become a good Christian and one of Fairfield's well-known citizens. He certainly spoke "the language of the English Bible," for his Yiddish-brogued father, who wrote his English name with labored care, had died (1758) when little Ansel was only eleven years of age. Ansel Trubee, Anshil's son, and David Judah were well acquainted with one another.[14]

Mordecai Marks—sometimes called Mordica or Mordeca —was born in London in 1706 and migrated to the colonies about 1726. Three years later he was in Stratford, Connecticut. On April 20, 1729, according to the record, "Mordecai Marks, Jew," was baptized in the local Episcopal Church. Eight months after he had accepted this new religion he married Elizabeth Yorieu, and when she died he selected, as his second wife, Elizabeth Hawkins, of Derby. It would seem that he had become a Christian in order to be accepted in marriage. Of these two marriages six children apparently survived, four boys and two girls. Abraham died in 1766 at the age of eighteen, during his father's lifetime; Nehemiah, born

14. George Bancroft, *History of the United States of America, etc.* (Boston, 1878), VI, 209. Trube in New York: *PAJHS*, XXI, 16. The 1722 bond: Connecticut State Library, Ms. Archives, Trade and Maritime Affairs, 1668–1789, Series I, Vol. I, Doc. 85. Details of marriages and births of his children may be found in D. L. Jacobus, *History and Genealogy of the Families in Old Fairfield* (1932), II, 971–72. Will: Connecticut State Library, No. 1949, Newtown district, December 5, 1758; proved, January 2, 1759.

in 1746, was a Tory and fled to Nova Scotia. Although the evidence is not conclusive, it would seem that Mordecai lived the rest of his life either in or around the towns of Huntington and Derby; certainly his last twenty years were spent in the latter place. As we know, he was an active member of the Episcopalian church in Derby not later than 1747; his children were reared as Christians, and his wife, of course, shared her husband's Christian faith. Four generations later, his descendants wrote of him as a Jew. There is no question that he lived as an observant Christian after he settled in Derby, for his tombstone says that he was "a useful member of society, an affectionate husband, a tender parent, and a constant communicant of the church, and on the 8th day of January, 1771, he departed this mortal life in hopes of life immortal."

One of his sons, Mordecai II (1739 or 1740–1797), was a well-to-do merchant and farmer who owned his own trotting and pacing mares, a Negro slave, and a small library. He was a man of some education and in his will, in which he invoked "our Lord and Savior, Jesus Christ," he provided for a "liberal education" for a minor son. A great-grandson of Mordecai I, David Marks, born in 1778, was a minister in the Calvinistic Baptist Church.[15]

We have followed the assimilatory process in the history of three of the four Jewish families and now turn to the Pintos of Stratford. Like the others, they had no doubt crossed into this county of Fairfield from neighboring New York.

---

15. *Memoirs of the Life of David Marks, Minister of the Gospel,* ed. by Mrs. Marilla Marks (Dover, N. H., 1846), further proves the Jewish origin of the family, Chapter I, p. 13. See A.S.W. Rosenbach, *An American Jewish Bibliography* (New York, 1926), No. 592, p. 417. For data on the Marks family, see Samuel Orcutt, *The History of the Old Town of Derby, Connecticut, etc.* (Springfield, Mass., 1880), pp. 153–54, 745; Orcutt, *The History of the Old Town of Stratford, etc.,* II (Fairfield, 1886), 980, 1243–44; E. J. Lines, *Marks-Platt Ancestry* (1902), pp. 33–34; *The Public Records of the Colony of Connecticut,* XIII, 148, 476–77. For the will of Elizabeth Hawkins Marks, see No. 6824, New Haven district, in the Connecticut State Library. For will of Mordecai Marks II, see No. 1316, Stratford district, Connecticut State Library. These nineteen documents in No. 1316, with their seven inventories, are useful for a study of the social background of the deceased.

By 1725 there were already two members of this family in Stratford, one of whom was Abraham Pinto. It is probably safe to identify him with that Abraham Pinto who later became a shohet or ritual slaughterer for the New York Jewish community. Abraham Pinto, of Stratford, had a son Jacob—or he may have been a more distant relative—who later moved the fifteen or so miles to New Haven and there, apparently, joined the Congregational Church.[16] We know that he was in New Haven as early as 1755, that he married a Christian—her name was Thankful—and for many years was to be the only "Jew" in town. For Ezra Stiles, our informant, a Jew was a Jew no matter what his religion was. Later, in the 1770's, Stiles referred to him as one who had "renounced Judaism and all religion." Evidently he and some of the other Pintos in town had become deists or possibly even atheists. After the death of Thankful, his wife, Jacob lived in a common-law marriage with another woman by whom he had four children. It was these four natural children who inherited his estate when he finally died in 1806. The three legitimate sons needed no help from their father because they had all been successful in life. Abraham—so called, probably, after his deceased grandfather the shohet—Solomon, and William were the names of the three sons, all students at Yale, two of them graduates of the class of 1777. All of them served with excellent records in the Revolutionary armies, Solomon as an officer. William, known for his ability to write a fine hand, was asked to make a copy of the Declaration of Independence for Governor Jonathan Trumbull and for President Daggett of Yale. None of these Pintos practiced Judaism.[17]

---

16. I say "apparently," for though he may have been compelled to pay taxes to the provincial church, he need not have been a communicant.

17. For older material on the Pintos, see *PAJHS*, III, 150; XI, 89–95; XIX, 111–13. Pintos at Stratford: *The Public Records of the Colony of Connecticut*, VI, 526, 577; IX, 406. Abraham Pinto, the shohet: *PAJHS*, XXI, 46–47, 54. Although we identify this Abraham with the Abraham of Stratford and as the father of Jacob, of New Haven, Orcutt, *History of Stratford*, II, 1269, does not know of a Jacob among the sons of Abraham, of Stratford. Jacob could then have been a son of Isaac Pinto, of Stratford,

There seems to have been a general trend toward religious assimilation and complete submergence in the local Christian community on the part of the individual Jewish families living an isolated life in the villages and towns. Jewish immigrants to New York in the first half of the eighteenth century, in search of wider opportunity and less competition, occasionally pushed across the border to the neighboring state of Connecticut. Naturally, the degree of assimilation to which they were exposed in their new environment varied with the individual and the circumstances. Anshil Troib re-

---

who may be the Isaac Pinto who translated the Hebrew prayer book into English, 1766 (*PAJHS*, XXX, No. 47, p. 58). 1757, August: Jacob Pinto supplied a horse for the defense of Fort William Henry and parts adjacent (Connecticut State Library, Ms. Archives, War, 1675–1774, Vol. VII, Doc. 36, pp. a–b). 1758, May: a committee of the Assembly was appointed to determine how many serviceable arms were available. Mr. Pinto, of New Haven, had ten weapons (*ibid.*, War, 1675–1774, Vol. VII, Doc. 213); Isaac Solomon(s) had one gun (*ibid.*, Vol. VIII, Doc. 15). This Jew, of whom we know very little, was a member of Shearith Israel in New York in 1749 (*PAJHS*, XXI, 60) and was engaged in litigation in Connecticut in 1748 (*The Public Records of the Colony of Connecticut*, IX, 522). He is there listed as dwelling in Middletown. Solomon also sold supplies to Jabez Hamlin, commissary for the troops of the Colony of Connecticut in the expedition against Canada, 1760–1761 (Connecticut State Library, Ms. Archives, War, 1675–1774, Vol. IX, Docs. 100, 261). 1759, October: Jacob and Solomon Pinto as part of the First [Church] Society in New Haven (*The Public Records of the Colony of Connecticut*, XI, 325). 1768: The Pinto store on the long wharf at New Haven (*ibid.*, XIII, 37–38). 1775, July: Abraham Pinto's service in the 10th Company, 7th Regiment, payroll (Connecticut State Library, Revolutionary War, 1763–1789, Series I, Vol. IIC, Doc. 43, pp. b–c). 1776, May: Pintos as land appraisers: *The Public Records of the Colony of Connecticut*, XV, 350. 1777, April 15–23: Jacob Pinto as appraiser of army blankets purchased (Connecticut State Library, Revolutionary War, 1763–1789, Series I, Vol. XI, Docs. 129, 130, 143). 1780, December 31: payroll of Capt. Hall's Company of the 7th Connecticut Regiment. Made up by Ensign Solomon Pinto (*ibid.*, Vol. XVII, Doc. 22). 1783, September 22: Jacob Pinto was among those who signed a petition asking for rights of incorporation for the town of New Haven (*ibid.*, Towns and Lands, 1629–1770, Series I, Vol. X, Doc. 1, pp. a–d). 1784, October: recommendations in report of committee on tax abatement for the New Haven sufferers in the Tryon raid of 1779. Relief given to Jacob Pinto (*ibid.*, Revolutionary War, 1763–1789, Series I, Vol. XXVII, Doc. 336, pp. a–c). 1786, October 4: interesting memorial of citizens of New Haven and Hamden with respect to catching and shooting wild pigeons for food and sale, signed by Jacob Pinto (*ibid.*, Industry, 1708–1789, Series I, Vol. II, Doc. 67, pp. a–d). 1787, September 11: will of Jacob Pinto. Codicil, January 14, 1806. Proved, 1806 (*ibid.*, New Haven district, No. 8285; includes inventory of February 17, 1806.)

luctantly surrendered most of his Jewish affiliations and
ethno-religious habits, and as Andris Trube was certainly
given a Christian burial. Of Mordecai Marks we know even
less. As with the Pintos and the Judahs, his children were
Christians or Gentiles by the second generation.

Michael Judah was hardly typical in his attempt to maintain himself as a Jew, even under the most difficult of circumstances. He could save himself "Jewishly," but not his child.
He stubbornly persisted, living and dying as a Jew. Among
the articles found in his pitifully meager inventory of belongings was a "killing knife," certainly a *halif* used by the shohet
in slaughtering animals. Apparently he attempted to provide
himself with kosher meat and poultry. In his will he left his
son, David, £5. Was this the bulk of his possessions? Or is it
too farfetched to assume that he was dissatisfied with this his
only child, his circumcised son, David, who had moved to
Fairfield, married a Gentile, and had broken completely with
the traditions of the fathers? Michael left his estate to the
Jewish people of New York: one half to the synagogue and
the other half to the poor widows and orphans of the community. His burial took place in New York and the expense
incurred was paid for by another dead man! Isaac Adolphus,
another Jew, had died owing Judah money, and when the
Norwalk merchant was buried in 1786 the congregation
merely asked Hayman Levy, the administrator of Adolphus'
estate, to pay the expense of Judah's burial. It was just like a
bill of exchange, no problem at all.

Even though Michael cut his son David off with £5, he
was hardly penalizing him very severely, unless there were
assets of which we do not know, for Michael died impoverished as a victim of the currency inflation caused by the Revolution. His inventory of household and other belongings
was appraised at £8. Just about the time the war was in full
swing, he found himself in possession of about £1,200, the
result of a lifetime's work and saving. With this tidy little
sum he was assured of a modest degree of comfort in his old
age. His wife, it would seem, had already died. But after the

war broke out and inflation set in he tried to protect himself by putting his money into goods, something substantial. With the permission of the authorities, he brought in a load of sugar in 1777, sold it at a profit, but decided this time to hold on to his paper money, confidently expecting that it would soon be stabilized. It was a vain hope. He lost practically everything he had . . . and now he was an old man. In his desperation he turned to the men who had helped him after the British raid of July, 1779, to Lopez and Rivera in Newport, telling them that his financial situation was very bad and that he could not go to New York for supplies: "You are gentlemen that has goods on hand and willing to do all the good you can to people under misfortune," he wrote. "I beg that you will befriend me to let me have a small assortment of goods." [18]

We do not know what Lopez and Rivera did for Judah. It is not safe to assume that following their natural bent they gave Michael a line of credit. The last years of the war were hard years for the Newport Jewish merchants. While they were trying to straighten out their accounts and to collect some of their debts, they found to their dismay that their

---

18. Michael Judah: *PAJHS*, XI, 90, 93; XXI, 47 (loan of money from the congregation, 1744–1745), 150; XXVII, 247; 1768, April 26: bond of Michael Judah as guardian of his son, David (Connecticut State Library, Norwalk district, No. 3496). Petition to bring in a load of sugar: July 7, 1777 (Hinman, *Historical Collection*, p. 459; *The Public Records of the State of Connecticut*, I, 344). 1784, December 31: will of Michael Judah; proved April 3, 1786. Inventory, April, 1786 (Connecticut State Library, Norwalk district, No. 3498). 1780, November 26: letter of Michael Judah, Norwalk, to Jacob R. Rivera and Aaron Lopez, Leicester (?), Ms. in archives of the American Jewish Historical Society; printed in Appendix III. For details of marriages and births in the Judah family, see D. L. Jacobus, *History and Genealogy of the Families of Old Fairfield* (1932), p. 559.

David Judah: circumcision: *PAJHS*, XXVII, 151. As soldier: *PAJHS*, XI, 92. As a leader of the Fairfield citizenry, petitioning the State Legislature with respect to road changes and bridge building affecting Fairfield: Connecticut State Library, Ms. Archives, Travel, 1670–1788, Series II, Vol. I, Doc. 73, pp. a–b, 1796–1798?; *ibid.*, Vol. XV, Doc. 77, pp. a–h, October 16, 1797; *ibid.*, Vol. XV, Doc. 81, pp. a–g, April 27, 1798. This last petition was signed only by David Judah and Walter Bradley as agents for the town of Fairfield. Mention is also made here of Beerses' and Judah's wharf at Saugatuck Stores.

clients and agents, instead of sending remittances, were seeking to borrow still further or to secure additional stocks of goods. For example, in August, 1781, Lopez was favored with a recital of hard times in a letter from one of his customers, Joseph De Pass, a merchant, now living in Woodstock, Connecticut.

De Pass, a Sephardic Jew, may have wandered in from Charleston, South Carolina, where there had been a family of this name since 1738. Finding himself unable to pay Lopez, he conceived the brilliant, but not quite original idea of asking for more credit. Whether he got it or not, he managed to pull through this economic crisis. Shortly after the death of Lopez, he was engaged in business in Newport—he may originally have come from Newport to Woodstock—where he became an active member and supporter of the local synagogue. He prospered in trade, for when the Lopez assets were liquidated about 1790, the shoe was found to be on the other foot: De Pass was now a creditor, and in order to satisfy a debt owed to him, the executors were forced to sell 14,473 Continental dollars. They brought in less than £4 in real money.[19]

Most of the refugees who crossed into Connecticut kept going until they had put a few miles behind them. Émigrés like to stay close, but not too close to the scene of their hurried departure. One of the men who fled and who was described by his contemporaries as "a decided friend of American independence" was an exception to this rule we have laid down. He hugged the border at Stamford from which vantage point he could watch what was going on and at the same time keep an eye on his holdings in the big city. This was the merchant Manuel Myers.

So far as we know, he was not related to the Myers-Mears-Simson clan, although, like them, he was of Ashkenazic origin. Fürth, in Bavaria, was very probably his original home;

19. De Pass: B. A. Elzas, *The Jews of South Carolina* (Philadelphia, 1905), p. 27; *PAJHS*, XXVII, 185; XXXV, 142. The letter of De Pass, Woodstock, Connecticut, August 15, 1781, to Aaron Lopez is published as Appendix IV.

his family was still there. Two sisters still dwelt in that town as did daughters and sons of two deceased sisters. In this distinguished and aristocratic community, his sisters had married into the best families. One of his brothers-in-law was a judge (dayyan), the other, a son of a judge and a descendant of Lipmann Heller, one of the greatest rabbinic figures of seventeenth-century Europe. Obviously, Manuel Myers himself came of an excellent and learned family.

It was some time in the early 1750's that he arrived in the colonies, and by 1759 he was both a naturalized citizen and a freeman of the city of New York. His first wife, Miriam, was a daughter of Abraham Pinto—the shohet, no doubt— and thus he may well have been a brother-in-law, or a relative, of Jacob Pinto. But what a difference in their religious careers! Jacob Pinto ended up a deist or atheist; Manuel Myers, who had some Hebrew training, ended up a synagogue president. By the time of his death in the year 1799, he had served more terms as parnas than any of his predecessors; by 1776, he had already served in that office for three terms.

When he left New York to go to Stamford, he was already a man in his fifties who had made his mark in life. It was no easy decision for him to leave his business, his property, and other valuables, and simply walk out. It would have been much easier for him as a man of substance to make his peace with the enemy, but he was too devoted a patriot to do this.

Exile in Stamford was worse than he had anticipated. Because it was almost impossible to earn a livelihood, he finally decided to make the attempt to return to New York and collect in wares and merchandise the debts due him. Some of the best people in the city owed him money: Nicholas Low, Roger Morris, one of the DePeysters, a Livingston, a Pintard, and a number of others less notable in name. In order to bring in goods from a neighboring state, however, it was first necessary to procure authorization from the General Assembly, the state legislature. Accordingly, he wrote to the Assembly, pointing out the fact that much of his property had

been destroyed by fire in New York and that he had an aged
mother and a brother-in-law to support. He fortified this request with a strong letter of recommendation signed by a
high state official, by the justices of the peace, and by the
selectmen of Stamford. Yet in spite of his need and the need
of the community for supplies, his appeal was negatived in the
Lower House. But in his case all things turned out well in the
end. He survived to return to his beloved New York, where
he occupied the finest and most expensive pew in Shearith
Israel and there again assumed the presidency for another
seven terms, finally dying in office. It was a pleasant ending
for the octogenarian patriot.[20]

After the war was over, Manuel Myers, it seems, was
rather slow in settling his affairs in Connecticut, for his return
to New York is not documented till the spring of 1785, over
a year after Guy Carleton had evacuated the city. By the
spring of that year, Myers was back in his beloved syna-

---

20. Biographical data for Manuel Myers: *PAJHS*, VI, 102; XIII, 6;
XVIII, 105; XXI, 85, 147, 168, 211; XXVII, 122. His brother Jacob lived
probably in Philadelphia during the Revolution. Jacob died in 1782 or 1783
(Ms. minutes of Mikveh Israel, Philadelphia, for 1783; copy of minutes in
American Jewish Archives, Cincinnati, Ohio).
Like other Jews in colonial times—Samuel Jacobs, of St. Denis, Canada,
for instance—Manuel incorporated his name in Hebrew script in his civil
name as a sort of cryptogram. Andris Trube, of Fairfield, did it also, only
he wrote his name in Hebrew script above his Latin script name. The Hebrew signature for Manuel Myers reads *Menil*, which is the transliteration
of his English signature "Manel." Manuel Myers' official signature may be
found in an interrogatory or deposition he signed (*Isaac Gomez, etc.* vs.
Louis Le Guen, etc., dated January 10, 1799, Library of Congress, Division
of Manuscripts, Hamilton Legal Papers, No. 94329). See also *PAJHS*, XVII,
66. 1782, January 7: memorial of Manuel Myers, Stamford, to the Connecticut General Assembly (Connecticut State Library, Ms. Archives, Revolutionary War, 1763–1789, Series I, Vol. XXIII, Doc. 286; accompanying letter
of recommendation, *ibid.*, Doc. 287; list of debts due him, *ibid.*, Doc. 288).
This memorial is printed as Appendix V. 1799, May 13: will of Manuel
Myers; proved May 28 (*Abstracts of Wills on File in the Surrogate's Office,
City of New York, Collections of the New-York Historical Society*, XXXIX,
156–57). This will indicates his wife's name was Judith, obviously a second
wife, since Miriam Pinto Myers had died in 1781 (*PAJHS*, XVIII, 122). He
had no surviving children. His Fürth connections are also described in the
will. For the importance of his Fürth relatives, see *Jahrbuch der jüdisch-
literarischen Gesellschaft*, VIII, 140–41. Ephraim Hart, Manuel Myers' executor, one of New York's outstanding merchants, was also a Fürth compatriot.

gogue, complaining that the functionary then in power had refused to grant him the religious honors to which he was entitled. After a protest was made, a committee was appointed to study the matter. In the narrow little world in which those men lived, such slights assumed huge proportions. The report which the committee brought in suggested that the injustice be corrected. The three men who made this recommendation were Abrahams, the mohel, who was also a businessman, Myer Myers, the silversmith, and his brother-in-law, Solomon Simson, the highly respected and wealthy merchant.

As far back as 1706, there was a Simson doing business in New York. In that year, Nathan Simson had come from London. A number of years later, initiating or continuing a pattern which was typical of American Jewish life, he brought over his twenty-two-year-old nephew, Joseph, the father of Samson and Solomon Simson. Samson, who seems to have been the real builder of the family fortune, died in 1773, at which time Solomon took over the conduct of the company which concerned itself with furs, shipping, candle manufacturing, and a general merchandise business which offered almost anything from a package of sarsaparilla to a cargo of mahogany.

During the war Solomon and his aged father, Joseph, had lived and wandered and done business in half a dozen Connecticut towns rather than remain in Tory New York. One of Solomon's sons was born in Danbury; Wilton knew the family for a time, and it was in nearby Norwalk that the Simsons were plundered in the raid of 1779. The eternal pursuit to make both ends meet during those troublous times brought Solomon to Stamford in the western corner of the state and to Lebanon in the east.

It was no small concern that led Simson to come to the little village of Lebanon in 1782. The town was by no means obscure in those days. In a way it was the unofficial capital of the state during the war years, for this was the home of Governor Jonathan Trumbull. Here in the little red two-room

house, the War Office, the Council of Safety met to deliberate on matters of import, and here it was that the New York
merchant came to see the governor. They had probably met
before this; both were active businessmen, and—this is only
a guess—the governor may have sought enlightenment from
Simson on some knotty problem of Hebrew grammar. Solomon's father, Joseph, was a good Hebraist.

It was not Hebrew, however, but salt, precious salt, that
brought the merchant to this distant village. He had some
time before this received a permit from the Council of Safety
to ship goods into the state but now felt that this certificate
would not give him the protection he needed to bring in a
cargo of salt. The British patrols were too numerous to risk
running the blockade; equally bad were the Connecticut privateers who seized ships first and asked questions later. He
was between the devil and the deep blue sea. There can be no
question that he was well aware of the anguish—and this is
literally true—which almost crushed the urbane Lopez as he
fought to rescue his valuable cargo in the *Hope*, which had
been seized by the voracious Connecticut prowlers in 1778.
That was four years before and in spite of favorable Con-
gressional and state court decisions, Lopez, by October,
1782, had still not received his schooner or merchandise. Simson wanted to take no risk like this on his precious shipment
of almost 1,500 bushels of salt. The solution to this problem
was clear: let his salt be brought in under a flag of truce. This
was more easily asked than granted, for in one of his numerous letters to his friend the governor, Washington had
frowned upon a too liberal use of this device. The flag was
not granted in spite of the fact that Nathaniel Wales, an important member of the Council of Safety, had assured him
that he would be doing his country a service by bringing in a
quantity of this valuable commodity at a time when it was so
sorely needed. It was up to Simson now to drop the project
or to risk his cargo between the Scylla of British cruisers and
the Charybdis of Connecticut privateers. He gambled and
lost. The privateers grabbed his prize and brought it into

Stamford harbor. In order to secure redress he wrote to the governor from New Haven, October 9, 1782, seeking his help to recover his boat and whatever was left of its load. He had now learned the lesson—if he needed to learn it—that fellow-patriots may often be as troublesome as the enemy . . . if not worse.

Two days later, back in Fairfield, he wrote again to Trumbull, but this time he was not seeking justice for himself, but mercy for another. He pleaded with the governor to permit the return to the state of an Episcopalian lay reader by the name of Henry Van Dyck. Some time during the war—it was in 1779—this man, who was opposed to taking up arms on either side, had left Stratford for New York with the permission of the Connecticut authorities, but while in that city had taken the opportunity more than once to help secure the release of patriots imprisoned there by the British. Now that the conflict was practically over—Cornwallis had surrendered almost a year before—Van Dyck wished to return and asked Simson to intervene with the chief executive on his behalf. Simson was only too happy to come to the aid of a man who, though not a patriot, was yet a person of character and integrity. It must have been a source of satisfaction to him when the State Assembly permitted Van Dyck and his family to return to their home in Stratford.[21]

---

21. Data on the Simsons in Connecticut: *PAJHS*, XI, 91; XVIII, 106, 209; XXV, 90; XXVII, 371; XXXIII, 202. Simson as possible part owner of the Middletown lead mine: see the Henshaw report quoted above. That the Simsons had business relations with the chemist J. S. Stephany—who was also one of the owners of the Middletown mine—is evidenced by the will of Joseph Simson, the father of Solomon (*Collections of the New-York Historical Society*, XXXVIII, 218–19. The will was dated November 5, 1781). Henshaw also consulted a chemist at Bound Brook, New Jersey: Ramsamen. This man is certainly identical with the well-known Bavarian chemist, Jacob Rubsamen, whom Ezekiel and Lichtenstein, in their *History of the Jews of Richmond*, pp. 336–42, consider a Jew. Judging, however, by the names of a sister and a brother, the family was Christian, unless, as converts to Christianity, they had taken on Christian names. The Simsons as merchants: Walter Barrett, *The Old Merchants of New York City* (New York, 1870), II, 2, pp. 234, 240. For Lebanon, Connecticut, during the Revolution, see *Connecticut* [American Guide Series] Boston, 1938), pp. 413–15. The letters of Solomon Simson, 1782: October 9, Solomon Simson, New Haven, to Governor Jonathan Trumbull; same to same, Fairfield,

Although no attempts were ever made, as far as we know, to build a permanent Jewish settlement in Connecticut prior to the mid-nineteenth century, Jewish merchants and traders had been establishing themselves in the different Connecticut towns and villages ever since the mid-1600's. In the next century, moving into the colony from Rhode Island on one side and from New York on the other, they dotted the landscape from Woodstock in the east to Stamford in the west. It is certain that most of these immigrants stayed but a short time —it is the accident of an obscure letter, a voucher, or a court entry that betrays their presence—and then returned to the neighboring Jewish communities of Newport or New York City. They realized that if they treasured any hope of remaining as Jews, of continuing a Jewish family life, there was no future for them in the monolithic religious and social life of Christian Connecticut. If they stayed—and a number of individual families did remain—they were destined to disappear as Jews in the overwhelmingly Christian environment in which they found themselves. They might struggle to maintain the cherished faith, and even to rear their children as Jews, but the struggle was a hopeless one.

The one chance to create a congregation came during the Revolution, when a number of patriots fled from Newport and New York and settled in Fairfield County. But these families of merchants and shippers remained in the state only for the duration of the war. There was no incentive to tarry in a community where they had no roots, no institutions, no great economic hinterland; there was every reason to go back to their original homes, to their synagogues, and to their communities: to Newport, the second largest town in New England, and to New York, the second or third largest port in the country. They did not hesitate to abandon their

---

October 11, 1782, in Connecticut State Library, Trumbull papers, M.H.S., 1631–1784, Vol. XVII, Doc. 127, pp. a–b; Doc. 132, p. a. These two letters are printed as Appendix VI. For Henry Van Dyck, see *The Public Records of the State of Connecticut*, IV, 305. Also, Samuel Orcutt, *History of Stratford*.

temporary asylum where their economic future was precarious in order to return to familiar surroundings where opportunity was sure and the future certain.

APPENDIX I

A

Norwalk, January 13th, 1779.

Dear Sir:

I hope this may find you safe at your journey's end, and that success may crown your undertaking is my sincerest wishes. Since your departure, I have made an inquiry relative to the sundry matters we were talking about, and I find that I may be able to purchase some flaxseed for two dollars, tho some people asks more. I found a person possessed of seven or eight hundred bushels of last year's seed, but he holds it at two dollars and will not take less. I offered him one and a half, but I don't expect to get it at that. However, if I find there is no probability of collecting it at less than your limitation, I shall not hesitate in giving it, as there is a person in this township that is erecting an [linseed] oil mill in a large way, and I expect he will give it a start [by buying this flaxseed and paying the price].

With respect to the velvets, I find there will be a chance to vend forty or fifty pieces. That which is wove plain thread will fetch from twelve to fifteen dol'rs, and that which is twilled, from twenty upwards. Middling and coarse cloths, woolen stuffs of every kind, trimings, worsted stockings, and all kind of men's ware will answer. The kind of salt you have will not sell for so much as the coarser and brighter sort, tho it will readily exchange for flaxseed.

I am informed of so many difficulties attending the geting flour out of New York State that I am apprehensive I shall not be able to procure any to send by the return teams you intend ordering this way, and there is no possibility of obtaining a permit to carry any out of this state that's raised in it. If it's possible to get it from New York State my endeavours shall be imploy'd.

My brother [-in-law Solomon] Simson and his family with the rest of my connexions here begs your acceptance of their respectful regard, and, believe me, none with greater warmth than your much esteem'd friend and most

Humble servant,
SAMSON MEARS.

Price Curr't
Sugar £60
Rum W[est]. I[ndia].: 18 dol'rs, ris[in]g.
Do. Cont[inenta]'l, 10 a 12 do-[llars].
Mad[eir]a. wine, 12 do.
Ten[erif]f.[e] and Fay[l] do. 8 a 9 dol'rs.
Best foreign salt, 40 do.
Home made 20
Tea 12 a 14 do.

To MR. AARON LOPEZ

B

Norwalk, January 20th, 1779.

Mr. Aaron Lopez,
Dear Sir:

Yesterday came here a team load of two h[ogs]h[ea]'ds of merchandize, one of spirits, and two barrs of lead, forwarded by Mr. Josiah Blakeley of Hartford. He informs me he could not procure a team to carry it further than this place. I have sent out to engage one to carry it on to you, which shall be done with all the despatch the nature of the season will admit of. Tho I had no acco[un]'t what the h[ogs]h[ea]'d of spirit should contain, yet I thought it necessary to examine the contents, and found by an inch rule (not having a gu'ging rod) a wantage of five and one-quarter inch's, of wh'h I advised Mr. Blakeley by the return of the teamster with whom he is to settle. I also discovered several spoil holes about the h[ogs]h[ea]'d and shewed them to the teamster who seemed to know nothing of it. However, if the loss is sustained between this [Norwalk] and Hartford, I make no doubt proper steps will be taken by Mr. Blakeley.

In my last of the 13th cur[ren]'t p'r post, to wh'h be pleased to be refered, I mention'd a person's having seven or eight hundred bushles of flaxseed, which Mr. [Solomon] Simson and self found to be very good. I have purchased it at two dollars, which I shall continue to do till I have got your quantity. The teamster delivered me two of your caps, a worsted and a linen one. He says Mr. Blakeley desired him to call at a place between this and Hartford for your overhalls and book where he had forwarded them, but he forgot the place and taking a different road has not brought them. If they come to hand before I send off the team (wh'h I very much doubt) they shall be sent along [to Philadelphia].

Mr. Simson and family joins in our best respects, and be assured I am, with esteem, d[ea]'r sir, your friend and h[um]'ble serv't,

SAMSON MEARS.

Rum is at 20 dol'rs and rising. A parcel of ready made buckskin breeches will sell well from forty-five to sixty dollars pr [pair], and some ready dress'd skins, some sheep skin breeches also will do.

C

Norwalk, January 28th, 1779.

Mr. Aaron Lopez,
Dear Sir:

My last of the 20th curr't p'r post advised you that I had sent out to engage a team to carry your goods forward, but I have met with no success yet. The badness of the roads at present and the distance of the journey are the objections made by those I have spoke to. My best endeavours shall be continued to forward them along as soon as possible.

I recollect you to have said when you was here that your motive for transporting a h[ogs]h'd of rum to Philad'a was purely to make up a load with the other goods. Concluding that to have been your stimulation, and not knowing the low market of that article there, to what it is here, and since it has come to my knowledge of the very great detriment it will be to you by sending it from so great a market as is here for it, to so poor a one at Phil'a, I should not think I discharged that duty due to our friendship if I was to persue your orders in sending it along, judging that if you thought your counter-orders would reach me in time, I should have had them.

From these considerations, togeth'r with the great risque attending such an article's going that distance, exposed to pilferage and adulteration (which I suspect it has already undergone), are strong inducements for me to embrace the prospect I have of obtaining twenty-two or twenty-three dollars a gallon, and perhaps more, in preference to what I am well informed it is at in Phil'a, by very late accounts, of eighty-seven shilling. So that I hope the step that I mean to take, to save a sacrifise of so considerable a sum as would prove a dead loss by the difference of prices, will be warranted by the principles of friendship (that in this case entirely dictates), tho I may stand condemned by the strict rules of mercantile matters. And I flatter my self so far with your indulgence as to avoid your censure and merit your approbation when I assure you the advancement of your interest was my sole object in deviating so far from the orders you left me.

Mr. James Jarvis told me he has about £2,500 in Phil'a which he would be glad to have in a bill [of exchange], and if you find the money will be of any service to you there, he will take your bill for it. On which subject he will write you and transmit an order if you chuse to make use of it.

The enclosed letter accompanied your goods here, and as I judged it only related to them, and having an expectation of forwarding them on immediately, was the reason I did not forward it p'r last post, reserving it to go with them, and as it's uncertain how long it will be ere they go on, and lest it might contain some other matter you may want to be advised of, I now forward it.

I have not since your absence been favor'd with any advice from your families. That I may soon have that pleasure from them and your self, is the wish of, dear sir,

Your faithful friend and most h'ble serv't,

SAMSON MEARS.

Mr. Simson and the rest of our families kind remembrance to you.

D

Norwalk, February 16th, 1779.

Mr. Aaron Lopez,
Dear Sir:

In my way to Stratford the 5th ins't I took up your esteemed favor of the 18th ult'o advising me of your safe arrival at Philadelphia and that your counsel'rs [James Wilson, later a Justice of the United States Supreme Court, and William Lewis] had given you some favorable expectations of success in your appeals [in the case of the schooner *Hope*], which I hope may soon be terminated agreeable to their expectations and your sanguine wishes.

A letter Mrs. [Isaac or Gershom] Seixas received while I was at Stratf'd from her husband, under date of 26th ult'o, by which she understood you was to have set out from Phil'a the next day, prevented my answer'g your letter p'r last post. And by a letter from Stratford yesterday I am informed it was a mistake Mrs. Seixas made in perusing her letter, which was instead of your seting out it was your going out if the weather was fair, after your confinement of which I was sorry to hear, tho hope your indisposition has been slight and only owing to the fatigue you say you underwent on your journey.

I observe you had ordered you[r] son to forward this way some salt, etc. When it comes it shall have my strict attention to improve it to your best advantage, tho the call for salt has much subsided lately. The additional arrivals to what was already here has made it a dull article at present, and has occationed it to fall something. Therefore I have stopt buying flaxseed for cash in order that I may the readyer get off the salt for it when it comes.

My letter of 28th ult'o will inform you I had anticipated your
orders respecting your h[ogs]h'd
of spirits and set forth my motives
that led me to it, and I am happy
to find my steps coincided so much
with your intentions, and previous
to the receipt of your letter, I embraced the opportunity I had of
dispos'g of it at twenty-four dollars. It guaged one hundred and
nineteen gallons, nine of which
was wanting. The lead I have had
no call for yet.

The remaining two h[ogs]h'ds I
have been constantly endeavouring
to forward and have rode a circle
of twenty miles round and could
not prevail on a person to under-
take the journey at this season. I
could get several to go so far as
the North River but not beyond
it, and they talk of having four
dollars a mile.

Unless your velvits will command an exceeding high price in
Philadel'a, I think they would neet
you an equal profit here without
that additional expence, for if they
are of the twilled kind they will
exceed your limitation on those
you have ordered here for sale.

Snuff and tobacco (some manu-
factured into pigtail) [twist] is
much wanted and will fetch:
twenty shilling, snuff, pigtail,
twelve shilling, if such a speculation is worthy your notice with
some other articles that you may
find answerable by the annexed
price current. Mr. [Solomon] Simson and I will join you in a purchase. The money Mr. Jarvis has
tendered at your service for a bill
on Boston will answer for the purpose.

Mr. Simson with his and families
best respects acknowledges the favor you was pleased to distinguish
him with in your address conjunc-
tively with my self, and we are
happy that the notice you justly
merited from us has been so kindly

received. We are wishful that you
will on your return home give us
a fresh occation to express the
friendsh'p and esteem with which I
have the pleasure of subscribing
my self and in behalf of Mr. Simson,
Your most ob't and very humble
serv't,

SAMSON MEARS.

Mr. and Mrs. [Moses] Isaacks's
best regard attends you with their
prayers for your prosperity, with
both the Mr. Myers's [Asher and
Myer] and their family's.

Price Cur't:
Sugar £50
Rum £6
Molases 72s
Foreig. salt £7.10
Tea 72s
Tobacco £18
Snuff 20s
Indigo 42s
Gineva [gin] (home made) 84s
Coffee 14s
Black pepper 30s
Writ'g paper £12

E

Norwalk, February 23d, 1779.

Mr. Aaron Lopez,
Dear Sir:
The bearer intending to set off
tomorrow morning for Phil'a just
gives me an opportun'y to acknowledge the rec't of your favor
of the 2d ins't and to advise you
I have this day engaged a waggon to set off tomorrow with your
goods. Having already wrote you
this day at large to accompany the
goods, have nothing further to offer than that if you have not got
any load to send back, nor are in-
clineable, either on yours or our
joint account, to send any, to let

Mr. Nathan Bush [of Philadelphia] know of it, as I have given him directions in your absence to procure a load on my accou't, which he can be geting ready by the time the waggon gets in. In case you sho'ld incline to benefit by it, it would be most agreeable to me that you should, and I will annex the articles I order'd him to procure, to wh[ic]'h be pleased to be refer'd, and accept of the cordial esteem of, d'[ear] sir,

Your assured friend and h'ble serv't,

SAMSON MEARS.

1/4 hund'd iron wire assorted from the size of a coarse kniting needle to the size of card wire and a less qu'ty of smalest size.
A small box of short pipes.
150 w't of best pigtail and 50 w't hogt'l tobacco, and the remainder in the best Scotch snuff.
If no pipes and wire to be had, that difficiency to be made up in snuff.

F

Norwalk, February 23d, 1779.

Mr. Aaron Lopez,
Dear Sir:

Yesterday your favor of 2d current came to hand. Mine of the 16th ins't will acknowledge the receipt of yours of the 18th ult'o with advice of the sale of your rum at twenty-four dollars, and for its further contents be pleased to be refered to the same.

From the sudden change and fall of the article of salt you need not regret that you did not order more of it this way for the present. It has become a great drugg for the cash which will, I apprehend, affect the favorable prospects I had some time ago of bartering it for flaxseed. The little call there is for the latter is the chief dependence I have of putting off the salt. The other articles I still have an expectation of vending to a good advantage.

I am glad to have your approbation of the purchase of the seven or eight hundred bushles of flaxseed and shall duly attend to your further instruction on that matter.

The uncertain situation your letter left you in with respect to your depending causes [before the Continental Congress in Philadelphia] must have been truly irksome to you. But I hope the grand contest between the two great courts [of the Continental Congress and the Connecticut Court of Admiralty] has been decided in such a manner as for the Court of Appeals [Committee on Appeals of the Continental Congress] to proceed on your matters, and that ere this you've reason to praise the Supreme Judge of the Universe for inspiring them with the principles of extending that justice to you (with an ample recompence for every difficulty you have been obliged to encounter) which the nature of your cause merits.

I have at last engaged with a person to carry your goods on to Philadelphia on as reason'ble terms as possible. He would go on no other footing than to have so much for his person and waggon and his expenc[e]ss bore. And not having any other prospect, and anxious of forwarding them along lest you should suffer by a further delay, I came to the following terms: to allow him two hundred and fifty dollars and pay the expences of his horses and self. With this reserve, that in case you should have any load for him to return with, he is to take it, and if not exceeding four hundred w't, he is to have one hundred and fifty dollars, and if it is six hundred w't, he is then to have two hundred dollars in addition to the two hundred and fifty. And as it is uncertain wether he will find you there, or that you have left anything to be brought back, I have wrote to my kinsman, Nathan Bush, that if any snuff or pigtail tobacco can be bought so as to yield a profit, to load him back with some. But by no means is that to be done if you are yet there and are inclin'able to improve it solely on your own acco't, or jointly with Mr. Simson and self, which I would prefer. In that case, I am not confined to those articles but any others that you may find preferable for carriage and profit.

Should this man return not loaded, his and horses expences you'll have to bear back, but if any other person or himself loads him back, you will be free from that charge.

Wishing that your goods may be safely delivered and that success may reward all your toils is, with Mr. and Mrs. Simson's and the rest of my connexions best regard, the ultimate conclusion of, dear sir,

Your esteem'd friend and h'ble serv't,

SAMSON MEARS.

P. S. In case you load the waggon back I must beg the favor you'll let Mr. Heyman Levy [the New York and Philadelphia merchant] know it who may have about fifty w't of sheet copper to send Mr. Asher Myers. Your indulging him with a chance of conveyance in the waggon will be gratefully acknowlelged.

Finding that the person I wrote by the 16th was not gone yet nor does not go this week, I have taken my letter from him and here enclose it.

The rec[eip]'t for your goods is enclosed in Mr. Hows's letter lest you mig't not be there when they arrive.

G

Norwalk, April 4th, 1779.

Mr. Aaron Lopez,
Dear Sir:

I have before me your several favors of the 16 and 23d Feb'y, 2d, 11th, and 12th ult'o. The first mentioned came alltogether to hand the 13th ult'o owing to the irregularity of the post, and your mentioning in y'rs of 2d ult'o your intention of leaving Phil'a in ten days after, prevented my acknowledging the rec't of them in due time.

Your goods geting safe to your hands renders a particular reply to your three first favors needless, and what respects the removal of your flaxseed in yours of the 11th ult'o, shall be duly attended to as soon as I can get a sufficient number of casks ready for its removal. The detention of your salt etc. from the easward (wh'h is not yet arrived) and your late orders to stop purchasing flaxseed for cash, has protracted my purchasing any more than wh't I advised you of, the 20th Janu'y. I've no apprehension at present of its rising above two dollars.

I was put in possession of yours of the 21th ult'o with your goods by Marvin [the teamster], *Bispre de Pesah* [Passover Eve]. 'Till that very day, I was daily looking out for you, and my disappointment therein leads me to conclude you will not leave Phil'a till after *Pesah* [Passover], and therefore will give you a chance of receiving this before your departure from there.

The badness of the weather and roads occation'd Marvin a long journey, of course a very expensive one. His bill of expences amounted to three hundred and seven dol'rs. Tho it's extravagantly high, I hope his load will yield an adeq[uate] profit.

One of Marvin's bladders of snuff got broke [and] powdered the whole hogsh'd. All the rest was in good order. [I] was a little apprehensive of some damage done to the con[tents] of the bonnet-box, which induced me to open it but I foun[d it] had sustain'd no injury. Hogsh'd Vs, have not ope[ned] yet. It appears dry and in good order.

I was happy to hear the sale of the rum you appr[ove] of.

That you may accomplish the object of your journey [to] Phil'a and afford us an opportunity of congratulating you s[oon] on the occasion is, with the united regard of our families, [the] conclusion of, dear sir,

Your respected friend and very h'ble serv't,

SAMSON MEARS.

H

Norwalk, April 18th, 1779.

Mr. Aaron Lopez,
Dear Sir:

Last evening your esteem'd favor of 29th ult'o came to hand, and if mine of the 4th ins't reaches you before you leave Phil'a (wh'h I hope it may) you'll be advised of the safe arrival of your goods p'r Marvin and that no goods had then, nor is yet arrived from Seixes. What occations the delay I cannot account for. I've not been favor'd with a line from there a considerable time.

I wish my present advice coincided with your expectations of my meeting with a ready sale of your skins and breeches. The season is rather too far advanced for an immediate sale. Had they been here a month or six weeks sooner, the sale would have been more expeditious. And snuff is not so quick as it was.

A quantity has been brought here that has plentifully stocked us abo[u]'t this part of the country, and of course will retard the sale something. However, no advantageous oportu'y shall be neglected to invest it into cash so as to enable you to have it circulating agreeable to your desire. And when ever I am in cash for you, the mode you point out for remittance shall be punctually attended to.

You have, d'sir, Mr. Simson's and my sincere congratulations on the successful essue of one of your depending causes [before the Committee on Appeals, April 10], and that we may soon have the like occasion in the other our ardent wishes attends you, and for every success that you can wish for in the speculation your leasure hours at Phil'a induced you to. But we have to lament that that has been productive of the disappointment you have prepared us for in the happiness we promised ourselves by your revisiting us in your return home. But since that cannot be complied with without interfering with your interest, our friendship for you directs us to submit to it in hopes some future occasion will afford us a personal interview when it may be more to mutual advantage.

In expectation of seeing you here kep me silent on a letter I receiv'd the beginning of last month under date of 10 Feb'y from Mess'rs Mendes's, relative to your draft on Mr. [Isaac] Werden [a merchant in the West Indies] wh'h I purposed shewing you. And for your investigation of what they wrote me on the subject I shall quote you verbatim that part of their letter which refers to it and is as follows:

"The 27 July last was handed us your favors of the 1st Feb'y, and 4 March, 1778. Did not answer the same in proper time, having ever since done all our endeavours to get the bill on Mr. Werden return'd or protested. Our trouble has been needless, and cannot obtain any plain knowledge wether its paid, protested, or in being. We are greatly surprised your mentioning that you can not acco't for Mr. Vance's backwardness, giving us to understand that before the definition of this bill we cannot expect payment from you. Our disbursements were for your account, and every risque untill paid must naturally be likewise, particularly whilst you can not alledge the cause of your disappointment to us, for we can always prove you that we sent th't bill to the principlest merch't at Dominico [the British West India Island] and never had an answer from him of the reception. Therefore can not oblige him (for want of proof) to deliver up the bill protested or otherwise. But in order to try the result of this troublesome and disagreeable affair, you will be pleased to forward us a second, third, fourth, and fifth of the same tenor and date, at the reception of one of them will commission some attentive and faithful person to present the same to Mr. Werden. If it's noted shall know the reason, and in case he really has paid the bill to Mr. Vance, we may then call on him with propriety. Must likewise observe to you that by what we can learn, Mr. Werden and Mr. Vance are very intimate and have many connections together, and they will both try to delay this affair as long as they can; [this information is] for your government."

It seems but one of those drafts have come to their hands out of the three you drew. One of them must have miscarried; the other one I have, wh'h I herewith return and beg you'll be so obliging as to renew your draft on Mr. Werden either in the same tenor, or for the balance he sometime ago advised

you was due, with the interest that you said might go with it, in consideration of my being disappoint'd in that remittance, wh'h will serve to go towards the payment of the interest Mess'rs Mendes's charges me with, 10 p'c't, for their advance, the lawful interest of their island.

As you'll have an opportu'y for the West Indies from some of the eastern ports before I shall from here, and if it will make no difference to you, I should esteem it a favor if you will draw a sett of four or five in favor of Mess'rs Gebroeders [Brothers] Mendes and remit them with a few lines to them, directing when received to place the amount to my credit, or if that should not be agreeable to you, please to forward them to me, as I am anxious to close that matter with them as soon as possible.

An other desire I had of seeing you here was to have some personal consultation with you upon the pres[en]'t times and to have had your advice what to persue to take me out of the inactive state I am at present in.

Mr. Simson's being fixed here with his family would be sufficient to transact any matter you might find your interest to employ him in, while I would wish to fix my self in some place that create more exercise than this contracted spot. Therefore if you can find any employ for me that may redound to your interest, either by my going abroad, or at any part of this continent, I will gladly accept of it. The confidence I place in your abilities to advise, and friendship to serve me, will determine my steps.

In hopes that your next may be dated at your happy mansion (to where this is directed in consequence of the tenor of your last) and that it may import your happiness of meeting your worthy families in health, to whom the resp'tful regard of all ours here are joined to that of, dear sir,

Your highly esteem'd friend and very humble servant,
SAMSON MEARS.

I

Norwalk, April 28th, 1779.

Mr. Aaron Lopez,
Dear Sir:

I wrote you at large the 10th current which I hope you'll receive at home and to which I beg leave to refer you.

Mr. Cannon, our neighbour, intends setting out tomorrow morning for Boston and is so obliging to take charge of y'r bonnet-box of plumes in which you'll find a worsted and a linen cap, with a small p's of new linen that the teamster left here last winter with your velvets, etc., and which I forgot to send you by Mervin [the teamster]. I hope they will reach you in good order. For want of a p's of linen I had the box sewed in two of your sheep skins. By them you'll see the trim the others is in by the break'g of a bladder of snuff.

I have made no progress in the sale of your consignment from Philadel'a yet owing to the advanced season for the principle articles.

The sales of your rum and lead I have the pleasure now to transmit which hope may prove agreeable. The neet proceeds of £827.0.5 is carried to your credit. Among the cash rec'd for the rum there was ten 40 dollar bills of the 11th Ap'l, 1778, which since receiving them that emission will not pass current. Therefore I remit them now by the bearer, and wish I was in more cash for you to augment the sum by so favorable an opportunity.

You have, no doubt, ere this been informed of the cause that has detain'd the goods you order'd this way.

If the salt comes now, there is so little call for it at this season that I apprehend I shall be slow in exchanging it for seed. From what I can learn I don't expect I shall be able to obtain above thirteen or fourteen bushles of seed for one of salt. What seed I have purchased, still remains here from the difficulty of geting cask[s] made to transport it in. I have got some done but not near enough. I have engaged more but when they will be ready is very uncertain. They ask five and six dollars a p's for them.

I don't apprehend much danger here from the enemy, especially as it's near opening the campain, and they will have greater objects to attend to than this insignificant place. However, when I have the seed ready to move, and you continue in the desire to have it moved, it shall be done.

With the pleasing expectation of hearing from you soon, this concludes me, with the joint respects of all our families here to you and your worthy connexions,

Your assured friend and most humble servant,
SAMSON MEARS.

My best regard awaits Mr. and Mrs. Rivera. Please to let him know I honor'd my self in address'g him lately by Mr. Jarvis.

J

Norwalk, May 10th, 1779.

Mr. Aaron Lopez,
Dear Sir:

My letter of 28th ult'o p'r Mr. Cannon will inform you of my intention of sending your box of plumes by him. But he could not make it any ways convenient to fix it to his sulky and was obliged to leave it behind.

Captain Whitney in a fast sailing boat presents this day for Providence, and judging you are desireous of receiving it, and no prospect of sending it by land, induces me to venture it by him to the care of Mr. David Lopez, Jun'r, through which channel I hope it will come safe to hand. I have only to confirm what I wrote you last, and add the respectful regard of all our families to you and yours from, dear sir,

Your assured friend and very humble servant,

SAMSON MEARS.

P. S. Nothing yet arrived from your quarter.

We are to the 20th May, and I find the demand increases for salt. It's got up again to forty dollars the coarse kind. There has been one or two persons here abo't purchas'g the snuff. It's not being of the best quality they declined it. No sale yet for the breeches and skins.

K

Norwalk, July 4th, 1779.

Mr. Aaron Lopez,
Dear Sir:

Our mutual friend, Mr. Ab'm Jacobs [a nephew of Solomon Simson], put me in possession of your esteemed favor of 21st ult'o and with concern I observ'd the pain you say you was under in replying to my several letters. I hope the affliction that occasion'd it is ere now intirely removed. Your silence I put a pretty just construction on in which your favor confirm'd me.

Happy I am that I made so slow a progress in the sale of your effects. Through a desire of investing your property as soon as possible into cash, agreeable to your last

instructions, I had offered the articles at a much lower price than you are likely to obtain for them where you are. Notwithstanding that, the articles were so much out of season that they have (luckily for you) stuck on hand. All that is sold is the tobacco, the gloves, a pair of buckskin breeches, a sheep skin or two and seven or eight bladders of snuff. As I have not the least prospect of obtaining prices near what you quote, and for the safety of your interest, I shall make it my study to get them on to you with all expedition. They would have been on the way now but the busy season makes it a difficulty to procure a team. I had some time back offered your snuff at twenty shilling and could not dispose of it, and no favorable appearance at present will induce me to send that on with the rest, tho that will not make up a load.

I confess I never was more perplexed in what to employ my self than I am now; sick and tired of an idle life and wh't to persue with any appearance of stability and advantage to take me out of it. I am at a loss, and now appears new difficulties arrising to the southward and eastward by the threatening of restrictions on trade that adds to the confusion of the times. Is there nothing abroad that I can serve you and Mr. Rivera in? If there is, with what little capital I can collect of my own it may be some inducement to me to leave this continent for a while.

My last accounts from [the Island of Eu]Statia and Amster'm advised me authenticated copies of Continental notes were negociable there. Others and I have had orders to transmit them to a considerable amount to both those places, from which circumstance I am led to think some advantageous speculation may be persued that way with no risque out. A capital employed that way among a company (which some of my acquaintance here would willingly join), I make no doubt, would answer some essential purposes. We have a parcel of spermaceti candles by us that might be included, either by invest'g them into cash or bills, as it might best sute. If you have a favorable opinion of it, please to let me know as soon as possible, and I will wait on you in person and form a plan I think will be attended with success after I once get into the West Indies.

Your good disposition to advise me, I accepted kindly; the embarrassng period alone, I am perswaded, is what denies one that mark of your friendship. I hope and trust the grand source of all knowledge will direct us all for the best. I am further obliged to you for your punctual transmission of your additional drafts on Mr. Werden from which I hope will flow every desireable purpose. Your reason for continuing them in the same tenor is satisfactory, and I make no doubt will answer every purpose, it being foreign to my desire to have you exposed to the least injury. I could wish your conjectures would prove true of the affair being settled between Mr. Werden and my friend but I can't entertain the least idea it is so unless it's been very lately.

Mr. Simson joins in thanks for your good intentions of a mutual improvem't of our situation if the times were encouraging. Until it is, we only can assure you of our anxious desires to have it in our power to convince you by our services the advancement of your interest would ever be the actuating principles we would be governed by, and that you may ever experience the smiles of Providence in everything that concerns you is, with our joint regard to you, your worthy lady, and every other branch of your family, the wishes of, dear sir,

Your assured friend and very h'ble serv't,

SAMSON MEARS.

L

Wilton, October 8th, 1779.

Mr. Aaron Lopez,
Dear Sir:

Your esteemed favor of 3d and 6th ult'o have received some time, which I should have answered ere now, but my time has been greatly taken up in riding about the country to procure convenient places to house our families for the ensuing winter, and notwithstanding our assiduous endeavours, we have not been so fortunate as to obtain a single entire house [away] from the sea-coast. And rather than to go any great distance in the country for the sake of a room or two in a house with other families, we have concluded to accommodate ourselves in that manner within a few miles of this house and within the same township.

Your indulgent disposition, I flatter my self, will from the above reasons plead an excuse for my protracted reply to your favors and [for] the benevolence of your generous family towards the relief of the unhappy suffer[er]s of Norwalk (who ever anticipates the occasions of the distressed and this large donation fully evinces it) with the great share you have taken in our losses and distress. I am authorized by every one your intentions extended to, in the most grateful manner, to return their unfeigned thanks for this great mark of your friendship and sympathizing feelling.

Agreeable to the confidence you was pleased to honor me with in the distribution of the same, I embraced the earliest opportun'y after the receipt of your letters to inform the suffering brethren in general of your generous contribution. In consequence of which, I am desired by my brothers [-in-law], Myer and Asher Myers, to assure you they retain a grateful sense of your friendly intentions to them. And altho their losses have been severe, they are yet blesst with some means of making necessary provisions for their families, and therefore hope their refusal to a part will not be accepted as a slight to your favor, but purely from a conscentiousness that they do not stand in that need of it as some others, and therefore think it their duty to join your contribution by giving up any part they might be entitled to receive, that the benefit may extend the farther to those who does, which will centre with Mess'rs M[oses]. Isaacs, S[amuel]. Israel, and M[ichae]'l Judah.

While on a visit to Mr. Seixas, came to his hands, the 4th ins't., Mr. Jn. [?] Wiley's draft for £ 500 in his favor on Samuel Loudon at Fishkill, which I shall endeavour to procure payment of as soon as possible. In the meantime I shall advance whatever may be required, and when the bill is paid shall advise you of it and how disposed of.

I noticed in your letter refered to by Mr. M[oses M.]. Hays [the Newport merchant] that the continued calls of business to this state [touching on the schooner *Hope*] deprived me of the satisfaction of having a reply to my letters with that leasure you wished for. To matters of greater importance I chearfully give way and content my self if I can only hear of your wellfare and prosperity. The additional blessing to your family of a son gives me great pleasure to hear, on which occasion our family

heartily joins in congratulating you and your worthy connexions.

I am extremely sorry to hear of the loss you met with by the damage of your goods by Wentworth who had my strict injunction to carry the casks on their bulge and which he promised me to do. It's a pitty they were not examined immediately in the delivery of them, as then his neglect would have been discovered and the damage less, and then you might have stopt the amo't of the damage out of his freight, which I think he ought to forfeit for his carelessness.

I must yet beg your patience for your acco'ts as we have not yet collected our scattered effects among wh'h is my books and papers. In my next I hope to be able to convey it. In the interim beg leave to command our families united regard to you and your extensive connexions, and with the greatest sincerity am, d'r sir,

Your esteemed friend and very humble servant,

SAMSON MEARS.

M

Newport, November 24th, 1779.

Mr. Aaron Lopez,
Dear Sir:

I arrived here the 19th ins't and flattered myself with having the happiness of seeing you and part of your worthy family before you return'd home. The difficulty of procuring a horse proved that disagreeable disappointment.

I brought with me your accounts, which I was in hopes to have handed ere this, with a balance of £ 116.1.11¼ Lmo [lawful money] which is now held at your disposal. Judging it unnecessary of sending the acco'ts where you are, and a flattering expectation of seeing you soon, is the reason of my not sending them by this conveyance.

In the meantime, desireous of availing myself of your being at Boston, and of your friendly services, I am induced to beg the favor of you to let me know if there is a probability of disposing of one hundred boxes of spermacity cand's deliverable at Norwalk for hard money or good bills of exchange, and what price may be obtain'd. They are as yet disingaged, which I shall keep so till I hear from you, reserving a preference to you or any of your friends. I understand there is a few boxes in this town which they ask six shilling sterl'g for.

If it will not interfere too much with your more consequential concerns, I shall be highly obliged by hearing from you as soon as possible, as I am make'g some preparation to leave the Continent [North America, for the West Indies] in persuit of better fortune than I have met on it, and if I should be so happy as to be able to render you any services abroad no one will be more devoted to your commands.

In expectations of seeing you soon, I remain, dear sir,

Your devoted friend and most humble servant,

SAMSON MEARS.

N

Wilton, January 31st, 1780.

Dear Sir:

The Tuesday morning after leaving you and encountering a severe cold journey I had the happiness of joining our families here, who I found in great anxiety about my long absence.

The means I took to advise them of the cause fail'd, and of course their conjectures were many, some not of the most favorable kind. However, my arrival put an end to every painful feelling and gave way to the inexpressible enjoyment of embracing each other in perfect health.

My intention of going to New London was obstructed by the information I rec'd at the place, where I was to take that road, of its being shut up. The only road I could then take was from Hartford, which would have encreased my journey seventy miles. My being out so long, and the great risque I run of being as much longer detained out by an other fall of snow, and the infirmity of my horse, were strong inducements for me to avoid that and proceed home immediately and defer my business at New London for a future journey.

From the information I obtain'd on the road of the price of produce that way, coffee was mention'd at six dollars, so that if I had got there there was no probability of effecting your order respecting that article.

I cannot pass over in silence yours and every branch of your worthy family's friendly civilities during my stay at your hospitable house. It fills me with every sentiment of gratitude while I offer my grateful acknowledgments for the many kindness I have repeatedly received.

Our families begs their united regard to you, your good lady, and the rest of your family, while mine in a most particu'r manner attends them and your self with the greatest sincerity of, dear sir,

Your assured friend and most humble serv't,

SAMSON MEARS.

P. S. Should Capt. [Benjamin] Wright [your factor] yet be with you, please to make my best regard acceptable to him, and let him know my warmest wishes are for the restoration of his health, and that I shall be happy in the continuance of his friendship.

APPENDIX II

Peter Betts and Myer Myers, both of Norwalk in the County of Fairfield, of lawful age, testify and say that some short time after the Continental troops retreated from Long Island they were at a public house in said Norwalk where they saw Ralph Isaacs of New Haven and heard him and a gentleman called by the name of Hazzard conversing and disputing about the times.

And that in said conversation they heard said Isaacs declare that in the battle on Long Island the ministerial [British] army suffered or sustained a very inconsiderable or small loss, and the Continental troops sustained a very great loss. And that the Continental troops will not stand fire but always will give back, and that the people to the westward had come in [to the British] and numbers more would come in, meaning they would come in in the same m[anner?] the people have done in Long Island.

And these deponents say that from the conversation and declaration of s'd Ralph Isaacs it evidently appeared that he was of the opinion that wherever the British troops should pass, the people there would readily submit to them, and that said Isaacs's whole conversation was very discouraging with respect to success on the Continental side, and these deponents further say not.

Myer Myers.
Peter Betts.

Fairfield County, SS., Norwalk, 16th October, 1776.

Personally appeared Myer Myers and Peter Betts, the signers of the above deposition, and swore to the truth of the same.

Before me Tho's Fitch, Justice of Peace.

Opened in the General Assembly at New Haven, October, 1776, by George Wyllys, Secr'ty.

APPENDIX III

Norwalk, November the 28th, 1780.

Gentlemen:

As I am under nesessety, I hope you will excuse my boldness in addressing my self to you. I have done but little business this four years, and what little I have done has been done to disadvantage on account of the depreation of the money.

When these times begun I had about twelve hundred pounds, good money, that I could call my own, and as I had nothing else to depend upon but a little traffick to git a support, I laid it out in the

artickle of suger, and at that time expected to advance my self greatly by it, and kept them by me some time before I disposed of them.

Soon after I dispos'd of them the money bigun to depreciate fast, and by the advice of my friends I kept the money by me for some time, I expecting it would be good in time. But to my misfortune it sunk so fast that I got but little or nuthing for the hool [whole], as low as a penny for a doller. So that I have all most sunk my hool substance so that I am not able to carry on any business, and as I cannot go to New York for supplyes, and you are gentlemen that has goods on hand and willing to do all the good you can to people under misfortunes, I beg that you will befriend me, to let me have a small assortment of goods. I am so far advanc'd in years that if I don't do something, I shall soon spend what little I have left.

You may relye upon me that I will be puntual to my engagements to you, either in money or any kind of produce that you shall chuse.

Goods will sell well hear and quick if I should be so fortunate that you will let me have a supply.

I beg you will favour me with an answer from you. I do not mention the quantity, more or less, but leve it to you to let me have as much as you think proper. This, gentleman, is the truth of my hool affairs. Please to ask Mr. Ralph Jacobs [of Newport, Solomon Simson's brother-in-law]. He is knowing to it.

No more at present but rain.

Your very humble servent,
Mical Judah.

To Mr. Jacob Dilevarey [De Rivera] and Mr. Aron Lopous.

APPENDIX IV

Woodstock, 15 August, 1781.

Honoured Sir:

By the arrival of Mr. Benj'n Jacobs [a nephew of Solomon Simson] I reec'id a verbal message from you which gave me great uneasiness to find it was not in my power to accomplish. You may depend on it that I have been very unlucky this two months as the trade has been very dull occasion'd by the people harvesting. When that's done, mine, I hope, will commence, God willing. Have been obliged to do my endeavours to raise some small matter to settle all my debts before I go from hence which will be to my new shop next week, when and where hope that my removal will be reciprocal both to myself and creditors. And as soon I have settled Mr. Jacobs, shall return to collect my debts of which you may depend on being the first person that I shall pay as far as I can.

I know you indulgence has been such that with shame to my self, may it be said, I did not nor could not perform my duty in my engagements, yet must crave your farther indulgence, and hope in a

short time after my removal to be able to pay a part if not all what I owe. The worthy Mr. Rivera [your father-in-law] can tell in what situation my shop is now, by which you may see if I have enough to pay my just debts. I cannot in conscience ask any more favours. But you know in order to attract custom we are obliged to furnish a shop as much assorted as is possible [with] the little of each article. Therefore, if I can crave a little farther of your help, I make no doubt it will enable me to pay you the old debt much sooner, as the place where I am going is more populus, and you are certain everybody comes to a new shop thinking thereby to purchase much cheaper. Therefore if I have such things as is most vendable [saleable] will then afford me a good assortment. The things that I shall want, Mr. Jacobs has a list, and if you chuse to let me have them, shall then think myself doubly indebted to you for your favors, besides paying you well for them.

Pray, dear sir, don't take it amiss what I write. You have been so good to assist me in my first beggining, therefore beg it is as a favour you'l continue it, and it shall be my chief study to forward myself by my assiduity and punctuality in paying you, all as soon as possible, for it gives me a great uneasiness to think have not been able to have settled with you before, but must tell you that instead of diminishing in my shop have added to it daily, so that having good sales may then be able to finish [paying] all my old accounts.

Cannot proceed without first asking after your good family's health; hope they are all well—as these leaves me at present—to whom you'll be pleased to tender my best regards in general and particular, you'l receive the same sincerely, and believe me to be,

D'r sir,

Your true friend and most h'[um]b[l]e serv't,

JOSEPH DEPASS.

[To Aaron Lopez]

APPENDIX V

To the honorable General Assembly to be holden at Hartford on the second Thursday of instant January:

The memorial of Manuel Myers of Stamford in Fairfield County and State of Connecticut humbly sheweth that he fled from the city of New York in the year 1776 to avoid the enemy and came to this place where he has resided till this time doing very little business, but living upon the little he saved from the city.

The memorialist further observes that his buildings since he left New York, the principal part of them, have been destroyed by fire, and that the memorialist has large sums of money due to him from persons living in New York who would be willing to pay him in good wares and merchandize of some kind and not in money.

And the memorialist further begs leave to observe to your honors that he is near sixty years of age, and has with him in Stamford an aged mother and brother-in-law who depend upon him for support, and that he has not much property of his own left in the country [Stamford].

He therefore prays your honors to grant him liberty to collect of debts due to him in the city of New York in good wares or merchandize to the amount of six hundred pounds lawful money, and bring them into this state to sell and dispose of, so that he may be enabled to support himself and family.

And your memorialist, as in duty bound, shall every pray.

Dated at Stamford, the 7th day of January, A.D., 1782.

MANEL MYERS.

APPENDIX VI

A

May it please your Excellency [Governor Jonathan Trumbull]:

When I had the honor of paying my respects to your Excellency in

person at Labanon, I then mention'd my having a vessel and cargo with salt which I expected daily, agreeable to permit from your Excellency and Council of Safety. Your Excellency's reply was that

Light

you was requested by General Washington not to grant any flags [of truce], and that I must act by the old permit. I afterwards applied to Nathan'l Wales Esq'r[22] on the same subject; related the difficulty I was under respecting the said vessel and cargo. That gentleman made the same reply, that your Excellency cou'd not consistantly grant a flag, that I must act on the old permit, that I shou'd do a piece of service to my country in introducing a quantity of salt at a time it was so much wanted.

Since which, the aforesaid vessel with a cargo of 1,448 bushels of salt purchased for and acoming to me, has been taken and carried into Stamford, and after being in the harbour, the greatest part carelessly lost.

As I am collecting every proof to shew that I have not acted in a clandestine manner but openly and publicly, I have requested my friend P. Edwards Esq'r[23] to git Squire Wales deposition, and your Excellency will add to the many obligations already confer'd in furnishing Mr. Edwards with such proof as may be necessary respecting my application and your Excellency's reply, which will not alone be doing an act of justice but rendering a person a most singular service, who will always gratefully acknowledge the favor, and

who is, with all imaginable respect and regard,

Your Excellencies
Most obed't h[umble]. serv't,
SOLOMON SIMSON.
New Haven, 9th Oct'r, '82.

B

May it please your Excellency:

I had the honor of paying my respects to your Excellency the 9th last [*sic*] instant. I have this day been informed that Mr. Van Dyck is applying for a permission to return. Very few indeed wou'd influance me to be troublesome to your Excellency, but I am constrain'd to do it on this occasion as an act of justice, that [since] the person is highly deserving, and that your Excellency take pleasure in serving such as are.

When I was in New York I was well informed of the real service Mr. Van Dyck had rendered many of his unfortunate country men by being instrumental to their release, and his readiness in serving others who wanted it, to the truth of which I shall be willing to declare whenever necessary.

I have the honor of subscribing, with all due respect,

Your Excellencies
Most obed't serv't,
SOLOMON SIMSON.
Fairfield, 11th Oct'r, '82.

---

22. Nathaniel Wales (1722–1783): influential Connecticut patriot, gunpowder manufacturer, member of Council of Safety, friend of Governor Trumbull (*Commemorative Biographical Record of Tolland and Windham Counties, Connecticut* [Chicago, 1903]).

23. Pierpont Edwards (1750–1826): member of the well-known Massachusetts Edwards family, New Haven attorney, member of Continental Congress (*Biographical Directory of the American Congress, 1774–1927*).

7

THE VALENZIN AFFAIR

Among the children of the well-known Revolutionary patriot Benjamin Nones was a son by the name of Solomon, who, so the family tradition runs, received a consular appointment in Portugal, probably early in the nineteenth century. While on his way to his new post—the story continues—the young official was captured in the Mediterranean by corsairs, and every man on board was executed with the exception of Solomon, who managed to save himself by giving a Masonic signal of distress. Too many people, particularly Jews, have been saved by their Masonic affiliation for us to accept these pious stories without generous reservations as to their authenticity. What is unfortunately true is that dozens of American sailors were seized by the Barbary pirates and ruthlessly sold into slavery or held for ransom. The situation became critical for American merchantmen in the summer of 1801, when the piratical Regency of Tripoli declared war on the United States. In discussing this subject years later, Mordecai Manuel Noah said that we had to fight back to save our ships, to abolish tribute, to free American captives, and, above all, to make our flag respected everywhere. These were the motivations, so Noah believed, that prompted President Jefferson to send a small fleet into the Mediterranean to wage war on Tripoli.

While engaged in this activity, the armed schooner "Enterprize," commanded by Lieutenant Andrew Sterett, seized the brig "Paulina" just after she had left Valetta, Malta, with a cargo of goods for Tripoli. Commodore Richard V. Morris and his officers did not hesitate to order the capture of this boat, for she was headed for Tripoli, a country at war with the United States. The captain of the "Paulina" knew full

This study appeared originally in Abraham Berger *et al.* (eds.), *The Joshua Bloch Memorial Volume: Studies in Booklore and History* (New York, 1960), pp. 140–50.

well that the port was blockaded, if only on paper, and the Americans had been informed by a British consul that the cargo was owned for the most part by a Tripolitan subject. For these reasons the "Enterprize" had no qualms about seizing the "Paulina" on January 17, 1803.

The "enemy" Tripolitan merchant who owned the larger part of the cargo of raisins, figs, cheese, silk, etc., was a young Jewish merchant in his twenties, named David Valenzin. Young David was held as a prisoner, his clothes and personal belongings were seized, and his cargo was speedily confiscated and sold at auction. It was in all likelihood a forced sale, and the goods, which he valued at seven to eight thousand dollars, brought a net of something over two thousand. The merchant who disposed of the goods seems to have been a friend of the American consul at Malta, and one may well believe that the consul—who was no doubt in business himself—saw to it that the cargo was sold very cheaply.

Commodore Morris, who had ordered the seizure of the ship as a prize and the arrest of her captain and Valenzin, as well as some others who were on board, soon discovered that neither the authorities on Malta nor those at Gibraltar would sit as an admiralty court in this case. The "Paulina" was a Hapsburg boat; its captain, a Hapsburg subject. By June, the commodore, in order to save face, restored the ship to its owner, and because no English admiralty court would try the case, he had, perforce, to ship Valenzin, impoverished, depressed, and destitute, still a prisoner, and still untried, to the United States for trial. About five months after his capture, Valenzin was brought to this country, but again there was no court that would try him. The commodore had bungled this matter as he had bungled his whole expedition, and because of his general ineptitude and his Mediterranean failure he was relieved of his command in June. In that very month, the Secretary of the Navy, Robert Smith, freed Valenzin and offered to return him to the Mediterranean on a government vessel. Smith's letter, offering to send Valenzin back, almost admitted that a mistake had been made.

No court would touch the case because the prize, the *corpus delicti*, so to say, could not be produced. The commodore and his eager men had acted arbitrarily without submitting their prize to the decision of a properly constituted court. They could not legally justify the procedure to which they had had recourse. Valenzin, as it turned out, was what he always said he was, a subject of the Hapsburg Emperor, albeit he also carried Tripolitan papers. The family was originally Venetian, and therefore Austrian, but on the death of the mother, the father moved to Tripoli and the sons went along with him, living in that country as friendly aliens under Hapsburg protection. When the boys reached their majority, they moved to Alexandria and Rosetta in Egypt, but maintained commercial relations with their father. This last cargo was undoubtedly destined for Tripoli. Morris and the American consular officers should have had Valenzin tried before a competent court before selling his goods, and should have determined his citizenship before imprisoning him. They had no right to rob him of all his personal possessions and to keep him destitute for a period of five months before taking him to the distant United States. It is extremely doubtful whether they were even justified in taking him as a prisoner to this country. Secretary of State Madison, in April, 1804, wrote to the United States minister at Madrid, Charles Pinckney, admitting that the proceedings were "marked with irregularities," and instructed him, in effect, to apologize to the Hapsburg imperial authorities and to promise them ample reparations. But even earlier, the American authorities here realized that it was all "irregular" and "illegal," and were willing to compound the case by freeing this young man and by sending him back home, but without any redress or restoration of his property. He was now given every encouragement to go back to the Mediterranean.

Valenzin almost returned, but some time toward the autumn he made up his mind to stay and to fight it out. It was a resolution of desperation. It is not improbable that he was given some help by Reuben Etting, the brother-in-law of the famous Rebecca Gratz, and at that time United States marshal for Maryland. Etting was a man of political influence, even if he could not hold office under *Maryland* law, and may have intervened, for we know that he was in touch with the unfortunate young Italian Jew. Early in November, 1803, Valenzin sent the following appeal to the House of Representatives:

To the Honorable, the House of Representatives of the United States of America:

The petition of David Valenzin *humbly sheweth* that your petitioner is a citizen of Venice and a subject of His Imperial Majesty, the Emperor of Germany [the Holy Roman Empire], by profession a merchant; that in the prosecution of his lawful concerns, about the close of the year, one thousand eight hundred and two, he departed from the port and city of Smirna on board of a Ragusan vessel, freighted by certain Turkish traders, in which vessel was also embarked all the property of your petitioner;

That in due time the said vessel with her cargo and equipage arrived safely in the port of Valetta, in the island of Malta, where your petitioner, in conjunction with certain Tunisian Turks, freighted and embarked his property on board of an Imperial [Hapsburg] *polacca* [a type of brig], destined originally for the port of Tripoli, but which place being at that time declared to be under blockade, the destination of the said imperial vessel was changed for Gerbi [Gerba, in Tunis], as might be seen by the charter party, and by the manifest signed by the master of the customs at the aforesaid port of Valetta, and witnessed by the seal of Great Britain.

Your petitioner begs leave in this place to observe that, at the time those arrangements were made, the squadron of the United States, consisting of three frigates and one schooner, under the orders of *Commodore Morris,* were at anchor in the said port; that just about the time when your petitioner in the aforesaid imperial vessel was ready to proceed upon the aforesaid voyage, the *schooner* "Enterprize," commanded by Lieutenant *Andrew Sterett,* one of the squadron of the United States above mentioned, made sail from the aforesaid port.

In due time, to wit, on the 25th [actually the 17th] day of

January, 1803, your petitioner and those others, being Turks
and subjects of Tunis, having concluded their lawful affairs,
departed from the port of Valetta, aforesaid, with the intention of proceeding on their before mentioned voyage to Gerbi,
on board of the said *Imperial vessel;* that a very short time after
losing sight of the said island of *Malta,* the aforesaid United
States schooner "Enterprize" was discovered to be in chase of
the imperial vessel, on board of which your petitioner had
embarked himself and all his effects. On approaching, the said
schooner fired a shot at the imperial vessel which latter immediately took in sail and lay-to for her. Soon afterwards the
said imperial vessel, though belonging to a neutral nation, was
taken possession of by an officer and several armed men belonging to the said schooner and ordered back to Malta, where
she arrived in a few hours afterwards, and on the same day on
which she had departed thence.

On the next day your petitioner, and the captain of the
imperial *polacca,* were conducted on shore, and at the health
office were met by the *commodore* of the American fleet
[Morris], James L. Cathcart, *Esquire,* a consular agent of the
United States, and the consul of the United States for the said
island of Malta. After answering various interrogatories, and
exhibiting his passport (which was declared by the above-
named gentlemen to be a forgery), your petitioner was re-
manded on board the said imperial vessel, under a rigorous
guard, with orders that no person should be permitted to
hold communication with him. In this situation your petitioner
was deprived of all his property, of his money, his clothing,
except those which he then wore, of all his books of accounts,
and other papers of consequence to him.

After twelve days, your petitioner, with the captain and
pilot of the said imperial vessel, and the before mentioned
Turks, were conveyed on board the said schooner "Enterprize" without having any part of his property or clothing
returned; and after a passage of fifteen days, the said schooner,
with your petitioner and others on board, arrived at the
Goleita [strait] of Tunis. At this place the consul of the United
States, William Eaton, *Esquire,* came on board the schooner
and set at liberty the Tunisian Turks before mentioned.

In the course of a few days (to the best of your petitioner's

recollection, twenty-five), the three frigates belonging to the
United States before alluded to, under the command of *Commodore Morris*, arrived at the Goleita, at which time, according to the belief of your petitioner, a full restitution was made
to the aforesaid Tunisians of all the property seized from
them on board the said imperial *polacca;* but your petitioner
in vain demanded either his liberty or his property. He was
transported, together with the captain and pilot of the imperial
vessel, on board the frigate "Chesapeake," which after fifteen
days arrived at *Gibraltar*. Here the two latter had permission
to land, but your petitioner was told that he must proceed to
the United States to be adjudged according to the laws of
that country. He was obliged to submit, and, after a passage
of thirty-four days arrived at *Norfolk*, and in a few days afterwards, to wit, on the sixth day of June, 1803, at this city of
Washington.

Here your petitioner hoped to have experienced immediate
justice; but for several days, during which the frigate was dis-
armed, no person came to examine him or place him in such
situation as he merited. Your petitioner at last so far overcame
the shame occasioned by his naked and degraded appearance
(he never having received back any part of his linen or other
wearing apparel taken from him by the officers and crew of
the said schooner "Enterprize") as to seek for William Eaton,
Esquire, formerly consul at Tunis, who immediately recognized your petitioner, and placed him in lodgings at the hotel
of Mr. Stelle in this city, and generously furnished him from
his own wardrobe with such raiment as was necessary to
shelter and cover his body from the weather.

From this place he wrote to the Honorable James Madison,
Secretary of State, representing the hardships of his case, and
requesting that the justice of the government might interfere
in his behalf. To this he had not any answer; but some days
subsequent thereto, he received a letter from the Honorable
Robert Smith, Secretary of the Navy, informing him that he
was no longer a prisoner, and that if he chose to return home,
free passage would be afforded to him on board a public ship,
to Malta or any other port in the Mediterranean. To this pro-
posal your petitioner could only reply that he had been deprived of everything he possessed by the officers of the United

States, and that until he should obtain some kind of restitution he did not think he would be justifiable in departing.

Not long after the receipt of this letter, all the ministers of the government departed from the city of Washington, and the condition of your petitioner becoming daily more and more distressing, he came to the resolution to go to Baltimore, where he exhibited himself at different times to the Honorable Mr. Smith, Secretary of the Navy, depressed with misery and burthened with debts which he had no means of discharging; but he [Smith] could not, as he said, consistent with his duty, grant any relief.

Having procured from the generosity of some persons the means of proceeding to Philadelphia, your petitioner arrived there, and by advice, entered a protest before a notary public against the proceedings of the said Lieutenant Andrew Sterett, etc., etc.; setting forth the value of the property taken from him . . . by the said armed schooner "Enterprize" to be between seven and eight thousand hard silver dollars. After undergoing various difficulties, your petitioner returned to this city of Washington, where the generosity of *Mr. Stelle* again offered him an asylum from hunger and want.

Since his return to this place, your petitioner, emboldened by the report of the great humanity and justice which characterize his excellency the President of the United States, addressed a letter to him, praying some *amelioration* of his unhappy condition. From that time to the present, your petitioner has not had the honor of receiving any notice.

Thus having been, in the pursuit of his lawful concerns as a merchant, and under the protection of the neutral flag of His Imperial Majesty, the *Emperor of Germany*, to whom as a citizen of Venice he is a subject, seized upon the high seas by a ship of war, under the authority of a commission of the United States, despoiled of all his property to the amount of between seven and eight thousand dollars, deprived also of his papers and books of accounts, robbed of his wearing apparel, made a prisoner, conveyed upwards of four thousand miles, and cast naked and destitute of friends, money, clothing or food, on a land to whose language, manners, and customs he is an entire stranger, a dependent for sustenance on the bounty of an innkeeper, denied any remuneration for his losses, ignorant of the laws and unable to seek redress, even if they are empowered to give it, reduced to the lowest depth of penury and wretchedness, your petitioner throws himself and his wrongs upon the justice of your honorable house, praying redress for what he has already suffered, and such provision as will enable him to bear up against the rigid inclemency of the approaching season, in a climate to which he is totally unused.

To this end, your petitioner, most humbly relying upon his just pretentions, and upon the principles of right which distinguish the government of the United States, begs that your honorable body may be pleased to take his case into consideration, and grant him such reparation as he may, in your wisdom, appear to be entitled to; and he, as in duty bound, will ever pray.

Washington City, Nov. 8, 1803.[1]   DAVID VALENZIN.

This petition was read in the House on the tenth of the month and was referred to the Committee on Claims. On December 12, 1803, the Committee reported that the petition should not be granted. Valenzin's papers, on which he depended to substantiate his claims, could not be found. Moreover, there is ample reason to believe that the officers who were cognizant of all the details preferred to stay out of sight: Were Valenzin's petition granted, they would not be permitted to retain their prize money! When finally the papers were produced, they were found to be in Arabic and in a Barbary-Italian dialect which was very difficult to translate. Some people believed that his story of German citizenship was a lie and insisted that he was a Tripolitan who deserved what he got.

---

1. The above petition, in printed form, is found in the Bixby Collection of Jeffersoniana in the Library of the Missouri Historical Society, St. Louis. It was preceded and followed by editorial comments which are reprinted below as an Appendix. The editorial and the petition are taken from an undated and unidentified newspaper clipping that appeared probably in an issue of January, 1804.

The writer of this essay wishes to express his thanks to the Missouri Historical Society, not only for sending him a copy of this clipping, but also for the many courtesies so graciously accorded him by the staff.

Strangely enough, the Committee on Claims, of the House, usually "hard-boiled," believed in this young man and were personally eager to help him, even with funds. Apparently from the very beginning, they were "apprehensive that other facts might exist material in the case," and when the petition and report of December 12th were ordered to be recommitted, they began to dig deeper. Among other "irregularities" they discovered that the prize master, Acting Lieutenant David C. Heath, had deposited the money received for the sale of the cargo in a Washington bank in his own name on December 17, 1803. The deposit was made *after* the Committee had begun its investigation, and, so Heath later testified, had the approbation of Secretary of the Navy Smith. Obviously the Secretary had warned the participants in this drama that their actions were being scrutinized. A day *later*, on December 18th, Secretary Smith wrote the Committee that he had no official information on the affair.

However, all the expressions of sympathy and the efforts to secure justice for Valenzin were insufficient to allay the fears of the frightened young man, rejected and alone in a strange country. All that he owned in the world had been invested in that cargo, and now it was gone; he had no clothes, no real friends, and he was cold. On January 20, 1804, despairing of a favorable decision, he committed suicide, stabbing himself to death.

After his death, the Committee on Claims made a supplementary report dated February 1, 1804, asserting that "the disposition of the prize was irregular and illegal." They recommended that the property taken from him be restored to his heirs and that provision be made to indemnify the persons who had contributed to his support during his imprisonment and who later had defrayed the expenses of his burial. The report was referred to the Committee of the Whole House, and the Committee on Claims was instructed to prepare a bill pursuant to its recommendations. That was done, and the bill was passed and approved on March 26th.

We have no doubt that the residue of his estate was finally

paid to his older brother Moses, in Alexandria. But how did they ever find Moses? That is an interesting story.

In December of 1804, almost a year after the suicide, General William Eaton, the Navy Agent for the Barbary Regencies, was in Cairo talking to a Jewish merchant whom he had just met, a fellow by the name of Leon Reubin (Reuben), and he heard the name of Moses Valenzin mentioned. Further inquiry and an official deposition elicited the whole story of David Valenzin's life in Europe and North Africa, and the existence of a brother in Egypt. Eaton at once sent the deposition and other details to his friend, Congressman John C. Smith, who had been on the Committee on Claims when the case had first come before it.

At first, when Eaton told Reubin of the death of the young Venetian, Reubin wept; later, when the General told him that the United States would surrender what was left of the man's property to his heirs, the Cairo Jew turned to a Jewish friend who stood nearby, raised his eyes to Heaven, "and laying both hands gravely to his breast, he exclaimed in Arabic: 'Great God! What an astonishing country that must be where the government takes so much pain to render justice to a Hebrew! Even at this distance to inform his heirs of cash in deposit, which might so easily have been concealed!' " [2]

---

2. For the reference to Solomon B. Nones, see H. S. Morais, *The Jews of Philadelphia* (Philadelphia, 1894), p. 401. For Noah, see *Naval Documents Related to the United States Wars with the Barbary Powers, Naval Operations* (Washington, 1944), V, 232 ff.

The details of the Valenzin Case are unfolded in the above cited series of *Naval Documents*, II (1940), 455, 461; III (1941), 1, 274, 341–46; V (1944), 217–19. The investigations of the Committee on Claims of the House of Representatives and the action of Congress are reflected in the following documents and works: Ex. Docs., 8th Cong., 1st sess., pp. 23–28, December 12, 1803: *Report of the Committee on Claims on the Petition of David Valenzin, Referred on the Tenth [of November] ultimo. 12th December, 1803. Read and Ordered To Be Recommitted to the Committee on Claims;* Ex. Docs., 8th Cong., 1st sess., 28 pp., February 1, 1804: *Supplementary Report of the Committee on Claims to Whom Was Re-committed, on the 12th of December Last, Their Report on the Petition of David Valenzin. 1st February, 1804. Read and Ordered To Be Referred to a Committee of the Whole House on Monday Next.* The above two reports were reprinted in *American State Papers,* Class IX, Claims (Washington, 1834), pp. 288–

APPENDIX

Spoliation—A man complains, with a very bad grace, of those faults or immoralities in another, of which he is glaring guilty himself. While the United States, from one corner to the other, resound with the cry of indignation against the encroachments on our neutral rights by the maritime powers of Europe, it behoves the government of the United States to give, in the management of its navy, an example of that justice which it demands. Our fleet is small and easily watched over; yet if we not only permit it to be guilty of depredations on the liberties and properties of other nations, with whom we never have been at war, and with whom, unless we provoke them by such acts, we will never be under the necessity of going to war, but if we refuse, when an appeal is made to the highest tribunal in the nation, to redress the wrong we have committed, with what face can we censure any act of a similar nature, where we are the victims of the injustice?

To exemplify this we have now before us the case of *David Valenzin*, a Venetian Jew merchant. This man was taken in the Mediterranean, almost within the jurisdiction of Malta, by one of our cruizers in January last, on board of an *Imperial polacca;* all his property was seized, and his baggage *plundered* from him. After being detained in the Mediterranean several months, without undergoing any trial, he was ordered to the United States, to be *tried and judged as a Tripoline*. He arrived here last June, destitute of money,

---

89, 292–96. The legislative record of the Valenzin petition and bill is found in the *Journal of the House of Representatives of the United States, etc.*, 8th Cong., 1st sess. (Washington, 1826), IV, 440, 484, 503, 561, 613, 615; *Annals of Congress*, 8th Cong., 1st sess. (Washington, 1852), pp. 278, 280, 288, 297, 1088, 1190, 1194–95; *United States Statutes at Large*, VI, 54–55.

A letter from the Secretary of the Navy to the Secretary of the Treasury, July 12, 1804, requesting a warrant for $500.00 to reimburse those who laid out money for Valenzin, is found in Treasury 2, September 3, 1803, to June 5, 1821, Naval Records Collection of Naval Records and Library, The National Archives.

Charles Prentiss, *The Life of the Late General William Eaton* (Brookfield, 1813), p. 244, contains a passing reference to the Valenzin affair.

friend, or food (for it appears that no care was taken to provide for him even as a prisoner). He frequently applied to the different offices of state, and even to the president, for redress, or for a trial according to our laws. These applications were made, as we believe, in Italian, the only language, except the Hebrew, known by the prisoner. We presume this is a language not unknown to Mr. Gallatin; and if the writer of this article recollects the information he had from Mr. *Mazzei* at *Pisa*, about two years ago, Mr. Jefferson also understands it. The only satisfactory answer he had to these applications was a letter from Mr. Smith, Secretary of the Navy, informing him that *he was no longer a prisoner*, and that if he chose to return home, he might have a passage in one of the public vessels. Mr. Smith is a *lawyer*, and certainly knows whether he possessed the right of *enlarging* [freeing] this man, without any trial, after he had been conveyed from Malta to Washington as a Tripoline prisoner, at the same time that he asserted himself to be an *Imperialist* [a Hapsburg subject].

Mr. Jefferson is a philosopher, the *study* of whose life has been to *ameliorate the condition of man;* why did he not apply his tenets to the condition of David Valenzin? Will he contend that it was consistent with the *fitness of things* that a *citizen of Venice* should be despoiled of all his property by citizens of the United States, and be denied even the forms of justice? Or will he suppose that the mere word of *James Leander Cathcart* (a man whose obstinacy will always be ready to support any assertion which his own self-sufficient, pompous, dogmatical ignorance may induce him to make) is conclusive evidence that the *prisoner* was really a Tripoline, and not, what his papers all shewed him to be, an *Italian?* It is impossible that *Mr. Jefferson* could think so; and when the *President of the United States* is applied to by any person, particularly by an oppressed and injured foreigner, it is the duty of his station to see that justice be administered, and not to turn him off with frigid indifference or disdain; it was doubly his duty in the present instance, as *admiral and com-*

*mander in chief of the navy from whence the wrong pro-
ceeded.*

Nothing, however, was done. All his letters, all his applications were ineffectual. He, at last (by the advice of a person
with whom he accidentally met at Mr. Stelle's in Washington; and who understood enough of the Italian to be able to
interpret his story), made his case known to Congress, as his
dernier ressort, in the following petition, which was presented to the House of Representatives by Mr. R. Griswold
[of Connecticut], on the tenth or eleventh of November.

This petition, as is usual, was, on the motion of the honorable gentleman who presented it, referred to the *Committee
on Claims.* It has now been before the Committee for two
months. We have attentively examined all the reports which
it has since made, but amongst them we have not yet discovered the name of *Valenzin.* His is a case of peculiar hardship;
and we did consider it as a claim of such a nature as would
have engaged the immediate attention of the gentlemen
whose duty it is to report upon it. The honor of the United
States is deeply concerned in the decision which they may
make upon the subject. If a favorable report should come
before the house, we have no doubt of its being confirmed;
and should it be unfavorable, we make no question that the
house will consider it as its duty to have the grounds of such
report well ascertained, before it is acquiesced in.

In mentioning this subject, we had in view to shew to the
people of the United States a sample of their own conduct,
while they are so bitterly declaiming against that of others;
and to convince them that they ought to set an example of
their own respect for justice, before they complain of others
treating it with neglect. The members of the *Committee on
Claims,* we would call upon to remember that *"this visitation
is but to whet their almost blunted purpose."*

8

THE *MODERN RELIGION* OF MOSES HART

In the year 1818, there appeared in the city of New York a sixty-one-page essay entitled *Modern Religion*. Its author was Moses Hart.

In presenting his ideal of a universal religious system to "the good people of this enlightened age," the writer said: "To harmonize the religious contentions of mankind; to heal the wounds flowing from religious intolerance, persecution, fanaticism, bigotry and tyranny; and to seat religion on the bed of truth, virtue and brotherly love, is the ardent desire which warms my breast. To proclaim religion the most noble, yet the most comprehensive science; the most sublime and magnificent, yet open to the meanest capacity; and to make religion the consoling prop of mankind, is the aim of my present undertaking." [1]

Moses was a member of the well-known Canadian Hart family. He was a son of Aaron, who originally came from New York City to Montreal in 1760 with the English as an army commissary, was very successful in his commercial ventures, and ultimately became a large landowner. He settled at Three Rivers in Lower Canada, and it was there that his eldest son, Moses, was born in 1768.

In dividing his property, Aaron gave the seigneury of Ste. Marguerite and the fief Marquisat-Dusablé to his first-born. Moses was also seigneur of Courval and Grondines, and was thus a very large landowner. Some time in the middle 1830's he established a private bank in Three Rivers and issued his own bank notes during the days when the French Canadians, urged on by their rebel leader Papineau, were reluctant to accept government paper. He also engaged in general com-

---

This study appeared originally in *Hebrew Union College Annual*, XX, 585-615.

1. Preface.

mercial actitivies, and was one of the first to bring the steam-boat to Canada. His chief competitor was John Molson, the pioneer of steam navigation on the St. Lawrence. A little over two years after Fulton's *Clermont* puffed her way up the Hudson to Albany, one of Moses Hart's steamboats was ploughing its way through the St. Lawrence. This was in October, 1809. During the Napoleonic wars he engaged extensively in the exportation of grain to Europe.

Hart was reputed to have been as ambitious, though not as able, as his distinguished father, Aaron. The traditions and stories that have gathered around his name show that he was undisciplined and eccentric, yet canny and clever. There is a story to the effect that an engineer on one of his steamboats was in love with a girl and was eager to see her as frequently as possible. He would repair to Moses Hart and inform him that the boat was tired! The owner understood the situation perfectly and instructed him to give it a rest at the mouth of the St. Maurice, where the girl lived! He died a wealthy man in 1847, leaving a number of legitimate and illegitimate children.[2]

This, in brief, is the biography of this rather undistinguished person who set out to establish (on paper, at least) a universal faith which would serve "to tranquillize the jarring religions under one banner." He began his work, in the Introduction, with a four-page statement of his theological beliefs, primarily his God concept, and then proceeded to outline the structure of his "ceremonial religion."

The book itself begins with a "solemn installation oath" for those whom we would call confirmands or initiates. This is followed by the "three superior duties obligatory," and the "twenty-five secondary duties obligatory." After this pres-

---

2. The data for the life of Moses Hart are found in Abraham Rhinewine and Isidore Goldstick, *Looking Back a Century* (Toronto, 1932); Benjamin G. Sack, *History of the Jews in Canada* (Montreal, 1945); A. D. Hart, *The Jew in Canada* (Toronto, 1926); personal communication dated December 4, 1946, from Alan J. Hart, of Montreal; Benjamin Sulte, "Les miettes de l'histoire," *Revue Canadienne*, VII, 426 ff.; Raymond Douville, *Aaron Hart, Récit historique* (Three Rivers, Que., 1938).

entation of the principles of the new faith, the author proceeds to describe and give the contents of the ceremonies of marriage and divorce. Life apparently begins with marriage, but by a natural association he takes the opportunity to write of divorce because the two are so intimately related. Then, influenced by the chronological scheme which he has adopted, he turns to the formal prayers recited by a woman lying in childbirth, and to those said by her husband on her recovery. Next comes the naming of the child, then prayers for children, for adults, for the Day of Rest and for the three major holy days of the year. Then come the occasional forms and blessings, such as petitions for the sick, prayers before meals, prayers in a storm, those said on going on a sea voyage, on returning safely to port, on undertaking a journey, on coming back from one, and on "making an enterprise." This is followed by petitions recited when in trouble, and on being released from trouble. Considerable space is devoted to war and peace; prayers are given for those about to engage in battle and for those who celebrate the end of the struggle. There are also supplications to be recited during the entire period of the war's duration. This war liturgy is followed by the author's own decalogue, which was recited on the weekly Day of Rest, on the three major festivals, and by the young man or woman who took the initiation oath. The liturgy closes with the funeral service for the dead.

Through an analysis of this brief religious system, we shall attempt to describe the ideas of the writer and the sources which he utilized. It is no less important to determine also whom he hoped to influence. He himself gives us our first hint in the all too brief advertisement which is inserted as the last page of his book. We are informed by him that this "ceremonial religion" of his, founded on natural principles, was submitted for the consideration of Jews and deists. The typical deistic character of his teachings is strongly reflected in the theology of the Introduction. He proves the existence of a Benevolent Creator through the argument from design, reflected in the perfect workmanship and harmony of the ce-

lestial system and in divine providence for the "wants of the
meanest creature." His essence is justice and order, truth and
charity; His virtues are ours to imitate.

The Beneficent Creator could not, by His very nature,
punish the wicked in any eternal netherworld. The evil are
punished in this world by the Greatest Creator and by the
laws of the land. (The author never uses the word "God.")
There is immortality in the future world, "further benefits"
there, but apparently no punishment. The good we do finds
its reward in this life. To express gratitude unto Him, it is
incumbent upon us to serve Him through a ceremonial and
rules of conduct which will enable us to live "a virtuous and
honorable life."

Thus, in this brief theological outline, Hart follows the
classical deistic tradition of a belief in a unitarian God, in immortality, and in the practice of "charitable actions to each
other."

The actual liturgy of this new religion begins with the
"Solemn Installation Oath" administered to a male at fifteen
and to a female at fourteen. The person rendering the oath
does so kneeling, with hands raised in a position of adoration,
and then recites the new decalogue. These ten commandments do not show much dependence on the traditional biblical decalogue. In the first precept, the initiate promises
gratitude to God; in the third, he vows honor and respect to
parents. In the other eight, the speaker—always speaking in
the first person—declares he will be loyal to the state in the
spirit of freedom and justice, that he will not defraud his fellowman, commit any crime or violence, or communicate
any deadly disease, and that he will judge his fellowman with
mercy, equity, and justice. The neophyte in this decalogue
openly proclaims the belief that he will be rewarded and punished in this life for the good or the evil that he does.

This initiation or confirmation ceremony shows Christian
and Jewish influence in general, but the details are surely non-
Jewish: traditional Jewish "confirmation," of course, was at
the age of thirteen, and the kneeling position has no place in

bar mizvah ceremonial. Hart is incidentally careful to avoid the use of the term "rabbi" when speaking of directors, priests, ministers, and the authorized leaders of a community. He writes of churches, chapels, rooms, temples, edifices of public worship, but only once in the entire essay does he mention the word "mosque" or "synagogue." He does not attempt to deny that he is a Jew—in the advertisement, he informs us that he had received a Jewish education—but he does not wish to identify his religious system with anything Jewish. That is obvious. Perhaps he believed that this would serve to prejudice people against it, or, on the other hand, perhaps he realized he had departed from any intellectual relationship to the synagogue.

One nurses the impression that the theological prescriptions in his decalogue are perfunctory; he has moved to the left from the theological position he took in the Introduction. In these ten commandments, he says nothing of immortality; he speaks only of gratitude to the Almighty Creator, and of reward and punishment in this life, probably through society, not through God's providence. The emphasis throughout his decalogue is on social ethics. We are dealing here with a sort of early nineteenth-century ethical culture society.

The sixth commandment runs as follows: "I will not persecute any person on account of his or her political or religious opinions or belief." This specific commandment will take on added meaning in the light of the history of the Hart family. Political and religious liberty meant a great deal to them. As early as 1770, Aaron Hart, the father, was among those who besought the British authorities to grant the people of Canada a representative legislative assembly. After the successful revolt of the American colonies, a petition of 1784, asking for a government in Canada founded on "fixed and liberal principles," carried the signature of Moses Hart. (It is possible, however, that this Moses Hart may have been an uncle of our Moses Hart.) Sometime before the death of the father, Aaron, in 1800, our Moses Hart nursed the hope

of becoming a member of the Legislative Assembly of the
Parliament in Lower Canada. His father, however, dissuaded
him from running, warning him that as a Jew he could not be
successful in this aspiration.[3] Apparently, a younger brother,
Ezekiel, was not so easily dissuaded. At any event, the father,
who might have stopped him, was already dead when, in
1807, Ezekiel ran and was elected to the Legislative Assembly of Lower Canada for the Borough of Three Rivers.

The election of Ezekiel Hart in 1807 was the beginning of
a long struggle for religio-political liberty that ended only in
1832 when the Jews of Canada were finally granted political
and civil rights. When Ezekiel Hart appeared in the Provincial Parliament on January 30, 1808, he was not permitted to
take his seat. The issue was involved. Although the French
element in Three Rivers had elected him, the French leaders
in Parliament resented him because of his strong pro-British
sympathies and because of his close friendship with the un-
popular and inept governor, Sir James Craig. *Le Canadien,* a
French-language newspaper, had attacked Ezekiel Hart as a
Jew; *The Mercury,* an English organ, had denounced the ex-
pulsion of the Jew from Parliament as an "act of tyranny of
ignorant fanatics" and had scoffed at the "idolatrous worship
of the Catholics." Hart was in part the victim of Anglo-
French political and religious rivalries, but he was actually
refused his seat because he was a Jew. Ezekiel ran again in
1808 and took his seat in 1809. This time he took the oath,
not according to the Jewish custom, with covered head and
with hand on the Book of Moses, but with head bared, on the
Evangels. In all probability, he thought he owed this conces-
sion to his constituents. Although he was always a practicing
Jew, he took the oath "on the true faith of a Christian," for
he had prior to this time assured the authorities that he was
prepared to take it in the "usual form." [4] His going to Ca-
nossa was evidently not enough for his opponents, for they
proceeded to identify him officially as a Jew and then to ex-

---

3. Douville, pp. 124–25.
4. That is, the Christian form.

clude him legally because of his Jewishness, and thus to deny the validity of his Christian oath. To preclude the hostile legislature from taking final action, which would make it impossible for Jews in the future to become members of Parliament, Governor General Sir James Craig dissolved the Assembly on May 15, 1809. Ezekiel Hart had by this time learned his lesson; he never again stood for election in the Legislative Assembly, although he was nominated again in October.

This cavalier treatment of a member of the family must have rankled deep in the hearts of the powerful Hart clan.[5] Is it too much to assume that Moses Hart was influenced by his own experiences, and particularly by those of his brother Ezekiel from 1807 to 1809 to believe that a new religious system should be evolved, which would not countenance political and religious persecution? "Alas! how many millions of people have fallen victims to religious intolerance, bigotry, and tyranny," he laments in his Preface. He was speaking not only of the world, but from bitter personal experience that was reinforced by another rebuff to the family three years after Ezekiel had been expelled from Parliament.

Benjamin Hart, still another brother, sought a commission in the militia in 1811. There was no legal objection to this aspiration. The request was referred to Colonel Thomas Coffin, the commander, but was rejected by him in the summer of 1812 on the ground that the men would not serve under him because of his religion. In August of that same year, Benjamin Hart wrote a detailed letter to the governor, Sir George Prevost, explaining that the issue here was a personal one—that other Jews had held positions in the militia, but that Colonel Coffin had been one of the men defeated by his brother Ezekiel Hart in the election of 1807 and was now taking advantage of the situation. Apparently, his protest

5. *The Mercury,* Feb. 22, 29, 1808, quoted in Sack, pp. 88–90. The political rebuffs of Ezekiel Hart are described in the above mentioned works of A. D. Hart, Rhinewine, and Sack. Further details may be found in *Publications of the American Jewish Historical Society* [*PAJHS*], I, 119 ff.; XXIII, 43 ff.

was of no avail: there is no record that Benjamin received his commission at this time.[6]

Years later, during the troublesome days that preceded the Rebellion of 1837 and 1838, Moses and Ezekiel Hart, unlike brother Benjamin (who was a staunch defender of the English system), were at first sympathetic to the French patriots in Lower Canada, who were now protesting against the abuses of the regime in Quebec. Moses, apparently, still held liberal views. He had not forgotten what he had written in 1818: "I will not persecute any person on account of his political or religious opinions or belief."

The "three superior duties obligatory" which follow after the decalogue are merely an expression of the first, the ninth, and the tenth commandments: they are the duty of offering thanks to God "when we may reasonably hope to be rewarded in a future life"; the duty of living an honorable life and the reward to be expected in this world; the duty of abhorring evil, which will assuredly be punished in this world.

The "twenty-five secondary duties obligatory" which follow stress the ethics and morals necessary for a happy society. The first three—following Catholic and Jewish patterns—forbid the use of the Almighty Creator's name thoughtlessly, require a slight inclination of the head when He is mentioned, and ask for thanks to Him "on lying down and rising from rest, at meals, and every other particular occasion." The fourth duty is to appropriate edifices for purposes of religion, to appoint a clerical leader who will also serve as the school superintendent, and to set up district ministers who are to supervise the individual clergymen.

The people are enjoined to set aside one day of the week to serve as a rest day; three grand festivals are also to be kept during the year. Among the remaining twenty-five duties are the commands to be loyal to the rulers "if their conduct merit respect"; to honor and to support indigent parents and relatives; to love one's fellowman, to avoid riots, to aid the

6. *PAJHS*, XXIII, 137 ff.

sick, encourage the sciences and the arts, etc.; to be honest
and hospitable, to judge our fellow creatures with mercy, to
practice cleanliness, avoid incest, to make an effort not to
communicate infectious diseases, and to keep far from every
type of crime.

Among these "twenty-five duties" is the prohibition
against enslaving a fellow creature for life without his "full
approbation." Castration is forbidden, and one-third of the
property of a convicted murderer is to be turned over to the
nearest heirs of the victim. Lawsuits are first to be submitted
to the clergy for amicable settlement—suits for debt excepted—before resorting to the civil courts. No woman is to
cohabit with a man when menstruous. This latter commandment, of course, reflects Orthodox Jewish practice.

The ceremony of marriage follows. As implied by the "installation" oath, majority is attained at fifteen by men, and at
fourteen by women. Polygamy is tolerated, for the author
no doubt hoped that his system would be adopted in lands
where plural marriages were practiced. For this reason the
man is not required to offer his bride the oath of fidelity
which she is required to offer him. In order to protect the
wife, she is to receive a copy of the marriage document
which she is to turn over to her nearest relative. If the couple
have any children born out of wedlock, they are to be placed
between the parents during the wedding ceremony.

The approach to marriage here is a realistic one in view of
the frequency of extramarital relations and common-law
unions in Canada at this time. The seigneurs of Canada were
notorious for the "establishments" they maintained. Moses
Hart—as seigneur—was, as we know through his will, no exception in this respect and was therefore dealing with a problem that touched him very directly. Typical of the marriage
abuses of this generation is the story of Bernard Hart, who,
by the way, was not related, as far as we know, to the Harts
of Three Rivers.

Bernard Hart, an American merchant of English birth,
married Catherine Brett in Canada in 1799 and then sepa-

rated from her after a year or two. Whether there was a formal marriage or divorce is very questionable. He returned to New York, remarried in 1806, and became a pillar of society. Before they parted, Catherine Brett had a child by him, Henry, born in 1800, who was the father of Francis Bret Harte, the famous American writer.[7]

Divorce was permitted—in this *Modern Religion* of Moses Hart—after a preliminary six-month period of absolute separation and after a trial by jury sitting in the presence of the district or superior clergyman. If the divorce was granted by a majority of the jury, then a further lapse of eighteen months was to intervene before remarriage would be permitted; if the divorce was not granted by the church-appointed jurors, then there was to be no divorce by the state in less than five years.

Final decrees of divorce are in all cases to be secured from the civil courts, provided the parties have not had sexual relations during the entire period of separation. If they have, a further prohibition to remarry for three more years may be imposed by the ecclesiastical court. Divorce was certainly not to be encouraged.

Returning to his chronological scheme—now that he has surmounted the hurdle of divorce—Hart presents a series of brief prayers: for a woman lying in childbirth, for her husband, and for herself on her recovery, for naming a child, and brief petitions to be recited by children and adults, morning and night. In a rather vague way, these prayers follow the traditional pattern laid down in Christianity and Judaism. Hart, who enjoyed a very fine social position, had ample opportunity to observe Christian religious practice at first hand. He was also well acquainted with Jewish ritual observance. We know that this is true, not only through his own statement in the advertisement appended to his ritual, but also by virtue of the fact that his father Aaron was an observant Jew and had very early subscribed to several copies of David Levi's edition of *The Order of the Daily Prayers in Hebrew*

7. *PAJHS,* XXXII, 99 ff.

and English, according to the Custom of the Spanish and Portuguese Jews, etc.[8]

Occasional phrases in *Modern Religion* show a faint reminiscence of the traditional Christian and Jewish liturgies; as a rule, however, the rather florid phraseology is the author's own. Typical is the priest's prayer at the ceremony of appellation, or naming the child: "May the Almighty Great Creator, the artist of that most noble and mysterious faculty, by which we are endowed to propagate our species; the author of those high refined rapturous sensations which bind parents to the care of their offspring; who causeth his divine providence to shield the young and helpless, and that we may be distinguished by different appellations, may he be pleased that the infant, now about receiving its appellation, may grow up and walk in the path of honor and truth."

The author is apparently very careful to avoid the adoption of any rite or ceremony that is specifically Jewish or Christian; thus there is no intimation of baptism or circumcision.

Hart does not concern himself about one fixed day of rest to be observed by all. Evidently, he has a society in mind which is to include Jews, Christians, and Moslems. It was immaterial, he said, which day of the week is selected for rest—Friday, Saturday, or Sunday—as long as one abstains all day from unnecessary work and devotes it to thanksgiving, reading, exercise, and virtuous actions.

The morning service of the Day of Rest gives us a good concept of the ritual of this deistic religion. The ceremony begins at 9:00 in the morning with a hymn sung by a group of young women. Then the priest or director of the service prays for the welfare of land and king, for the sailors at sea, for the sick, for the privilege of rest, for divine favor, for protection against violence, for the gift of health, the light of truth, for literature, the arts, the sciences, and for the professions which adorn and honor our lives. The aid of the Almighty Creator is then invoked to help every individual flee

---

8. *PAJHS*, VI, 155.

with abhorrence from the commission of crime. Sex crimes
and crimes of violence are evidently very distressing to the
author and very much on his mind, for more than once
throughout his liturgy he refers to them as great evils to be
zealously avoided and shunned. These prayers are followed
by a vocal solo, the repetition of his "decalogue," and then
by a hymn sung by a number of young male voices. While
this last song is being sung, alms are collected for the poor by
a young man and woman. Then follows the sermon, followed by "any private ceremony or prayer," an additional
oration by any young person who may feel the urge to
speak, and finally, the concluding anthem. Afternoon services
on the Day of Rest and the holy days are optional.

The first of the three major holy days is the Spring Festival
observed on the first Wednesday of the Sowing Moon
(April or May). This is called the First Moon. The second
holy day is styled the Harvest Festival and is to be celebrated
on the first Wednesday of the Harvest Moon (August or
September). The third and final holy day is called the Winter
Festival and is observed on the first Wednesday of the Ninth
Moon (December).

The liturgy of these three holy days follows, in general,
the pattern established for the Day of Rest. The theme of the
first is a rhapsodic apostrophe to "the High Almighty Great
Creator and the matchless artisan" who manifests Himself in
spring agriculture. The reference to the Creator in the spring
as an "artisan" and as an "architect" in the golden harvest
reflects the Masonic terminology which many of the eighteenth-century deists employ. Moses Hart's father, Aaron,
had been a member of the Masonic Trinity Lodge No. 4 in
New York, in 1760, before he came to Canada. No doubt,
his sons were also members of Canadian Masonic lodges.[9]

The officiants at the spring service are young boys and
girls who sing the songs, collect the alms, and deliver an oration, in addition to the one usually made by the clergyman.
One of the high points of this service is the grand spring pro-

9. *PAJHS*, XIX, 28.

cession during which the young participants carry typical emblems of the season and scatter flowers and perfumes while the priest bears aloft a small tree in bud. The youthful singers are garbed in uniform attire.

The theme of the second festival is the harvest; the chief officiants are mature men and married women who have borne children. The Creator's bounteous providence is reflected in nature and in the boundless favors He bestows on mankind, and even though this providence manifests itself in reward and punishment in this life, we may also assume, says Hart, that those favors which are to be our lot in a future life will be immeasurably greater than those which we at present enjoy. The symbolism of spring and budding youth in the first festival is continued in this holy day dedicated to ripeness and maturity. In this grand procession, emblems of the harvest are carried and married men and women strew flowers and perfumes, while the priest offers to the view of all a small branch or vine with fruit.

The third or Grand Winter festival, to be observed in December, is dedicated to the old men and women, the imitators of the divine attributes of justice, mercy, truth, charity, order, and benevolence. Even as there is no cruelty or malevolence in the Almighty Bountiful Creator, so must we "fly with horror and detestation from the commission of crimes toward our fellow creatures." In the Grand Winter procession, the emblems of winter, of trades and commerce, and of the arts and sciences are carried about the temple to an obbligato of vocal and instrumental music, while the old men and women strew perfumes and decayed leaves.

As a good deist, Moses Hart had to cope with the problem of the efficacy of prayer in the various occasional blessings and petitions that now follow in his liturgical system. Does the Almighty change the order of nature when we appeal to Him during periods of great danger and impending calamity? The answer, of course, is that the Almighty Creator does not work through miracles. In his advertisement, Hart stresses the fact that his religion "contains no flattering miracles to gratify the ear of the credulous." The Almighty Supreme Creator effects his purpose by causing the sick and the troubled to pursue such rational means as will tend to relieve and help them in their distress.

Hart's book, published only four years after the fighting had come to an end in Canada in 1814, reflects the horror of war and the need for peace. Services are to be held daily in the places of public worship as long as the war lasts. In these supplications the people are warned not to wage war except in defense of their rights and liberties, and only after every attempt to obtain satisfaction by negotiation has failed. They are enjoined to evade war by every honorable means, to distinguish themselves by mercy to the unarmed, women, children, and prisoners, and to pledge themselves to a reasonable peace. Daily collections are to be made for those who have suffered in the conflict, and in the ceremonial procession men are to march about carrying emblems of the evils of war. Heroism is to be lauded and the conspicuous defenders of their land are to precede or to follow the priest under a canopy supported by young females in mourning.

When peace is finally declared, a grand celebration is to take place in every temple, with hymns sung by young women dressed in white and with uniform wreaths of peace. In his thanksgiving from the pulpit or altar, the priest is to invoke the "benign and bountiful Creator . . . who cementeth nations together in the bonds of intercourse and esteem," who has caused "the calamities of war to cease," and who is responsible "for the smiling canopy of peace, which spreadeth gladness throughout our land, renovating the arts, sciences, agriculture, and trade."

If marriage is the beginning of life, bringing with it children, death is the end: the funeral services complete the liturgy, although the author does digress for a moment to suggest that the state may date the year from its founding or from the founding of its government.

At the interment, the priest recites a series of brief prayers all centering around the theme that death is necessary in order to make room for those who follow. Hart had evidently read and approved of Malthus' *Essay on the Principle of Population*. Our author is nothing if not a thorough rationalist and would-be scientist, but he does temper this rather unhappy, if not prosaic reason for dying by voicing the promise of "new life in some other hemisphere" where, endued "with other intellects," man will be able to gratify and complete his "adoration, acknowledgments, and thanks" to the "holy and sovereign Creator of worlds."

The requirements for mourning are rather severe: no person who has lost a father or mother is to speak audibly for four weeks after death. There is a descending scale of silence for lesser relatives which reaches its bottom in the cousin who merits but two days of this silent treatment. The mourner is not to feast or "to drink any spirit, or juice of any grain or fruit, unless permitted by a doctor of physic."

These forty-seven pages of liturgy, described here, are but one-third of the material that is to be prepared. This is only the moral part of the ceremony; the poetical and musical parts, which are to be optional, are not as yet completed, we are informed.

We are interested in the description of the ideas and of the structure of this new religious system; we are even more interested in determining the sources and patterns which influenced it.

Is it possible that this is the first attempt to create a Reform Jewish "church" on this continent? The initial efforts to establish reforms in the Jewish synagogal system in North America were made at Charleston, South Carolina, in 1824, six years after the appearance of *Modern Religion*. There is nothing Jewish about the Hart religion; the Charlestonians, on the other hand, stayed well within the periphery of traditional Judaism in their original "memorial" and merely asked for minor changes, such as the introduction of the vernacular and the English sermon, the elimination of repetitious prayers—which Hart also recommends—the shortening of the services, and the emphasis on understanding what one prayed

". . . in fine, we wish to worship God, not as *slaves of bigotry and priestcraft*, but as the enlightened descendants of that chosen race, whose blessings have been scattered throughout the land of Abraham, Isaac, and Jacob." [10] Hart and the South Carolinians have very little in common theologically and liturgically, but they both share and enjoy common deistic prejudices, and it is by no means improbable that the appearance of Hart's pamphlet may have stimulated the Carolinians to begin their reforms.

The Charlestonians of 1824[11] admitted that they were influenced by "the reformation which has been recently adopted by our brethren in Holland, Germany, and Prussia." Is it possible that Hart and the Charlestonians were both influenced by the recent Jewish Reformation in the Germanic lands? The Hamburg Jews had promulgated their reforms in 1818, the very year that Hart's book appeared, but here, too, there is no evidence of similarity or spiritual influence. The deviations from Orthodox Judaism in Hamburg in 1818 are minor and inconsequential: introduction of the vernacular, use of the organ, more decorum, etc. The changes are primarily aesthetic. The orthodox fundamentalist theology remained unchanged except for a tendency to deny the hope for the coming of a personal Messiah. Behind the Hamburg Reformers of 1818 stood the example and the teachings of the Westphalian banker Israel Jacobson (1768–1828), who was the founder of the Reform Movement in Judaism. He, however, was certainly not the spiritual father of Hart's new system. Jacobson's modest changes were solely aesthetic and expressed themselves also in the eagerness for decorum and the introduction of the vernacular into the first "temple" which he built in 1810.

Closely associated with Jacobson, however, was his friend David Friedländer, who achieved a great deal of notoriety in

---

10. L. C. Moïse, *Biography of Isaac Harby, with an account of The Reformed Society of Israelites of Charleston, S.C., 1824–1833* (n. p., 1931 [?]), p. 59.
11. Moïse, p. 58.

1799 through his anonymous *Sendschreiben an Seine Hoch-
würden Herrn Oberconsistorialrath und Probst Teller zu
Berlin von einigen Hausvätern jüdischer Religion.* In this
"epistle" to William Abraham Teller, a distinguished Protestant churchman, Friedländer, apparently speaking for a small
group of cultured Berlin Jews, proposed that he would embrace Protestantism under certain conditions. These conditions are practically a demand that Protestantism become a
deistic faith in which the belief in Jesus as the Son of God
would play no part. Protestantism was to become a system
of "eternal verities," a religion which did not offend "reason" and "morals." This new Protestantism was to be
founded on five basic principles: (1) belief in one God, the
creator of the world; (2) the soul of man is incorporeal and
is capable of infinite growth; (3) the destiny of man here
below is to strive for higher perfection, to further the happiness of all, and thus attain it for himself; (4) the soul of man
is immortal; (5) reason is given man to further himself; punishment is the result of the violation of reason.

As far as basic principles and ideals are concerned, Hart
and Friedländer have much in common. Both were prepared
to reject traditional Judaism. Friedländer (p. 8) denounced
historical Judaism as an irrational faith which was not to be
confused with the original Hebraic religion. Hart, too (last
page), believed that the original Mosaic faith was deistic but
that the present "Mosaic" works were a late—and presumably
corrupt—compilation by Ezra on the basis of contemporary
oral traditions. Both are, obviously, thoroughgoing deists;
their theology revolves around the typical eighteenth-century
concepts of a unitarian God, immortality, reward and punishment as a rational mundane procedure, the perfectibility of
man, the sovereignty of reason and morals, and the inesti-
mable value of education.

Friedländer had no new system, no liturgy to offer; at
least he published none. We have no evidence that Hart had
ever seen or read the 1799 "epistle" of Friedländer. It is true
that their fundamental concepts of natural religion are alike,

but Hart could have acquired these same principles from any
and all deistic writers and thinkers of his day. It would be far
more probable to assume that Hart, a subject of Great Britain, would have turned to the English deists for his religious
patterns.

Our search in England, however, for a more direct source
of the Hart system does not carry us much farther. It merely
confirms what we already know—that he is a typical deist.
Hart would certainly have been willing to accept the five "innate principles" of Lord Herbert of Cherbury, the father of
English deism. He would certainly have been willing to go
along with the English rationalists of the eighteenth century,
who emphasized the strong relation between religion and
morality, the eternity of the moral law, the basic oneness of
all religious ideals, the rejection of miracles and of irrational
revelation, and the ultimate appeal to reason.

The English and other eighteenth-century deists held fast
to the conviction that these principles and ideas which we
have just mentioned are held in common by intelligent
people, that all "modern" people are prepared to reject the
"superstitions" of the historic churches and creeds. It follows
from these common beliefs and from the common hope for a
moral and ethical order that men should unite to attain their
goals. This hope expressed itself, particularly in early eighteenth-century England, in the flowering of the Masonic
movement and its liturgy, a movement and a ritual with
which Hart was, as we have seen, probably well acquainted.

A non-Masonic effort in the same direction in contemporary England (1720) was documented in the *Pantheisticon,
sive Formula celebrandae Sodalitatis Socraticae* of John Toland.[12] This English deist had hopes of creating a Socratic
Society, for which his *Pantheisticon* was to serve as a liturgy.
It is a liturgy of a sort, yet this work has little, if anything, in
common with *Modern Religion*. The atmosphere is Socratic

---

12. I have used Ludwig Fench's German translation of *Pantheisticon—
Das Pantheistikon des John Toland* (Leipzig, 1897)—for want of an available copy of the original.

or Hellenistic and is modelled on the Platonic dialogues, particularly the *Symposium*. The whole approach is philosophic, not theological. Horatian odes are sung, reason is glorified, superstition is denounced, death is rationalized. There are no reminiscences of the standard forms common to the Jewish and Christian religions. It is a very popular, simple, philosophic ritual that sets out deliberately to ignore the liturgical background of the great historic religions of the European world. When all the illustrious worthies of the past are invoked, from Solomon to Hypatia, Moses and Jesus are pointedly omitted. There is very little, even in content, which Hart could have borrowed from this work of Toland, certainly nothing of form. In the latter part of the century, the quondam English preacher, David Williams, opened a deistic church in London, and, with Basedow, of Dessau, became one of the precursors of the French theophilanthropist movement which we shall soon discuss. The French theophilanthropists, in turn, found enthusiastic followers in the English Friends of Morality in the last decade of the same century. It is by no means improbable that Moses Hart may have been influenced by this English manifestation of an original French deistic movement. However, before we attempt to make a decision, it may be advisable to determine if he was exposed to some North American manifestation of French or English deism, and it is to colonial America that we now turn.

Because of the religious radicalism of present day Unitarianism, the student is tempted to seek for some influence of early Unitarianism, particularly American Unitarianism, upon the thinking of Moses Hart. This would be a gross error. Outside of their concept of God, the Unitarians of the late eighteenth and early nineteenth century were poles apart from the teachings of *Modern Religion*. The Unitarian leaders of Hart's time were comfortably ensconced behind the wall of a traditional Christian theology. They had rejected the divinity of Jesus, but the conservative theology and the authority of the Bible still remained. The cultured and wealthy Bostonians and their immediate neighbors, who were now the core of the new, evolving antitrinitarian church, would never have accepted the deistic religion of *Modern Religion*, completely divorced as it was from the historic Christian faith. Joseph Priestley, whose works were probably not unknown to Moses Hart, would have been regarded by the latter as a rather conservative Christian, theologically at least. It is true that Priestley wrote against war (1769 and 1774) and attacked the slave trade (1788), and it may be that Hart in his attitude toward these institutions was influenced by Priestley's writings. It is just as probable that both men were influenced by the growing enlightenment and the social humanitarianism of the century which gave them birth. Hart could not have been unaware of the fact that it was the French National Convention that abolished Negro slavery in the French colonies on February 4, 1794.[13]

If we are to lay bare the roots of Hart's *Modern Religion*, we shall have to look farther to the left than Priestley and his friends. The heart of that "left" was reflected in the work and the influence of Elihu Palmer (d. 1806), a deistic preacher and organizer.

In 1794, under the influence of French political and religious radicalism, Palmer, a former Christian minister, established in New York City a Deistical Society which had certain "church" qualities. There was apparently no liturgy, but there was preaching every Sunday night. Following the example of the New York City fellowship, a somewhat similar one was organized by anti-Christian Masons in Newburgh, New York. They called themselves The Society of Ancient Druids. This was in the late 1790's, for Palmer was preaching or lecturing to them in 1799. By 1801, there was a deistic society in Philadelphia calling itself the Theophilanthropists —the lovers of God and man—after a similar organization of that name which flourished in the days of the French Revo-

---

13. See Joseph Henry Allen and Richard Eddy, *A History of the Unitarians and the Universalists in the United States* (New York, 1894); G. Adolf Koch, *Republican Religion* (New York, 1933), p. 295.

lution. This Philadelphia group attempted to build or buy a hall which was to be "not a house of prayer nor a house of any sort of ceremony." It was to be "a house of Reason and the one God is to be the sole object of mental worship and veneration in it." This was in 1801. During the weekdays— when there was no lecture—this building was to be used for the instruction of the youth, primarily in mathematics. This Philadelphia organization was more of a society than a "church." Its meetings, except for its public lectures, were held in secret. The members, like the Masons and the European Illuminati, were divided into grades; the discussions were philosophic rather than religious. A similar group with the same name—the Theophilanthropists—was established about the same time in Baltimore, and probably in other cities, too. Palmer's influence was felt through the deistic magazines which he helped establish: *The Temple of Reason* appeared from 1801 to 1803 in New York and Philadelphia; *The Prospect: or, View of the Moral World* appeared in New York from 1803 to 1805.

Tom Paine, who had written his famous deistic and anti-Christian *The Age of Reason* in 1794, finally came back to the United States in 1802 and gave this deistic church movement a new impetus. He was an active member of the New York Deistical Society of 1804 and cherished the hope that it would some day develop into a Deistic Church. This hope was not realized, but the year after his death the declining deists summoned up their strength and in 1810 began publishing *The Theophilanthropist.* This was to be a deistic monthly "containing critical, moral, theological and literary essays." It is curious that the publisher, though not the "proprietor" of the magazine, was Henry Hart, of 117 Chatham Street, New York, a New York Jewish (?) deist who could well have been related to the Canadian Harts. It is very likely that *Modern Religion* itself was published in New York by this same Henry Hart.

Moses Hart had something in common with the Deistic Church of Palmer and Paine. This latter group, organized into a fixed society, had preaching and a hall; only the liturgy was absent. Palmer and Paine fought political oppression and religious bigotry. Both men were opposed to the traditional theology of organized Christianity; both were strongly influenced by the teachings and practices of the French Revolution. Hart, too, asked for political liberty, although much more circumspectly. He was not of the stuff of which heroes are made. He had something to lose, too. He was a wealthy man. He made no attacks on Christian or Jewish orthodoxy; he merely ignored both faiths in his liturgical system. They do not even exist for him in the body of his work, and in his advertisement he implies that both the Old and the New Testament deserve no credence because the former—in its present form—was not written by Moses, as commonly stated, and as for the latter: "We are ignorant whether they [the Evangels] wrote by inspiration, hearsay, or ocular demonstration: at what period they flourished, of what country they were, or even the language they wrote in." It is obvious that Hart, like Palmer and his rationalist friends, will have no truck with "religious superstition," the greatest bar to education and universal progress.

Like Priestley, *The Temple of Reason* fought for the unmarried mother; *The Theophilanthropist* opposed war. Hart, too, as we have seen, was concerned over these two social ills.

It is not too farfetched to assume that Moses Hart followed the Palmer and Paine deistic church movement from its rise in 1794, in the wake of the French Revolution, to its decline in 1811, when *The Theophilanthropist* suspended publication. He was a frequent visitor to the United States. No doubt, he attempted to profit by the errors and mistakes of the New York crowd. His own statement of beliefs shows no dependence on the "Principles of the Deistical Society of the State of New York." The failure of the American movement in 1811 was certainly obvious to him when, seven years later, he published his *Modern Religion*. Apparently, he was

prepared to develop his own system, independent of the ha-
ranguing deistic evangelism of Palmer and Paine.[14]

There is still one major source of influence on Hart which
we have not discussed, and this is the religious counterpart of
the French Revolution. The address of Robespierre on the
Supreme Being, delivered on June 8, 1794 (20th Prairial),
was reported in American newspapers; an address of another
leader, made in the Temple of Reason in France, in the second year of the Republic, was reported in *The Theophilanthropist*. There can be no question that Hart must have
known of these radical religious changes in France. All the
papers were full of them; he lived in a French-Canadian environment; he was well acquainted with the French language,
and he may even have had contacts with some of those
French priests who had fled to Canada. It may be no fortui-
tous circumstance that the distinguished French revolution-
ist, Bishop Henri Grégoire, wrote a short article for the re-
formist German-Jewish periodical *Sulamith*, III, 2 (1811),
426–27, excerpting the material on the Hart family of Canada from the work of John Lambert, *Travels through Lower
Canada*. Does this not imply that Grégoire may have been in
correspondence with Moses Hart or one of his brothers? A
further analysis of *Modern Religion*, however, will disclose
to what extent it was influenced by the religious revolution
which accompanied the political upheaval in France after
1789.

The leaders of the French Revolution, particularly during
the period from 1793 to 1802—approximately the time when
Elihu Palmer was most active in the United States—were determined to destroy the old state church, Catholicism, and to
set up a new religion which would strengthen the state and
help it attain its revolutionary goals. The leaders stumbled
about in this attempt, but never lost sight of their real aims.

14. For the American deistic movement, see Koch, *Republican Religion,*
and Herbert M. Morais, *Deism in Eighteenth Century America* (New
York, 1934).

During the days of the Cult of Reason (from about November, 1793, to about June, 1794), Reason was deified; in the spring and summer of 1794, the Cult of the Supreme Being was established by Robespierre and was continued even after his execution in July. In actual practice—certainly in the minds of many—there was little distinction between the two cults; they merged into one another. What is important is the fact that in these systems—until their abolition by Napoleon in 1802—the attempt was made to create a new religion with its own holy days, martyrs, liturgies, hymnologies, and the like. We shall attempt to show that it was this cult and its liturgy, rather than its English and American counterparts, that most directly influenced Moses Hart and his *Modern Religion*.

Robespierre, who was very much interested in establishing a rational religion built on the teachings of Rousseau and furthering devotion to France, felt that it was imperative to encourage belief in a beneficent Supreme Being, in the life to come, in reward and punishment for the just and the wicked, and in the sanctity of the social contract and its laws.[15] On May 7, 1794 (18 Floréal, Year II), a decree was therefore passed which was to establish this new religion on a firm foundation. The theology of the French people, we are told, is the recognition of the existence of the Supreme Being and the immortality of the soul. This Divinity is to be worshipped through the practice of the duties of man. These duties lie in the attempt to help the unfortunate and the oppressed, in crushing tyranny and injustice, and in the effort "to do to others all the good that is possible." To manifest their devotion to this theology and to these ideals, the French are called upon to celebrate festivals in honor of the Supreme Being and of the dignity of man. Four major festivals are to be observed; thirty-six additional festivals—one every tenth day of the new thirty-day month—are to be instituted, com-

---

15. See *The Social Contract* of J. J. Rousseau, Book IV, Chapter VIII, Civil Religion.

memorating the virtues of humanity and the gifts of nature.[16]

Like Voltaire, Robespierre believed that all these civic-religious ideals were of great social and moral value, but would not receive mass acceptance unless they were clothed in an attractive liturgical garb. The more appealing and aesthetic this religion was, the better it could cope with and ultimately supplant Catholicism. To accomplish this purpose, Robespierre, we may assume, was prepared to encourage the use and spread of an official liturgical ceremonial. Even before his death, these civic-religious rituals were already in use. After his fall in July, 1794, the spread of the new religion went on apace. His death brought no slackening of his religious hopes. There were services for the celebration of the recurring tenth day (*décadi*) which was to supplant the Saturday or Sunday day of rest. In some places the people venerated the great historic martyrs of the past and the present—Brutus, Marat, etc.—instead of the saints. Many important events of life, formerly associated with Catholicism, such as marriages and burials, were now observed with a secular ceremonial. The devotees of the new state cult stressed the significance of the decadary festivals, which they believed would win the hearts of the people away from the established forms of Christianity through dances, patriotic songs, and moral instruction.

The efforts of Robespierre and his successors to establish a ceremonial, patriotic religion devoted to the interests of the state were furthered by the rise, in 1796, of the semiofficial Theophilanthropists. This was a society closely related in content and form to the state cult of Robespierre and to the decadary festivals of the Directory. It rejected all creeds, dogmas, and forms of supernatural revelation—some of its members were atheists. Many others, like Tom Paine, were deists. Its followers gathered for worship in homes and in temples to pursue their moral teachings. When it reached the zenith of its influence in the fall of 1798, it held services in

---

16. For the Decree for Establishing the Worship of the Supreme Being, see F. M. Anderson, *The Constitutions. . . . of the History of France, 1789–1901* (Minneapolis, 1904), p. 137.

practically all the churches of Paris. Its ceremonial was reduced to a minimum; its shrines and altars were adorned with the products of field and garden. Like the devotees of the national cult, the Theophilanthropists had their hymns and addresses, and discoursed on the virtues of a Washington, Socrates, or Rousseau. Napoleon practically destroyed the waning cult in 1801 by refusing to permit it to use the churches and other public buildings for its services, but it still managed to drag out an obscure existence for a few more years. This society, which had its imitators in Germany, England, Italy, and the United States, was founded by a bookseller named Jean Baptiste Chemin-Dupontès, who enjoyed the support of Louis Marie de La Révellière-Lépeaux, a member of the Directory. Chemin's *Manuel* was sent into the provinces by the government, and the catechism of the Theophilanthropists was accorded official approval. But it remained the private religious society of a limited number of intellectuals and never became a state cult.

This, in brief, was the French Revolutionary background that must have impressed itself on Moses Hart. The points of correspondence between *Modern Religion* and these civic cults are numerous, and it is safe to conjecture that this whole development was known to him. In all probability, he had before him one or several of the local civic religious manuals of the state cult and the Theophilanthropists when he composed his own work.

In the decree of 18 Floréal, Year II, Robespierre had declared that "the worship of the Supreme Being is the practice of the *duties* of man." Hart's basic principles are conceived of as "*duties* obligatory." Tucked away in the back of Hart's mind is the ideal of the French Temple of Reason, and this creeps forth almost unconsciously when he describes the place of worship as the "temple."

Participants in the French national festivals were sometimes asked to take the oath (*serment*) of loyalty to the revolution; Hart prescribed a sacred installation oath for his devotees. French legislation attempted to make the *décadi* a real

Day of Rest. People were compelled to be present at the meetings and were forbidden to work or even to secure food in public places while the addresses were being delivered. Hart also asked for a complete cessation from unnecessary work on his Day of Rest.

The themes of youth, manhood, and old age were the occasions for three separate *décadi* festivals in the decree of the 18th Floréal, Year II. At the time of the Directory, some of the churches taken over by the State were called the Temple of Youth, Old Age, etc. Hart, too, dedicates his three great annual festivals to these same three stages of life, and like the *décadi* festivals these holydays are tied up with the corresponding seasons of spring, summer-autumn, and winter.

In the famous pageant of the Cult of Reason, on November 10, 1793 (20th Brumaire, Year II), and in the similar celebration of the Supreme Being on June 8, 1794 (20th Prairial, Year II), young women, dressed in white, marched in procession, carrying wreaths and singing hymns. In one of the ceremonial parades of the 20th Prairial, old men were shown on an oxcart, carrying sheaves and vinestocks to represent agriculture, and a rule and square to symbolize the arts and industries. In other pageants women carried flowers; men boughs of oak. Similar ceremonials are prescribed in the three festivals of *Modern Religion*.

The state religion as conceived by the Directory, if not by Robespierre, was to offer a common meeting ground for the citizenry where all men could worship together on a common platform. The republican calendar, with its tenth-day rest day and its Bastille Day and other celebrations, did not directly conflict with the Saturday-Sunday day of rest and the traditional Judaeo-Christian festivals. One could thus follow both the state cult and Christianity, and many did. Observance of the decadary festivals did not, therefore, preclude loyalty to one's ancestral religion, although the State hoped that its national faith would ultimately displace the traditional historic churches. Robespierre wanted all sects to "mingle spontaneously in the universal religion of nature."

Hart nourished somewhat similar hopes for his religion of nature and accordingly made provision for its observance by Jews, Christians, and Moslems. While he expected that his *Modern Religion* would be used exclusively by a specific group of Jews and deists, he also hoped that it would be followed by all religious groups, albeit separately, in their own respective synagogues, churches, and mosques. His three Grand Festivals, therefore, were set on Wednesdays, and the calendar for these days—which he appends to the liturgy—was, in all likelihood, so arranged as to provide a minimum of conflict with the traditional Jewish and Christian holydays.

The whole atmosphere of Hart's religion was akin to that of the French cults of Reason and of the Supreme Being, and that of the decadary festivals. Like them, it was very close to the State; Hart tells us the "legislature" has the power to compose and establish additional religious services. Like them, it is completely uncreedal in character. If it had any "orthodoxy," it is an emphasis on the eighteenth-century "trinity" of God, immortality, and ethics. Like the French, Hart did not advocate any theological change or modification of the established churches. He was not attempting a reform from within. *Modern Religion* was not part of an evolutionary development, such as in those English and American churches of the late eighteenth and early nineteenth centuries, which were cautiously groping their way out of orthodox Calvinism into the dawn of a moderate liberalism. Hart, like the French, was a revolutionary. After making a perfunctory bow to the respectable concepts of God and immortality, he placed himself entirely outside the periphery of established theological thinking. He repudiated it. He attempted to create a new religion, a deistic one.[17]

17. For the history of religious development during the French Revolution, see F. A. Aulard, *Le Culte de la Raison et le Culte de L'Etre Suprême* (Paris, 1892); A. Aulard, *Christianity and the French Revolution* (Boston, 1927); Albert Mathiez, *The Fall of Robespierre* (New York, 1927), pp. 84–118; Mathiez, *After Robespierre* (New York, 1931), pp. 137–55; Georgia Robison, *Révellière–Lépeaux Citizen Director 1753–1824* (New York, 1938), pp. 161–95; Pierre de la Gorce, *Histoire Religieuse de la Révolution Française* (Paris, 1924), IV, 269 ff.; Mathiez, *La Théophilanthropie et le*

The influence of the French Revolution is stamped on this booklet of Moses Hart; yet there are a number of marked differences which indicate that the author had consciously departed from the French civil religious system. In relation to the practices of the French state cult for the period from 1793 to 1802, Hart definitely veered to the right by returning to the traditional forms even though this was a return to externals alone. Why, we may ask, did Hart make these concessions, superficial though they may have been?

In 1818, when Hart published his work, the Metternich System of reaction and oppression was already in force. The ideals of the French Revolution, even in their diluted Napoleonic form, had been suppressed. In Canada, the Hart brothers had experienced religious bigotry and political discrimination in a very personal fashion during the period from 1807 to 1812. Although Viscount Castlereagh, back in England, had officially sanctioned the action of Sir James Craig in dissolving the Assembly in the Hart affair, nevertheless, in a personal letter to the governor, dated September, 1809, he pointed out that a Jew had no right to sit in Parliament.[18] In the United States, deism as a church had died a mute, anemic death in 1811. Protestantism had developed no great liberal church; William Ellery Channing's Unitarianism—a relatively conservative faith, at best—was not to burgeon forth till 1819. Canada was strongly Catholic and conservative.

Hart, obviously devoted to the promulgation of deism, believed strongly that the times required a liberal religious faith, but realized that the somewhat reactionary age would not tolerate marked deviations. It would certainly not be expedient to transfer the deistic state cult of France bodily to the atmosphere of a Catholic Quebec or to a religiously cautious and evangelically stirred United States. He resorted, therefore, to compromise. To be sure, he made no compro-

---

Culte Décadaire 1796–1801 (Paris, 1904); Julien Tiersot, *Les Fêtes et les Chants de la Révolution Française* (Paris, 1908).
18. Quoted in Rhinewine, p. 64.

mise in the rationalistic nature of his *Modern Religion*. It was
markedly unchristian and unjewish. There is no mention, no
intimation in the text, of an Old or a New Testament. The
traditional Bible was ignored. The Creator was there, in a
colorless fashion. (But even though he is described by a variety of attributes and synonyms, the careful Hart never once
refers to him *à la Robespierre* as the Supreme Being.) There
was a flabby immortality and a materialistic concept of reward and punishment here in this life. There was no burning
fire of fervor or mystic faith in the author of *Modern Religion*. He was spiritually cold; he was superficially intellectu-
alistic. There was no deep philosophic insight in him or his
ritual. He was a typical eighteenth-century deist, not a
prophet. Unlike that of the French revolutionaries, however,
his cult had a priest and ministers, and a hierarchy of a sort.
The French revolutionaries had attempted to create a civic,
national cult; he was seeking to create a universal religion.
The French, fearful of the hostile intentions of their neighbors, were trying to foster a patriotic cult; Hart, after a war
of invasion, was interested in establishing a religion of peace.
The occasional prayers, the structure of the service, the cal-
endation with its seven-day week, all this shows a departure,
for the most part, from the French revolutionary cults and a
dependence on the Jewish and Christian books of common
prayer and on the traditional Judaeo-Christian liturgical system. The three major holy days which he prescribed are,
roughly speaking, chronologically close to Easter-Passover,
to the Jewish High Holy Days and the Feast of Ingathering,
and to Christmas-Hanukkah (The Feast of Lights).

Did Hart really entertain the thought that the Catholics
and Protestants and Jews of Great Britain, Canada, and the
United States would take his manual seriously? Was it a mere
literary whim which he decided to publish? If we may take
him at his word in his advertisement, he intended this "ceremonial religion, founded on natural principles," for Jews
and deists alone. Evidently, he believed that the Jews of
the United States and Canada—there were only a few thou-

sand of them—were culturally ripe for his advanced religious system. Many of them, like his brother Ezekiel, who did not scruple to take the Christian oath, had no doubt assimilated themselves radically to their non-Jewish environment. Hannah Adams, a contemporary writer, points out: "It appears from authentic accounts that many Jews at the present day have imbibed the principles of infidelity, and no longer receive the writings of the Old Testament as divinely inspired, or expect the coming of the Messiah." [19] Yet it is curious that Moses still remained an occasional contributor to the Spanish-Jewish Congregation Shearith Israel, of New York, during this period.[20] His aid to this mother synagogue of American Jewry, however, may merely have been motivated by loyalty to the memory and wishes of his late father. He never surrendered his liberal views. This is confirmed by a letter, dated April 12, 1830, which his son Areli-Blake Hart sent from a France once more in the throes of revolution: "You can tell the Governor and Uncle Ezekiel that France is the land of political and religious freedom; all the French are Deists; the shops are opened the same as another day of a Sunday. The women sawing [sewing?] at the window of a Sunday. The revolution and Voltaire has destroyed the Christian religion in this country. . . ." [21] Nine years later, May 10, 1839, Moses wrote to the Canadian authorities asking for financial aid in the establishment of an academy "for the education of the youth of both sexes. . . . I do not mean that children should be divested of religious instruction," he added in this letter, "for this could be given them at some other place as their parents might think proper, but to make the Academy encourage every sect, no particular prayer should be used, so that virtue and respect for the Great Creator would be inculcated." [22]

Nowhere in this liturgy, it is true, does Hart specifically

19. *Historia Judaica*, VIII, 131.
20. *PAJHS*, XXVII, 78.
21. Douville, *Aaron Hart*, p. 191.
22. Quoted from Canadian records in *American Israelite*, June 14, 1917, p. 4.

ask the older faiths to scrap their systems; he does not even ask for a joint observance, yet he does offer a common ritual to be followed by the different faiths in their respective houses of worship. This ritual might well be accepted by all of them, so he thought, because he had sedulously avoided all historically motivated holydays and had proposed only mutually acceptable festivals of nature. Obviously, he is appealing to all religious groups, not merely to Jews and deists. Moreover, in his Preface, he does hold forth the hope that he might "tranquillize the jarring religionists under one banner . . . [and] harmonize the religious contentions of mankind." He probably nursed the hope—like his French forerunners—that his system would attract Christian and other orthodox religionists and ultimately supplant Christianity.

Yet there is apparently no evidence or tradition that he attempted seriously to implement his plan. Perhaps the "timing" was bad. Deism was dead, had been dead for almost a generation . . . but did Hart realize it? This work—if it has any importance—is significant as evidence of the penetrating influence of deism, eighteenth-century liberalism, and the French Revolution in the life of an individual Jew who lived in a quiet Canadian town. It is an evidence of the diffusion and spread of antiwar and antislavery sentiments in the life of this man. It is a demonstration that, in an age of expanding religious orthodoxy, individuals still nourished the hope of a universal rational faith. He saw the salvation of mankind in a common assimilation to common ideals. And it is fair to assume that he was not alone in the religious aspirations that he cherished.

But let there be no mistake: he was no unsung precursor of American Reform Judaism. Like the emerging Unitarians in the United States, the Reformers who first appeared in Charleston, S.C., in 1824 wanted to reform customs and to modify their creed, but they were equally determined to remain well within the field of traditional theology and well inside the magic circle of the ancestral faith. They were not revolutionists; they were not "assimilationists." Hart was.

Addendum

Since the above was written, the writer has had an opportunity to consult the Hart manuscripts in the Seminary of St. Joseph in Three Rivers, Canada, and takes this opportunity to thank the archivist, Abbé Tessier, for his courtesy in making this material available to him.

Investigation of the Moses Hart papers shows that as early as December 11, 1794, Moses Hart was experimenting with a type of radical prayer or a prayer manual. In 1815, he published *General Universal Religion*, By . . . ., New York, printed for the author, 1815. This is practically identical with the 1818 edition of *Modern Religion* except for pages 20–21 in the 1815 edition, which makes provision for half-marriages and half-wives and the legitimation of children resulting from such unions. This material was omitted in the 1818 edition. The ceremony for this type of semimarriage is also given in the 1815 edition. The 1815 edition, like that of 1818, contains 58 pages of text. The printers in 1815 were Van Winkle and Wiley. *Modern Religion* was reprinted by Johnstone and Van Norden in New York in 1824. The Three Rivers records also disclosed that Moses Hart made a systematic effort — at least during the period 1816–1826 — to establish his religion in Canada and the United States, particularly in Vermont, the home of that known religious radical, Ethan Allen. As late as 1825, Hart was in close touch with the associates and followers of Tom Paine.

The writer of this essay also had an opportunity to examine copies of various French catechisms and manuals issued by French religious radicals during the period of the French Revolution. The writer is more than ever convinced that Moses Hart was influenced by the religious trends of the French Revolution and by the attempts of J. B. Chemin-Dupontès and other Theophilanthropists to offer "natural religious" prayers that would substitute for the Christian liturgy. However, the actual wording of the prayers in *Modern Religion* (and *General Universal Religion*) are apparently original with Moses Hart.

The Three Rivers archives also included a ms. anti-Catholic polemic by Moses Hart.

9

FROM PEDDLER TO REGIMENTAL COMMANDER IN TWO YEARS: THE CIVIL WAR CAREER OF MAJOR LOUIS A. GRATZ

Early in 1861, a German Jewish immigrant, not yet twenty-two years of age, landed in New York City. The name by which he was to be known in this, the land of his adoption, was Louis A. Gratz. Judging by the surname, which was Grätz in German, the original home of his family was either in the Austro-Silesian town of Grätz or in the German-Polish town of the same name in the province of Posen. Although there is no conclusive evidence by any means, the likelihood is that the Louis A. Gratz family stemmed from this latter town, the same city that in all probability once sheltered an ancestor of Heinrich Grätz, the classical Jewish historian, and an ancestor of the Gratz brothers, notable Philadelphia merchants of the eighteenth century.

We do not know where Louis A. Gratz was born, but we do know that some years before his emigration he went to live with an uncle by the name of Kurtzig in the Posen town of Inowrazlaw. He made his home with this family for several years, and when later he joined the long stream of wanderers to these shores, he wrote back to his beloved relatives, describing his life and adventures in the new world. These German letters—some of which have been preserved and are appended to this article in translation—are the source of our knowledge of his career during the years 1861 to 1869.

Uncle Aron Kurtzig and Aunt Emma Kühlbrand Kurtzig were engaged in the manufacture of oil from rapeseed, and it

This study appeared originally in *Publications of the American Jewish Historical Society*, XXXVIII, 22–44.

was in the pursuit of this task that Kurtzig introduced the first steam engine and modern industry into his district. This was no mean task, for the nearest railroad was at Bromberg, twenty-six miles away, and all the heavy boilers and machines had to be dragged over the miry roads. The sticky mud of this part of the country was far-famed, and tradition had it that when Napoleon I was once bogged down in the neighborhood, he is reported to have said ironically: "And they call this a fatherland!"

Inowrazlaw, situated in the midst of a rich grain district, was a typical isolated German-Polish town. There was very little water in town—just a few wells—and the luxuries of life were conspicuously absent. When the children in the Kurtzig house once received an orange from one of the neighboring gentry, they did not eat it, but put it under glass where they could look at it as much as they wished and inhale its wonderful perfume. The town, in the decade of the 1850's, sheltered some 5,000 people, almost half of whom were Jews. Most of the latter were Orthodox and observant; the Kurtzigs we know were, and it was in this rigidly religious environment that young Gratz spent considerable time. We may safely assume that he was given the usual Jewish education and hence enjoyed some familiarity with the Hebrew language and ritual.

What induced this young man to leave Inowrazlaw for America? Although he lived under rather comfortable circumstances at home—he was by no means faced by want—he was induced by a friend to go to America in the hope of becoming rich. This was the lure that led him to say yes to the solicitation of his companion; the realities he found on his arrival were a grim disappointment.

The eight-week voyage on a sailing vessel almost took all the starch out of him; bad food and bad quarters left him shaken in body and soul when he arrived. He visited a cousin but was shabbily received and probably never called again; he knew no English, had no trade, and soon became so discouraged that he was almost disconsolate. His one friend, the

man who had accompanied him here, soon left him in the
lurch to take a job with a relative. His total fortune was ten
dollars, not a great deal for a stranger in a strange land, a
frightened, lonely young man of twenty-one. His board in a
good Jewish family, where the dietary laws were no doubt
observed, cost him two and one-half dollars a week, and at
that rate he knew his little nest egg would not last very long.
The eager immigrant tried desperately to get a job, but nobody had anything for him; everyone with whom he spoke
discouraged him, and finally he turned to the last—if not the
first—resort of every unskilled, but intelligent German Jewish immigrant: he became a peddler.

He invested part of his meager store of money in a basket
of shoelaces, thimbles, and stockings, and started climbing up
and down stairs, and knocking at doors in the great metropolis of New York. By dint of hard labor he earned enough to
pay his daily board. That meant he earned about thirty-five
cents a day. By this time—his first week in the country—he
knew the names and prices of the goods he carried. One of
the merchants who sold him his supplies helpfully suggested
that he would do better peddling in the countryside and even
offered him five dollars' worth of goods on credit. The
young man accepted the kind offer, trudged out to the farms
in the outlying districts, and did a little better until he ran
into rain. There could be no peddling while the mud in the
roads was knee-deep; he had to go back, and he walked the
twenty-five miles to the city carrying his pack on his back.
The net result of this first expedition on the road to fortune
was a bad fever and an infected leg.

Now his troubles really began. Instead of resting—how
could he afford to do this?—he started peddling again until
he was confined to bed with a constant fever. In the meantime his money was dwindling away because of his expenditures for food and medicine. There was but one thing to do:
go to a public hospital reserved primarily for the poor, a hospital where conditions were indescribably bad and where the
surgeons operated experimentally on his legs twice a week.

There is no indication that he went to Jews' Hospital—later Mount Sinai—and it is difficult to understand why he did not take advantage of its resources, unless, of course, he did attempt to do so, but was refused admittance for one reason or another. For six weeks he lay in the hospital, and when he was finally discharged, he returned to his former quarters, uncured and depressed. Fortunately he soon found a physician who did cure him, and again, for lack of something better, he took up his peddler's pack. The scene of his new labors was Carbondale in the coal country, and here he went to work in partnership with a New York clerk, originally a compatriot from Inowrazlaw, who had a capital of fifty dollars. During his nights and spare time, Gratz devoted himself to the study of English, for he realized the importance of a fluency in the vernacular, and like other ambitious men he was resolved to get ahead.

All these experiences were crowded into a few busy months, a half year at the most. In the meantime war broke out, and Abraham Lincoln issued his call for volunteers. Young Gratz—Lewis he then called himself, no doubt for the homonymous Löb or Levi—joined up in Pittston, Luzerne County, where many of his fellow Germans were to be found. What had he to lose in a ninety-day enlistment? Everyone was excited; there was wild enthusiasm, and the war would certainly be over in a few months. It could all be a very pleasant interlude, and so he enlisted as a volunteer in the Fifteenth Pennsylvania Infantry Regiment some time in late April or early May, 1861, telling the recruiting officer that he was twenty-two years of age. His biography, published during his own lifetime in the Goodspeed *History of Tennessee*, indicates he could have been only eighteen years of age.

It is questionable if he really thought seriously about the issues at stake; the war was for him probably a relief after the weary toil of peddling—an adventure. He was determined to make of it an opportunity. Unlike the vast majority of his fellow soldiers he now sat down to study the language in earnest; in a relatively short time he became a noncommissioned officer, a corporal, and then began to aspire to the lieutenant's bars of a commissioned officer. Day and night, when the opportunity presented itself, he studied English and military tactics; he had no money for private instruction. Our information is not adequate to trace his career in every detail, but we do know that he was a good soldier, stood out in action, if only in a modest sense, acquired influential friends, and was finally presented to Simon Cameron, then Secretary of War. Cameron, a consummate politician, was the Pennsylvania political boss and was willing to look kindly upon this attractive, ambitious, and brave young German who wanted a commission. Upon the expiration of his period of enlistment he reentered the service on October 7, 1861, as first lieutenant in Company B of the Ninth Pennsylvania Cavalry, the Lochiel Cavalry, which was sent West the following month to the Kentucky and Tennessee front. His regimental commander was Colonel E. C. Williams; his company commander, E. G. Savage. This was not a bad start for a young immigrant not yet a year in the country. Yet let it be remembered that it was not luck that had brought him this far; he had accomplished what he had through laborious and intensive study and under difficult circumstances. He was a young man of character.

As far as we know he had not written back home to the Kurtzigs since his arrival. No immigrant who set out for the American land of promise to pick up the gold lying in the streets ever cared to admit—certainly not to his relatives—that he had been a failure. Some immigrants, we know, deliberately lied about their disappointments and wrote home describing in detail the good fortune that existed only in their imagination. Gratz had preferred thus far to remain silent, but now that he had mounted the first rung of the ladder to success, he felt like crowing—just a little—to the folks at home. He had been promised a captaincy, and he set out to earn it; he was proud of what he had accomplished. Just a few months back, he was a struggling peddler barely making both ends meet; when he had peddled around Carbondale, no one wanted to know him; now he was on special duty as a recruiting officer with headquarters in Scranton, in the same neighborhood, and the best Jewish and Gentile homes were thrown open to him. Not many Jews could show a similar record of speedy achievement, he wrote. In this he was quite wrong. There were a number of German Jewish immigrants who had earned rapid promotion or made a brilliant career for themselves as speedily as this young man from Posen; a notable example was the gallant major of the Twelfth Alabama Infantry, Adolph Proskauer. "My dear ones, I beg you with all my heart not to be angry because I have gone to war," Gratz wrote home. ". . . And should it be my destiny to lose my life, well I will have sacrificed it for a cause to which I am attached with all my heart, that is: the liberation of the United States." The Americanization of Louis A. Gratz was proceeding apace, yet it would be false to infer that, even though this young soldier had already risked his life on the field of battle, and even though he was ready at the moment to do it over and over again, he had forgotten his native land. His heart still lay in Germany with his father and his relatives and his dear friends. It is almost asking too much to expect a man—even a young man—who has been in a country less than a year completely to disavow and surrender his past. There is such a thing as indecent haste. Gratz wrote home that, if he survived the war, he intended to return to Germany!

On August 4, 1862, Lieutenant Gratz was discharged from the Ninth Pennsylvania Cavalry, now fighting in Kentucky, and on the 16th of the same month accepted a commission as major in the Sixth Regiment Kentucky Cavalry. The Sixth was short of officers, and this able young lieutenant was jumped to a majority, probably never holding a captain's commission. During the fall and early winter of 1862, he was busy with his regiment, scouting and fighting around Cumberland Gap and chasing General Morgan, the Confederate raider; by December, he was already in command of the regiment, although only a major. The other regimental commanders in the brigade at this time had at least the rank of lieutenant colonel. He was now twenty-two or twenty-three years old according to his service record, possibly only nineteen.

The spring of 1863 found the Sixth Kentucky Cavalry and Major Gratz in Tennessee protecting the right flank of Rosecrans, and on September 19th and 20th, he was in the bitter battle of Chickamauga. It was probably during the action at Crawfish Springs that he nearly lost his liberty—and his life. Through the inept leadership of the Union general, the Northern front was opened up and the Confederates under Bragg poured in. The Sixth was repeatedly flanked, and at times almost if not completely surrounded. Gratz had to make the difficult decision of surrendering or fighting his way through. He dreaded the prospect of rotting away in a Southern detention camp—every Union soldier knew of the horrors of captivity—and made up his mind that he would rather be shot in battle than be taken prisoner: he gave the order to his men to break through the encircling forces which heavily outnumbered his. It was a desperate dash for safety, and a costly one. One hundred and twenty of his men were captured, several—surprisingly few—were killed; the regimental chaplain was shot down at his side; his adjutant, ten paces behind him, was captured, and his orderly, three paces behind him, was shot dead off his horse.

The courageous conduct and presence of mind of Gratz at Chickamauga may have been one of the factors that induced General Samuel Powhatan Carter to place him on his personal staff on December 25, 1863. Carter was now stationed at Knoxville, and in all probability it was at this time that Major Gratz learned to know the young lady whom he was ultimately to marry. In the summer of 1864, he made the march through Georgia with Sherman, and the following spring, in March, he was in North Carolina serving as Acting Assistant Inspector General at the headquarters of the Second Division of the Twenty-Third Army Corps; in April, at

Raleigh, he was appointed Acting Assistant Adjutant General for the Third Division. Three months later, on July 14, 1865, he was mustered out of the service at Edgefield, Tennessee, near Nashville.

In December, 1863, when Gratz was appointed to the staff of General Carter, he was already a seasoned cavalry officer who had seen a lot of service. Judging from a letter written to the folks back home a few months later, he was not only seasoned, but hardened. With all the bravura of the dashing cavalry officer who had earned his spurs on the field of battle, he talked toughly of exterminating the rebels. "Our army is standing on the soil of the South, our flag is waving in every rebellious state." We would have won this war before had it not been for the traitors in our own midst, right in the cabinet itself. If the patriotic feelings of the people would be appealed to, the war would be soon over. The call for 500,000 and the threat to draft the unwilling was a wise move. We shall yet wash away the stains of dishonor with our heart's blood. But even this magniloquent outburst of youthful patriotism could not help the young soldier hide from himself the distress and the suffering about him. He bitterly attacked the people of the South and exulted for a moment in their despair—was he trying to hide his own sense of guilt as one of the ravaging troops?—but in the next moment he wrote contritely: "I can assure you that I am often heartsick thinking of the distress of the people." In his thinking, in his feeling, he was completely at one with those with whom he had thrown in his lot. It is "our cabinet," "our army," "our battles." His Americanization had taken deeper root. There is no talk or postscript of returning permanently to Germany after the war. This land was to be his home.

This sentiment of "belonging" was reflected even more fully in General Orders, No. 34, issued on June 17, 1865, at the Headquarters of the Third Division of the Twenty-Third Army Corps, at Greensboro, N.C. It was General Carter's valedictory to the men of this division as they were about to be mustered out of service, and was countersigned by the Acting Assistant Adjutant General, L. A. Gratz. It is safe to assume that this adjutant—like most adjutants since time immemorial—wrote General Orders, No. 34, for his commanding officer, and that it expresses the sentiments and words of Major Gratz as much as those of the Major General. "Three or more years ago," the valedictory reads, "you left all that was dear to you to respond to the call made upon you by the country, to save it from disunion and to overthrow a wicked rebellion. . . . Nobly you rallied around our starry banner and vowed to save it, and by unfurling it over every inch of this great country, secure liberty to all and for all time to come. Gallantly have you kept your vow. Through your exertions and deeds of valor our country stands today more glorious than ever, the proudest among the proud, and the first among the free." In every sense of the word, this immigrant was now an American.

Ever since Gratz had been detailed to the staff of General Carter—the famous sailor on horseback—he had had more time for himself. This mature and thoughtful young man realized the war would soon be over and knew that he would again have to go out and hustle for a living. When he was mustered out, he was offered a colonelcy in the new army, but refused to accept it; he was interested only in active service and was beginning to tire of a soldier's life: he had been in for over four years. His English had improved, so much so that frequently he was taken for a native American. During his leisure moments at staff headquarters in 1864 and 1865 he had studied law religiously, on the promise of fellow officers, practicing lawyers back home, that they would prepare him for the bar examination in the shortest possible time.

The close of the war found him back in Knoxville, his old headquarters. There, in 1865, he soon hung out his shingle; and on October 18, he married Elizabeth Twigg Bearden, whom he described to his family as a beautiful and virtuous woman related to one of the oldest and best families in the state. Her father, Captain Marcus D. Bearden, was to be mayor of Knoxville from 1868 to 1870. Like many of the other lawyers of the early postwar period, Gratz had to do a lot of circuit traveling. Apparently he had plenty of work offered him, although the people were frequently too poor to pay; hard cash was scarce, and he had to be content with promissory notes which were as good as the harvest that was yet to come in. Judging from his letters of this period, the struggle was not too onerous, for he was a man of more than ordinary capacity and was soon making a modest, but comfortable living. Years later he found lucrative clients, like the Knoxville Water Company and the Grabfelder interests of Louisville. By the fall of 1867, he already owned his own home on the outskirts of town, had a large lot with a fine garden on it, and the beginnings of a fast-growing family. Ultimately, Lizzie Bearden was to bear him five children.

Like other veterans of his day—and a later day!—he went into politics. He was twice elected city attorney of Knoxville, was the first mayor of North Knoxville after it was incorporated in 1889, served for four terms (1889–1892), and worked hard to establish adequate public schools in this new village. He saw that Knoxville was a growing town and anticipated its growth by laying out the Gratz addition to the city; Gratz Street still recalls this early enterprise.

He was also active from the seventies on in the national fraternal and benefit society, the Knights of Honor, an organization numbering hundreds of lodges and including many thousands of members, and in the 1880's he became its Supreme Dictator. By 1893 he was living in Louisville where he represented this order and served, at the same time, as private counsel for Mr. S. Grabfelder, the well-known whiskey dealer who also had hotel interests in Knoxville. It was while on a business mission for Mr. Grabfelder that Gratz died of a heart attack on a train going from Louisville to Knoxville, on the night of September 19, 1907. At the time of his death, his first wife had already died, and he was survived by his second wife who also bore him several sons and daughters. All told, he left twelve children. His widow, the former Miss Fiddler, had once been a Mrs. Kempshall.

The career of Louis A. Gratz, after he was mustered out of the service, was not atypical. It was the normal success story of the competent American lawyer who worked hard, acquired more or less wealth, attained a considerable degree of recognition from his colleagues, and left a family of sturdy, church-going children. As students of American Jewry, however, we are not primarily interested in the typical career of this American citizen. Louis A. Gratz was not only an American, he was also a Jew by ethnos and originally, at least, by religion. In Inowrazlaw, as a boy in his teens, the "Jewish" part of him was not inconsiderable. In the 1850's, the Jews of this town had little to do with the Poles, and the German Gentiles still looked askance at Jews. Years before Gratz left town, during the post-Napoleonic period, Aunt Emma's father, a physician, had distinguished himself fighting an epidemic of typhus, and the Prussian authorities, as a reward, had offered to make him a district physician, but only on condition that he become a convert to Christianity. Conditions had improved somewhat since then, but complete civil and political rights—on paper—were not to be granted to Prussian Jewry until the 1860's. During this period the majority of the Jews in town still spoke a German Yiddish, kept kosher, went frequently, if not daily, to the synagogue, and, no doubt, many of them still sported the earlocks of the pious religionist. This was the outer form of the heritage that Major Gratz brought with him to these shores. What happened to it in America?

In September, 1867, the Major wrote home that since he had decided to remain in Tennessee, he was determined to become one with the people. This sounds almost like an apology to his Orthodox Jewish relatives for marrying out of the faith. His "Jewishness"—that undefinable, but not indefinite something—had been gradually slipping away from him. As far as we know, the noun and adjective "Jew" and "Jewish" do not occur in any of his letters after that of November, 1861. He had ample opportunity, had he so desired, to maintain close religious contacts with the Jewish community in the town of Knoxville in 1865. There were at least fifteen families there, and just about that time—it might have been a year earlier or a year later—they had established a confraternity, the Hebrew Benevolent Society, which also conducted religious services. The Knoxville Jewish records—woefully inadequate, it is true—offer no evidence that he joined the Jewish group. No doubt he had to make some sort of decision in his own mind as to whether he would affiliate himself actively with the Jewish religious group, and apparently the decision was in the negative. There is no indication in his obituary, in the *Knoxville Sentinel* for September 20, 1907, that he was even born a Jew. All this does not mean that he had no social relations with the little Jewish community; he could not have avoided meeting some of them every day, and, as a matter of fact, one of his friends was a cultured Bavarian Jewish immigrant, Squire Julius Ochs. Captain Ochs—he had served in the Fifty-Second Ohio Volunteers, a militia regiment—had come to town in 1864 and gone into business, but had never achieved any degree of economic success. One of his boys, Adolph, had been compelled to go to work to help the family eke out an existence, and at eleven years of age he was already getting up every morning at five o'clock to deliver newspapers on his route. Louis Gratz, who knew the family well, must have seen the boy frequently, but certainly hardly dreamed that this little fellow was one day to become the owner and builder of *The New York Times*. Another son of the Squire, Milton B. Ochs, was acquainted with the Major, but never knew that he was a Jew.

Captain Ochs was a justice of the peace from 1868 to 1872, and Gratz must have brought some cases into his court during this period. The Squire was also the unpaid volunteer rabbi in town, but, as we suggested above, we have no way of knowing if the Major ever came to services even to hear his friend preach on the High Holy Days. We do know that Gratz reared his children as Christians. We may assume that the Squire and the Major met in the Grand Army of the Republic posts where they were both active, and when the former died in Chattanooga in 1888, the Major went there to serve as one of the pallbearers.

In the course of time Gratz forgot much of his native German—for his wife and children did not speak or understand the language—although for a few years he still cherished hopes of securing a diplomatic post in Prussia in order to be able to see his family once more. These hopes were never realized; he never returned to the land of his birth.

The following German letters sent by Louis A. Gratz to Uncle Aron and Aunt Emma Kurtzig in Inowrazlaw were published—with certain omissions of a more personal nature —by Aron's son, Heinrich Kurtzig, in *Ostdeutsches Judentum* ("East German Jewry") in 1927. These letters, which are the chief source for our knowledge of the career of Gratz for the years 1861–1869, are given here in translation:

Scranton, November 25, 1861

I will start from the moment I came to America, and you will learn from my short biography that America is the only country where one can make his fortune although in a variety of ways. When I came to this country all my property amounted to ten dollars. In addition, I did not understand the English language, and I had neither relatives nor friends. By pure accident I was introduced by a young man to a poor Jewish family of good reputation with whom I lived as a guest paying two and a half dollars a week. Living in this way did not solve my problem; however, I had at least found some people who did not cheat me and who provided me with cheap though poor food.

I wasn't particularly happy, and I felt also very depressed, for I had not learned any trade. I could not expect to become a bookkeeper, even to get a very small position in a business, for who would accept a young man without any other recommendation than his good looks, a young man completely unfamiliar with the language and the customs of this country? In addition, eight weeks on a sailing vessel under every imaginable deprivation had very much weakened my physical and intellectual strength. Although I had the intention of forgetting all my comfortable and easy past after my departure from Europe, and of concentrating my efforts towards the single goal of becoming a rich man — a goal only possible by hard work, toil, and economy — the execution of this plan was harder than I had thought. Everybody whom I asked for advice gave me a discouraging reply. I began to realize, only too clearly, that there is money lying around on the streets of America, but that it is very difficult and hard to pick it up. A young man, who had induced me to emigrate, and who, despite the fact of having more money, promised to work together with me, deserted me after a few days because he had found a position in a shop through the recommendation of one of his relatives. I visited my cousin Louis Basch, but I was coolly received; a question as to how things were at home was his only interest in me.

However, it was necessary for me to do something. My ten dollars was sufficient for four weeks; after that I would be without a penny. During those days I approached one person after another, willing to work for almost nothing, but, unfortunately, people believe that a young man cannot be any good who looks respectable and pretends also to be respectable, but yet is willing to take any small job.

Having spent two and a half dollars for board and lodging during the first week, I was compelled to buy some notions for the remaining seven dollars — fifty cents had been spent for small expenses — and to peddle them. My "splendid" stock in trade consisted of shoelaces, stockings, thimbles, needles, and pins. This was to be the cornerstone of my fortune of the future, and besides I would have to make enough to eat, drink, and buy clothes, especially shoes.

The first day's attempt at peddling was made in New York. From early in the morning until late in the night I climbed up and down stairs, until finally I made enough to pay for board and lodging for a single day. You can imagine how difficult it was for me to make even that much dealing with notions, for I could barely memorize the English names and prices of my stock, and I could not answer any other question. After having peddled for a week in New York, I had scarcely made enough for my board and lodging. The merchant from whom I bought my articles, seeing how I struggled, advised me to go to the country, and was even willing to loan me merchandise to the value of five dollars. Naturally, I accepted this offer and started at the beginning of the next week.

The first day I did well; I made a little more than I needed for food, although I ate only breakfast and supper, and as cheaply as possible. On the second and third day I also earned the money I needed for my living, but it rained on the fourth. I was compelled to spend the entire day at the inn. When the rain still did not stop the next day, I returned to New York, because it wouldn't cost me so much to live there. There are not as many good roads here as back home. The roads here are of sand and clay and a little rain is sufficient to transform them into mud. It was on a path like this that I had to walk twenty-five English miles with my pack on my back, and sinking into the mud up to my knees.

My dear friends, for the first time in America it was difficult for me to endure these hardships and privations. I finally dragged myself into New York, and the result was a fever and an injured foot which, however, I ignored. I was well aware that my material conditions did not permit me to become sick. So the next day I peddled again in New York. Although I had not eaten during the whole day, I felt too sick in the evening to take any food. In addition, my foot was so badly hurt and swollen that I could not walk. I went to bed, and a full eight days passed before the fever disappeared. But the foot! The people with whom I lived did not know, naturally, that I was so poor, otherwise they would not have kept me any longer. My financial situation did not permit me to stay in bed for six weeks. That period, according to my doctor, was absolutely necessary for the recovery of my health. I did not have money enough to pay for my food, and even less to pay for the doctor and his expensive prescriptions. I had to make up my mind to go to a hospital for the poor where medical treatment, medicines, and food were free of charge.

My dear friends! You cannot imagine what I suffered during the six weeks which I had to spend in the hospital among sick people of all kinds and under loathsome conditions. Twice a week the doctors of the hospital operated on my foot, and, in my opinion, made it only worse. I could not understand their reason. Probably the doctors did it in order to find out how a negligible wound could cause so much irritation and swelling. I can only stress that after six weeks I left the hospital on my own initiative, physically and mentally more ill than before I had entered it. From the hospital I returned to the people with whom I had formerly lodged. There a doctor promised to cure me completely within four weeks, and all that for a fee of five dollars. I preferred to spend my last penny for such treatment and even to go into debt rather than to stay longer in the hospital. And so I submitted myself to this treatment by Dr. Berg. To put it briefly, after four weeks I had recovered, but was as poor as a church mouse. I had to pull in a notch in my belt, for my hosts had reduced the cost of my board, and therefore I had to eat less.

During this time I met a young man whom I had known before in Inowrazlaw and who worked as a clerk in New York. After my complete recovery we agreed to peddle together. I was very happy, since the young man had about fifty dollars, and I was entitled to fifty per cent of our common profit. Eight days later I left New York with my young companion for Carbondale, a city in Pennsylvania. In the meantime I had improved my English somewhat, studying with great zeal until late in the night. Our stock had at least a value of fifty dollars. We had some success working very hard, but then suddenly war broke out in America. You must have learned about this war from your own newspapers, so it is not necessary for me to go into detail.

Business came to a standstill, all public works were stopped, and after the call of the President to defend the country with arms, all the young folks flocked to the colors. Carried away by the general enthusiasm, I became a soldier. I studied English with great zeal until I could talk fairly fluently. Since I had the good will of my superiors, I became a noncommissioned officer in a few weeks. However, the way to a higher position was barred to me, because I had to write and read English perfectly to get such an appointment. I started again, sometimes studying through the better part of the night, and all this without any help, since I did not have enough money to hire a tutor. Now I am able to speak, read, and write English well. In the meantime our enlistment term, fixed for a period of four months, expired. Everybody had

believed that this war would last only four months. We had
been sworn in for this period only and were discharged on its
expiration. However, the war was far from being finished,
and therefore the President issued a second proclamation asking for soldiers for a period of three years.

Through the intervention of several high-ranking personalities, who had become interested in me, and possibly also
because of the fact that I had shown courage several times
during my first enlistment, I was introduced to Secretary of
War Cameron and was examined by him. I had used my time
profitably to study military tactics whenever I had a moment,
and so I became a first lieutenant in the cavalry of the United
States. The name of my regiment is the Lochiel Light Cavalry.
The name of my colonel is E. C. Williams, and that of my
squadron commander is E. G. Savage. I have been given the
promise of a captaincy as soon as possible, and therefore I am
doing my best to make myself worthy of the commission.

We are now with our regiment in Washington; in a few
days we will leave for the theater of war. Formerly a peddler,
barely able to make a living, I have now become a respected
man in a respected position, one filled by very few Jews.

I have been sent by my general to enlist new recruits and so
I am today in Scranton, a city in Pennsylvania only twenty
miles away from Carbondale, where I had peddled before.
Before this no one paid any attention to me here; now I move
in the best and richest circles and am treated with utmost
consideration by Jews and Christians.

My dear ones, I beg you with all my heart not to be angry
because I have gone to war. The dear Lord can also save me
from this as He has saved me from many other perils. And
should it be my destiny to lose my life, well I will have sacrificed it for a cause to which I am attached with all my heart,
that is: the liberation of the United States. My beloved parents,
brothers, sisters, and relatives will be taken care of. Should I
fall in battle, use the enclosed address of my bank, where I
have deposited my salary; should I survive, well, I shall return
to Germany and live with you.

                                  Knoxville, February 7, 1864
Our situation has changed very much since I wrote you my
last letter. Although we have not yet entirely exterminated

the rebels, nevertheless we are gradually reaching the goal we are aiming at. You have probably heard about our recent victorious battles under the command of Rosecrans, Grant, and Burnside. The South has been deeply affected by all this because it has destroyed the hope that foreign "European powers" would intervene in their favor. England and France are declaring themselves clearly against the South. "Cotton is not king," as the South always maintained, and because of which it hoped to rule the entire world. Now if the cabinet in Washington would simply forget all political maneuvering and would work unanimously and patriotically for the Union, then this once happy country would again speedily regain peace and harmony. The President has once more called 500,000 to the colors, and, if they are not willing to come, they ought to be drafted by force. This step is wise.

In September the President issued a proclamation reprieving all the rebels who would lay down their arms voluntarily and who would take the oath of loyalty. The higher ranking ringleaders were excepted. Thousands upon thousands have left the army of the enemy and have laid down their arms. Thousands more would do the same if they had not been told a lie by their commanders, that all this was only a trick to bring them over into our lines in order to throw them into jail and dungeons. It is not necessary to stress that we had no such intention. Now, having stretched out the hand of mercy, we must also extend the hand of power in order to demonstrate that we are strong enough to punish when kindness fails.

If you were well acquainted with the conditions of this country — that is only possible if you live in the midst of the people — you would easily understand why the powerful North took so long a time to overwhelm the South. To pretend that the North would not fight was nothing more than vain boasting on the part of the South. At the same time the North was mad to believe that a rebellion could be suppressed within three months. And why? We have traitors in our midst, even in our cabinet, who, ever since the beginning of the war, have fought with all their energy against the application of drastic means. At a time when we had 100,000 soldiers at the front, the South had 300,000. When the people, the widows, and the orphans screamed that the thousands of the

slain must be avenged, these scoundrels tried to prevent the
South from being vanquished at one blow. They speculated
that the North would become tired of mobilizing soldiers and
money, and that foreign powers would intervene. However,
they had forgotten that the Americans — even though of the
North — have a sense of honor in their hearts which no man
and no force can extinguish. While the South has mobilized
men from sixteen to sixty-four — naturally only through the
draft — we have an army equal to this number, which consists
of men who left their homes and farms voluntarily in order to
cleanse, with the blood of their hearts, the blemish that defiles
their honor. When nothing but poverty and famine characterized the South, industry and prosperity were flourishing in
the North.

In the South the soil is unploughed and deserted; all men
physically able to lift even a finger are drafted into the army;
their slaves are deserting them. Their elegant ladies who once
had been too lazy even to dip a finger into water, and who indeed were unaccustomed to work, are now forced to enter
our lines in order to beg literally for bread from a government
which they had once treated with contempt. So deep has the
proud South fallen.

Our army is standing on the soil of the South, our flag is
waving in every rebellious state. However, my dear uncle, I
am not able to give you, in writing, a description of the misery
now dominant here. I am now in a position where I can better
understand the circumstances of this war, and I can assure you
that I am often heartsick thinking of the distress of the people.
Although the battle [of Chickamauga] under the command of
General Rosecrans seemed to have been a real success, in my
opinion the very contrary was true. I had the command of my
regiment which had been separated from our army by a mistake of our general. Before we had time enough to discover
that mistake we were attacked by 3,000 enemy cavalrymen.
We fought as long as we could, but when I saw that nothing
was left to me but to become a prisoner, I thought that it
would be better to be shot than to spend years in a Southern
prison. Accordingly, I rallied my men and we broke through
the line of the enemy and reached our own army about mid-
night. Of course, we were compelled to abandon our baggage

wagons to the enemy. On this occasion I lost all I had saved during the past months. My clothing, money, and jewelry, which I had in my suitcase, and which, as I believed, were better preserved there than on my person, were taken by the enemy, in addition to my three horses. However, I am grateful that I have escaped and that I am living. I lost 200 of my regiment. The chaplain of our regiment was shot down at my side; my orderly, a young German, dropped from his horse, dead, no more than three steps behind me. My adjutant was made prisoner no more than ten paces away from me. God has held His hand over me. Although I regret my material losses because of my poor relatives, I am not discouraged from making a new start.

Thank God, I have always been in good health and strong, although I have passed through periods which were so difficult that I thought I would succumb. Now I have easier duties since I have received a slight promotion, for I am now Chief of Staff to General Carter. My address is: Major L. A. Gratz, Chief of Staff to General Carter, Knoxville, U.S.A.

Knoxville, February 25, 1864

The prospects are now very favorable that the war will soon end. The appeal of the President, calling for 500,000 new soldiers, will be answered almost entirely by volunteers. All measures have been taken in order to carry out a brilliant battle plan during the spring and summer.

I learn from the newspapers that there have been clashes between the Prussians and the Danes. Poor Denmark, what can a crow do against an eagle? I fear that under the present circumstances your business will suffer. However, if you hope for the best and are prepared for the worst, you will be happy and content in all of life's circumstances.

Recently I have received several propositions, and since I am not quite sure which I shall choose. I would like to have your advice. When I left Germany my knowledge was not very great, and because I was well aware of this fact, I have utilized every free hour to improve my education. I have learned the English language so well that many do not believe that I am a European. I have studied law because I think it is necessary to become acquainted with the laws of the country where I have my residence. I enjoyed my studies so much that my interest was stimulated. I have made the acquaintance and even acquired the friendship of many civil servants of high rank. Questioned by me, these gentlemen promised me solemnly that they would train me within three months after the war, so that I could then pass the bar examination. Many distinguished and prominent people have promised to use their influence on my behalf. I am firmly convinced that I can pass the examination and that I can, in all probability, guarantee my future career after one or two years of practice.

Knoxville, September 4, 1867

I hope, dear uncle, that you have received my letter. However, I did not go into detail; therefore I now wish to tell you briefly what has happened to me. After I had written to you and had spent some more time in this place where my chief, General Carter, was commander (this part of the country — East Tennessee — belongs to the conquered part of the South), we finally received the order to join the army of General Sherman. Our Army Corps, the Twenty-Third, finally joined up with the general army, and we participated in the brilliant campaign under the leadership of Sherman. It would be the task of an historian to describe in detail the adventures which we experienced, and the brilliant results of this campaign. Certainly you have read of the most important events in your papers. In August, 1865, my regiment was brought up to full strength so that it could continue in service, and I was offered a commission with the rank of colonel. However, I turned the offer down, partially because the war was over and, consequently, active service was over, and partially because I was fed up with the life of a soldier. At that time I had served four years and three months; the necessity which previously existed was no longer existent; therefore I offered my resignation, which was accepted.

I was compelled to make a living because the war with its ups and downs had left me very little. I had the intention, as I have already written to you, of taking my examination as a lawyer in order to dedicate myself to a career in law. Consequently I followed my instinct and entered this profession.

Having passed my examination rather well, I received my diploma and opened an office as lawyer and counselor.

During my stay as a soldier at General Headquarters in this place I made the acquaintance of Lizzie Bearden, a young American lady. She was beautiful, virtuous, well-educated, and related to the oldest and most influential families of this state. I met her often, and as destiny would have it, acquaintance became friendship, and friendship, intimacy. Briefly, I had selected this place for my future residence, and I thought it necessary to tie myself more closely to the people living in this town. Since I loved Lizzie with all my heart, I asked for her hand, and I was accepted. My marriage took place on October 18, 1865, and now I have a little girl, a little angel, who is almost one year old. Her name is Frances, the name of the mother of my wife, and Henriette, the name of my late mother.

Although the war is now terminated, conditions at home here have improved very little. The South, with the exception of our state of Tennessee, is not yet represented in Congress. Recently the civil authorities were replaced by military authorities. In reality the war is terminated but we are still far from peace. Naturally, all this has brought very bad consequences in its wake, and the present circumstances are so lamentable that even the oldest inhabitants cannot remember when they had suffered through such bad times. To pay the taxes and interest on the war debt (3,000 millions) is a gigantic burden. In addition, the expenses of the Federal and the State Governments are enormous. The war has left the South in a terrible condition. Many years will pass before the country can recover.

Now I will describe to you briefly my own profession. The jurists, that means the judges, are of course paid by the state. The lawyers and advocates, however, receive nothing from the state. We receive also no fees as part of the court costs. If anybody wants to go to law or to be defended, he hires the services of a lawyer who demands a certain fee according to the circumstances and the importance of the suit. Our profession would be brilliantly recompensed if the people were not so impoverished by the war. Under the present circumstances

we are compelled to accept bills of exchange from them and
to wait until they can meet them.

The state is divided into districts, and approximately every
five or six districts have a judge who holds court in every
district three times a year. Many, nearly all districts, have no
lawyers with fixed residence, and so, together with the court,
we visit the different districts and are hired and paid by the
litigants. Lawyers do live in the large towns; however, we
are compelled to spend a great part of our time in the circuit
courts. This town, Knoxville, which is my residence, has four
railroad lines, is the seat of a court of appeal, and is a rather
important city. About thirty lawyers live here, and from here
we visit the different towns in the district.

After my marriage I built a nice house, around which I
have about sixty rods of land. My house is about 300 paces
distant from the outskirts of the town, and a quarter of a
mile from the courthouse and my office. I have already started
a nice garden which I intend to improve and enlarge. The
more I practice as a lawyer the better are my prospects, because the people become better acquainted with me and I
acquire more experience. In our profession we work under the
same conditions as a physician in Germany. The more numerous his patients and the greater his knowledge and his experience, the more he gains. Cash money is very scarce;
therefore I am very satisfied if I get enough money to cover
my personal expenses and those of my household.

My social position is excellent. I would be more than happy
to have you for some time with me in order to show you that
the good principles and the education that I have received in
your home have borne their fruits. I hope you will not mis-
understand my speaking about my own success, and I hope
you will not call it pride or boasting. I am convinced that my
success will please you. Since I have nobody here who could
relieve me of the difficult task of speaking of myself, I myself must perforce do it, or I must renounce the pleasure of
pleasing you with my achievement. My profession as a lawyer
requires a profound knowledge and infinite study in order to
master the law, a subject of gigantic proportions. Through
industry I have succeeded so far in my profession that I have
not been overshadowed by old and experienced lawyers. The

judges praise my humble achievements more than they merit. The number of cases given to me has the effect that my aim is always to become worthy of this sort of confidence. Since all discussions, speeches, etc., are presented, naturally, in English, it is imperative that I have a profound knowledge of the language. At home we speak only English, because my wife is an American and does not understand German. Therefore I have almost forgotten the German language. I imagine you have learned this fact from my bad style and spelling. I hope you will kindly overlook my many literary and other mistakes. I would like to practice the German language in order to become proficient in it, but I have neither time nor opportunity for this. I hope that I have discussed my own matters enough.

Now what are you doing? I am almost afraid to hear from you about the vicissitudes at home. Are all of our friends and relatives still alive? If this constant worry concerning my father, my aunt, my brothers and sisters, and all of you would not gnaw at my heart and cause me many sleepless nights, I would be as happy in my family and social life as a man could be.

I have often thought of going to Europe, if only for a visit. However, I cannot do it because of my profession. I have a chance to become the secretary of the American Legation in Prussia as soon as I can leave my practice for a year or more. This would enable me to see all of you again.

Knoxville, April 30, 1869

As you see from the date of my letter I am still living in Knoxville, practicing my profession as a lawyer and counselor. I am sending you a picture of my wife and my two little daughters. The older, Frances, will be three years old on the first of August, and she is charming and clever. The younger, now almost sixteen months old, runs around all over the place, and her evident German good nature would surely give you all a great deal of pleasure.

I make enough for the moment to live without any worry, but also without luxury and pretension. I am very content with my social position. With regard to political affairs I am not ambitious, and because my opinions do not quite go along with the party now in power, I do not face the danger of being overloaded with political honors during the next four years. By the way, I have but one desire, namely, to be connected officially with the American Legation in Prussia in some way so that I may have the opportunity to be with you for some time. I send my love to all, and in this my wife and my children join me. I feel a great affection for you, and my children include you and yours in their daily prayers to the Lord.

My dear aunt, I learned some time ago that a person by the name of Rudolf Neumann is in Liverpool. Is it our Rudolf of Inowrazlaw? How do you like rural life? I myself live a short distance from the town, although my office is in town. I would not change my home, where I now am, for the best in town. While I am writing this the roses in our garden are blooming wonderfully, strawberries are beginning to redden, and we have been enjoying vegetables, such as lettuce, radishes, spinach, and the like, for several weeks already. The climate is wonderful. East Tennessee, of which Knoxville is the capital, is traversed, or rather surrounded, by gigantic mountains, which are only a little lower than the Alps. From my house you can see the Unika Mountains in the south — almost piercing the clouds at a distance of at least fifty English miles, and in the northwest we can see the Cumberland range clearly and distinctly before us. This part of America is justly called the Switzerland of America. My life would not be lacking a thing if I did not live so far from you and my other relatives, but fate put us here and I am compelled to be content with the situation. The dear Lord, who causes everything to turn out for the best, will bring all of us together at the fit time. For today I close. Farewell, may the dear Lord protect you and give you all that your heart longs for. Kiss your dear little children for me and teach them to love me and my family.

SOURCES

The Gratz letters and the Kurtzig family material are in Heinrich Kurtzig, *Ostdeutsches Judentum* (Stolp, 1927). I am indebted to the late Dr. Joshua Bloch, of the New York Public Library, for drawing my attention to this work. For a study of the Orthodox Jewish background of Inowrazlaw in the mid-nineteenth century, see A. Heppner and J. Herzberg, *Aus*

Vergangenheit und Gegenwart der Juden in Hohensalza (Frankfort on the Main, 1907).

Further biographical data on the life of Gratz may be found in the following obituaries: *Knoxville Sentinel,* September 20, 1907; Louisville *Courier Journal,* September 20, 1907; *The Times* (Louisville), September 20, 1907; will of L. A. Gratz in Jefferson County Court, Kentucky, Will Book 28, 307; *History of Tennessee . . . with an historical and biographical sketch of the county of Knox and the city of Knoxville* (Nashville: Goodspeed Pub. Co., 1887), p. 968; communication from Milton B. Ochs, of Chattanooga, dated January 13, 1948; W. Rule, *Standard History of Knoxville, Tennessee* (Chicago, 1900), pp. 125–42; M. U. Rothrock, *The French Broad-Holston Country* (Knoxville, 1946), p. 378; *Directory of the Knights of Honor in the United States for . . . 1877* (Greensburg, Pa., 1877).

For the military record of Gratz, consult also his service record in the War Department, Adjutant General's Office, Washington, D. C.; F. B. Heitman, *Historical Register and Dictionary of the United States Army . . . ,* 2 vols. (Washington, 1903); *War of the Rebellion,* consult the general index volume under "Louis A. Gratz" and "Samuel P. Carter," particularly the following references: Series I, vol. XX, Part I, 144–46; Part II, 186; XXIII, Part II, 580; XXX, Part III, 275; XXXIX, Part II, 75, 220; XLVII, Part I, 995; Part III, 189, 252, 398, 650–51 (G. O., No. 34), 669; LII, Part I, 361, 386–87. Consult also Thomas Speed, R. M. Kelly, and Alfred Pirtle, *The Union Regiments of Kentucky* (Louisville, 1897), for the history of the Sixth Kentucky Cavalry; *Report of the Adjutant General of the State of Kentucky . . . ,* Vol. I, 1861–1866 (Frankfort, Ky., 1866), pp. 136 ff.; Samuel P. Bates, *History of Pennsylvania Volunteers, 1861-5 . . . ,* Vol. I (Harrisburg, 1869), pp. 142 ff.; Vol. III (Harrisburg, 1870), pp. 234 ff.; *Annual Report of the Adjutant General of Pennsylvania . . . for the Year 1866* (Harrisburg, 1867), p. 499.

For the Ochs family and Knoxville Jewry, see *Temple Beth El 80th Anniversary Celebration* (Knoxville, Tennessee, 1947); *Inventory of the Church and Synagogue Archives of Tennessee, Jewish Congregations* (Tennessee Historical Records Survey, Work Projects Administration, Nashville, 1941); G. E. Govan and J. W. Livingood, "Adolph S. Ochs: The Boy Publisher," *East Tennessee Historical Society's Publications,* No. 17 (1945); Gerald W. Johnson, *An Honorable Titan* (New York, 1946); *American Israelite,* May 23, 1873; October 17, 1873; November 2, 1888, quoting the *Chattanooga Daily Times* for October 29, 1888.

10

THE AMERICANIZATION OF
ISAAC MAYER WISE

BIOGRAPHY

Isaac Mayer Wise was born in Steingrub, Bohemia, March 29, 1819. After a brief career as a rabbi in Radnitz, Bohemia, he came to the United States in 1846, and was elected rabbi in Albany, New York. He entered upon a career of religious reform, and soon became one of the outstanding Jewish religious leaders in this land. In 1854, he was elected rabbi of Congregation Bene Yeshurun in Cincinnati, and occupied this position for the rest of his life. The very year of his arrival in Cincinnati, he founded *The Israelite*, an Anglo-Jewish newspaper; the following year, *Deborah*, which was published in German. He was a prolific writer: belles lettres, histories, theological works, polemics, and rituals flowed from his fluent pen. Wise's efforts were chiefly directed, however, toward the organization of American Jewry and, after years of intensive labor, were marked by success. In 1873, he inspired the founding of the Union of American Hebrew Congregations, and two years later this association of Jewish synagogues established the Hebrew Union College, a rabbinical seminary for American Jews. Finally, in 1889, the alumni of the College, now decidedly Reform, and other rabbis joined to create the Central Conference of American Rabbis. In all three institutions Wise's will was influential. He was easily the most distinguished organizer and leader of American Reform Jewry. He died in Cincinnati, March 26, 1900.

* * *

In February, 1850, Isaac Mayer Wise visited Washington. He was on his way South in search of health. Although only

This study, an address, was delivered in honor of Isaac M. Wise on Founder's Day, March 28, 1931, in the chapel of the Hebrew Union College, Cincinnati, Ohio. It was privately printed that year.

thirty-one years of age, he was already a neurotic, torn by morbid fears, racked by an incessant cough. He visited and impressed the President, Zachary Taylor, chatted with Senator Seward, and dined with Daniel Webster. The topics of conversation at that dinner were Unitarianism and Herbartian psychology. When that young rabbi left Washington, America had become for him "my" country; its people "my" people. What was this Americanism of Wise, one of the most eminent American Jews of the nineteenth century? Was it a complacent conceit engendered by the flattering attention of the great, or was it reasoned conviction? What had brought him to America?

This young Bohemian came here because to him America was the source of all political liberalism. His every intellectual and political experience conspired to bring him to this land. He was very unhappy in the Austrian Empire. He was born in the decade that marked the downfall of the Napoleonic system and of French liberalism. The year of his birth, 1819, saw the "hep-hep" riots, a wave of anti-Jewish hatred that swept through the Germanic lands, bringing destruction and even death in its wake. In 1830, when he was but a child of eleven, the people of Central Europe protested in vain against the monarchial conservatives who governed them. It was then that young Wise began to sense the full humiliation of his civil and political status; it was then that he discovered the writings of Gabriel Riesser. Riesser, a young liberal, twenty-four years old, had been refused an academic post because he was a Jew, and with a heart full of bitterness wrote *The Condition of Those Who Acknowledge the Mosaic Faith in Germany. To the Germans of all Confessions*. The boy Wise heard this cry of an outraged soul with tears in his eyes. "I was quite a boy when that book appeared and most likely understood it quite poorly," he later said, "still I read it for nine long weeks every evening, as long as the stump of my candle would hold out and moistened each page with my tears."

The whole life and thinking of Wise are foreshadowed in

Riesser's essay. The devil, said Riesser, could not have invented a more diabolical system of law than that which subjects the rights of citizenship to religious conformity. The great principles of our century are equality before the law, the natural right of all men to humane treatment, and unlimited opportunity for all our moral and intellectual development. This book and the other writings of its author were of the most profound influence on this young lad. Wise was begotten politically by Riesser, and the liberal views he acquired from him were supplemented from other sources.

The greatest influence throughout South Germany at this time was exercised by the two historians Karl Wenzeslaus von Rotteck and Friedrich Christoph Schlosser. They wrote the bibles of German liberalism. This didactic school went back to Rousseau, the American and French Revolutions, and Kant for its political ideals and its moral judgments. It evolved a philosophy of history that conformed to its own prejudices; it preached popular sovereignty, government by the will of the people. It insisted on the right to revolt and hoped for a coming liberal revolution everywhere.

Practically all of Wise's intellectual forbears had their roots in the Enlightenment movement of the eighteenth century. Their political guide was Rousseau; their literary light was Lessing; they preferred cosmopolitanism to nationalism; they demanded full, unlimited political and religious liberty for all, without regard to established tradition. Their political philosophy was that of the middle class, which had for the first time successfully effected a revolution in France in 1789. The American state was their ideal.

Wise early turned with affection to this school of thought. Its glorification of the new American republic especially impressed him. Moreover, he learned to understand America at first hand through the novels of Cooper and the political writings of Richard Henry Lee. "I was already an American in Bohemia," he once said.

He was determined to leave the country. Conditions were unbearable. He chafed at every restraint, for he was by nature fiery, restless, earnest, fearless, without tact or moderation. He lacked perspective. Like most self-taught vigorous men he envisaged his ideals in an absolute sense, apart from their relation to society—ideals to be realized without qualification or hesitation. He was by instinct a fighter.

After the failure of the revolution of 1830, the political reaction increased in severity. The Jew in Bohemia was hampered in his choice of residence, was subject to ignominious Jewish taxes, limited even in the human right of marriage, and withal compelled to profess a fervent loyalty to an emperor who tolerated these inhumanities. Wise was galled by these indignities. He was reprimanded by the officials for his lukewarm loyalty. They were right. He felt no loyalty to the Austrian Empire; he felt that it was immoral to be loyal to a land that denied him the "rights of man," that encouraged a bigoted State-Church, that "treated its serfs worse than the slaves in the South." He bitterly resented his status as an imperial-royal Bohemian Tolerated-Jew. "My father," he said, "was not permitted to call even a handbreadth of land his own, therefore I never had a fatherland." He was too impatient waiting for the revolution that might never come to recognize that his disabilities were the result of historic conditions having their roots in the centuries. Many of his later German rabbinical colleagues who came to America as a land of refuge were so woven into the texture of German life that they never surrendered their love for the state that virtually exiled them. Wise, who was never subject to a systematic public school education, escaped the German political influence and had the courage to break with his Germanic loyalties. Refused a passport, he smuggled himself across the border. He came to America as a political pilgrim; he came to these shores not to found a new religion, but to live as a free man politically. He landed in New York with two dollars in his pocket, and a wife and a child. The first Americans he met were German hack-drivers, who demanded six dollars for the trip to the East Side and reviled him as a Jew because he refused to pay it.

When he came here in 1846, he was not really open to new political influences. Most of his thinking had already been done in Bohemia. He came here to find his ideas in practice, and took note only of that which was in consonance with them. He found much that pleased him: American Revolutionary ideals and Jeffersonian democracy were professed by every man. Wise knew these same teachings as French and German liberalism. They meant much to him; he had suffered to realize them. As rabbi of Albany, he associated with political liberals and religious radicals, and out of the broad arena of American political life he chose as his heroes those men who gave him what he came here to find. Senator Seward, of Civil War and Alaska fame, Stephen A. Douglas, Daniel Webster, Henry Clay, and Horace Greeley were his friends or models. Seward influenced him to stand alone and to fight for principle; Douglas preached the great eighteenth-century doctrine of popular sovereignty; Webster encouraged him to admire the Constitution; Greeley was sympathetic to aliens and Catholics. All of them loved the Union, and most of them were determined to hold it together even if it meant the continuance of slavery.

Wise began as a Whig, but developed into a fervent States' Rights Democrat. He became a true Jeffersonian. At one time in the 50's, in Cincinnati, he almost joined the new Republican party, but held aloof because of German atheists who were associated with it. He had an almost worshipful attitude to the Constitution, that democratic instrument which guaranteed civil equality and religious liberty. America's great contribution, he believed, was its separation of Church and State, its promise of freedom of conscience to all. The dominance of the Catholic Church in old Austria had made of him an implacable opponent of any sectarian influence in the state. "This is a democratic republic," he reiterated, "and must be governed without God's special police." To maintain religious liberty in this land, he was willing to pit Catholics against Protestants until they had learned to become liberal American citizens. "We want the democratic republic, now and forever, no Christian stock company."

It is not surprising that Wise, who worshipped the concept of liberty and lived most of his life on the border line between the North and the South, laid the utmost stress on personal and states' rights that were not to be limited except to hold the Union together. He was a free trader. He was opposed to partisan politics and the vicious spoils system. It was inevitable that he should join the Democratic party, though it, too, did not always escape his criticism. Yet he was not such an extremist. He looked askance at the uncouth Jacksonian democrats, as he did at the mild socialism of the intellectuals. He had much in common with the typical American radicals of his day like Emerson and Lowell, who were largely antiwar, antislavery, antiliquor and antipoverty; but he could not go the whole way with them, for he was essentially a middle-of-the-road man, not only in religion, but also in politics. The only exception was where politics touched Jewish emancipation and liberty. Then he was an implacable extremist and demanded immediate change. He refused to wait placidly for a dilatory evolution to solve the Jewish problem. The State and the Jew must do it now.

The early Wise was not a nationalist; he was a cosmopolitan. "We do not love one section of the earth or one class of people better than others," he once said. "The world is our country and humanity is our politics. Cosmopolitanism is the highest object of humanity. We love this country's institutions, because they approach nearest to the principles of absolute justice . . ." He was an eighteenth-century European liberal on nineteenth-century American soil. Young America, nationalistic, looked West. Wise, here in America, looked eastward, to Europe, and dreamed of a universal republic.

When in 1848 all Europe was aflame with revolt, Wise thought for a time of returning to aid in the establishment of a European republic. He was not altogether happy in America. He was looked upon as a radical religious agitator, and for a while Temple Emanu-El of New York even closed its

pulpit to him. In order to be absolutely free he determined to
give up the rabbinate and study law. His insistence on secular
education for the young and modern music in the service had
aroused his own people against him. In this conservatism,
Jewry was at one with Christianity. It was only fifteen years
before Wise's arrival that the most intelligent Gentile group
in Albany had even tolerated a choir. The choir leader then
had dared to bring a tuning fork into the loft in order to give
the correct pitch. "An old, gray-haired pillar of the Church,
who heard and saw the unfortunate tuning fork, arose in the
midst of the service and cried out with a loud voice: 'I demand that this instrument of hell be removed from the house
of God.'" And it was.

Seward, Greeley, and others prevailed on the impetuous
Wise to remain. He stayed because he realized that Europe
was not ripe for freedom. Moreover, he cherished the hope
that the principle of liberty coming from America would ultimately make the whole world free. "America," he declared,
"is the most perfect realization of the idea of human rights in
the world." This land, he taught, has a mission: "Providence
reserved this sea-girt continent for the last and highest tri-
umphs of humanity; no power on earth can change this manifest destiny." Possibly before the end of the nineteenth century, all monarchies will be gone and there will be but "one
mankind, one liberty, one fraternity." These are the dreams
of a young man of thirty, an impractical doctrinaire if you
will, but one deadly in earnest.

He was very anxious for all Jews to be thoroughly Americanized, that is, to possess an understanding of the principles
of political liberty. He believed it necessary above all for
them to know the vernacular. In his day, over two-thirds of
the German Jewish immigrants spoke no English. Wise tells
us that the only phrases many of the peddlers knew were:
"You fant to puy somdink? Can I shtay mit you all nacht?"
These phrases were written on a slip of paper, and it was no
minor tragedy when the unfortunate peddler lost his "English language." English was necessary, Wise believed, not

only to bring the Jew into contact with American ideals, but also to restore his self-respect. The Jew in Europe had been crushed through long oppression, and it was now urgent that he divorce himself from the German tongue with its rich vocabulary of anti-Jewish invective, which only served to recall the old disgrace. This explains his impatience with the great German-American rabbis of the 60's who Germanized instead of Americanized, and, as he said, "made Israel a stranger forever in this country." Through English, the immigrant Jew can again "gain the proud self-consciousness of the free-born man." His political thinking colored his religious practice. It is not improbable that his religious liberalism sprang from his political orientation. He had a horror of religious despotism and thanked his God that in America there were no petty tyrants, like the chief rabbis of England and Germany; and he cherished a cordial hatred for the old-fashioned autocratic parnas.

While the concept of America's political mission was running through his head, he went to Washington in 1850. The democratic attitude of the leaders toward him, an alien of only four years' residence, convinced him that his ideals were possible in this truly democratic land and sealed his loyalty to America. This new American never seemed to realize, however, that his political idealism, so childlike and humane, was already antiquated on the American scene. He failed to understand that America in this middle period was already in transition from a liberal state built on cosmopolitan ideals to an Anglo-Saxon conservative republic. The new tendency was a self-centered nationalism. Wise's teachings were obsolescent.

It would be unfair to assume, however, from the naive enthusiasm of young Wise that he was completely enthralled by American life and culture. He was a discriminating critic, for in Europe he had experienced not only autocracy, but also efficient government and a broad culture. Public morals, he preached, were poisoned by centralization of power, church influence in politics, high tariffs, and that to which he

later refers as "the disgrace of the great nation"—corruption
in office. Like Emerson he had little faith in parties. "The
country is safe," he said sardonically, "whoever shall be nominated or elected. The main question is, who shall divide the
spoils and how it shall be divided." He had a profound contempt for the party in power. "If we had not here and there
an honest man among them," he said curtly, "the whole crew
would be ripe for hell, and the sun would shine on them only
by virtue of the horses, dogs, and cats depending on them."
He stormed against demagogism and the ignorance of science
and literature. "That thing which the Germans call *Bildung*,
real and thorough culture, is at a considerable discount here."
And in a sterner mood he writes: ". . . it appears to some
observers that the nation which chews tobacco, drinks whiskey as a common beverage, swears most unenlightened, bets
on elections, horses, fighting-men, dogs and cocks, has so
many and so well-filled jails, penitentiaries, gambling houses,
brothels and other low dens, is none too enlightened."

But he reserves his most bitter indictment of America for
its worship of money. "It cannot be the destiny of a nation to
make money," he said. Like James Russell Lowell and others,
he was unsympathetic to the industrial revolution that was
transforming America. Wise had grown up under a *klein-
buergerlich* economic system of live and let live, and did not
really understand the inevitability of the machine civilization. He saw its bad results, and wanted a return to a more
primitive economic system, where, he imagined, huge fortunes and dire poverty were both unknown, where tradition
and custom and law protected the economic status of the
lower middle classes. His concepts of extreme political indi-
vidualism, on the one hand, and of economic protection of
the middle classes, on the other hand, were completely at var-
iance. His uncritical economic philosophy was inspired by
democratic considerations. The rich were bad; "we have already an alarmingly large number of millionaires, much too
large for a sound republic, and much too influential for the
public welfare." "In the *HaMagid*," he said facetiously, "we

find the phrase: *ish 'ani abal yashar,* poor but honest, but how would you render in Hebrew or in any other language: rich but honest?" He saw no reason to be proud of the wealth of the Rothschilds, for their money was no proof of the excellence of Judaism. He was opposed to the building of factories, large mercantile establishments, and the proletarianization of the workers. Like the dramatists and liberals of his day, he stood with the masses against the classes. Yet Wise did not favor a social revolution, because he saw no need for it. His interest, too, lay primarily in political improvement. Emerson believed that free trade and "the access of the young and poor to the sources of power and wealth" would aid the people materially. This was the attitude of Wise also. America, he said, was rich enough to provide for all, and the unions "would redeem the laboring man from the oppression of hard labor and the despotism of capital." He saw no solution in the "serpent" communism or in socialism, for he was opposed to extremes. He resented the economic teachings of the radicals, probably because they jeopardized the political goals of the liberals. Yet later in life, he was frank to admit that some day the Socialists Marx and Lassalle might be considered the greatest among nonreligious Jews, and he once said prophetically: "Possibly the future lies largely with them."

Wise's economic and political liberalism had little influence on his contemporaries because as men of trade their fortunes were bound up with the new party of centralization and "big business." His plea, however, for cultural adaptation and religious liberalism was eagerly received by a generation of Germanic immigrants who recognized in him their first articulate leader.

In the 50's, Wise, now in Cincinnati, turned his attention to the impending Civil War. He saw it coming. It depressed him, because he felt that it was unnecessary. He was of the opinion that all differences could be settled if the extremists were disregarded—the secessionists of the South and the abolitionists of the North who preached "the irrepressible conflict." The issue of slavery, he insisted, was only a pretext of the new Republican party to get into power, and get at the spoils of office; speculators, both slavery and antislavery men, were creating strife in order to line their pocketbooks in the new western and southern territories. But his keenest suspicions were directed at "the grand chorus of black coats and white cravats," the Protestant clergy, who, he feared, were using the slave question to gain political control and Christianize the American Constitution.

He had gloomy forebodings as to what this war would do to his ideals. "Liberty never suffered a more fatal blow than this," he mourned, when South Carolina seceded. He saw clearly the dangers of disunion, for he knew the fate of disunited Italy and Germany. In his mind's eye, he saw the rise of three or four republics here; his feverish imagination saw standing armies in these small states, despotism, bureaucracy, huge taxes, poverty, European mockery. The war threatened to shatter all his hopes of bringing democracy to a Europe that was still largely monarchical and autocratic. In 1860, he wrote again on his favorite theme: "America has a great future"; it must grow to such heights that all nations may see us and learn the great lesson of liberty. "Our country's future, for this reason, is the future of all humanity." A compromise, he pleaded, can and should be made. Wise, like his Kentucky neighbor Henry Clay, was a great compromiser. Like Vallandigham and thousands of other Ohioans, he was a Peace Democrat. The problem of slavery was not insurmountable. It was a "political question." Though Wise was correct in laying bare many of the material causes that drove the North and South to war, he failed altogether to sense the outraged moral indignation of the masses in the North against the institution of human slavery. He begged that constitutional guarantees be given to the South to protect slavery, or the Union would be dissolved. Here we have the motive of Wise's attitude: with so much at stake no price was too big to pay for union and peace.

The tragedy of disunion was a real one to him, for it endangered the liberalization of all the world; only a powerful United States of North America could bring liberty to Europe. To some of his Democratic friends, only the future of America itself was involved, and they, like Stephen Douglas, had a solution: force, war. This was no solution for Wise. He was opposed to violence, he abhorred the idea of war. Not only did he have friends and relatives on both sides, but as he said: "We are the servants of peace, not of war." It was "depravity to admire the bravery of the warrior who kills scores and to condemn the murderer to the gallows." Not only was he opposed to war, and saw no solution on that score, but he believed that free states must not be coerced. Free states have the right to secede when their rights are infringed upon. His studies of Richard Henry Lee's writings back in Bohemia had made him an anti-Federalist. Here was his dilemma: Success to his hopes could come only through a united America, but he refused to encourage the only means whereby the Union could be held together—war. Here are his words: "Force will not hold together this Union; it was cemented by liberty and can stand only by the affection of the people." When the war broke out, he had no recourse but a sullen resentful silence. When his patriotism was suspected, he answered that the "pulpit is no place for star and stripeism"; it was his business to teach religion.

Wise was gratified by the results of the war; the Union was saved, and slavery was abolished. Although he would have been willing to tolerate slavery in order to save the Union, he was by no means in sympathy with slavery. He was now anxious that the United States manifest its high purpose as an exemplar of equality, not only abroad, but here at home; that it allow no abuses of the Jew. For there were such abuses. The Civil War had demoralized the nation; the new political cliques in Washington, recruited from the towns and villages, brought in prejudice and contempt for the Jew. Wise turned his titanic energy and enthusiasm to combating this danger. His zeal in the fray was all the greater because

the target of many of his attacks was the political party he
detested.

In defense of the Jew, his policy was one of unbridled bel-
ligerency. He was determined that no man should dare to
attack the Jew with impunity. Wise protested against the
boorishness of the German-American press, the brutality of
Boerne's polemics, but it is obvious that he had read them all
to good advantage. He had learned much from the embittered Riesser, and he admits himself that his articles were
"filled with fire and brimstone," and that he fought like a
wounded boar. The *Cincinnati Gazette* had called a Jewish
merchant a Shylock. The first paragraph of Wise's answer
to these "scrofulous mongers," as he called them, will not
bear repetition, but he continued in a milder vein: "We will
. . . square accounts with the *Gazette*. We only wait for
an opportune time to chastise again that priest-ridden, cod-
fish aristocracy, designated the Cincinnati Gazette Co., who
are British in politics, Henry VIII in religion, and Peter
Amiens in fanaticism. Our time will come again to pay 'eye
for eye and tooth for tooth.'" "These tactics proved effi-
cacious," he once said of his vigorous journalism.

Wise believed that the source of prejudice lay in the teachings of Christianity, "for every child was taught in school
that the Jews had crucified 'our Lord' and every parson re-
peated it as often as possible." The realization of the consequences of this age-long accusation induced him to make the
strong statement: "The world has sinned more against the
Jews than a hundred Christs could atone for on the cross."
But he felt that the Jews were at fault, too, because they did
not encourage intelligent leadership, because of the low cultural plane of the newly rich among them, and because of the
lack of Jewish pride. When in June, 1877, Joseph Seligman,
one of America's wealthiest Jewish bankers, was excluded
from the Grand Union Hotel in Saratoga, Wise wasted little
sympathy on him. He was impatient with Jews who patron-
ized the eastern water resorts and associated with "gam-
blers," "hollow heads," and "the scum of society." "It is not

indispensable to show one's marriageable daughters at Saratoga." "Keep away from places where you are not wanted." Wise had little sympathy for Seligman, the "money-prince," but he was indignant at the insult offered to the Jew, and preached an economic boycott against the offending owner, a boycott that was apparently effective.

Even as he tolerated no social discrimination against the individual Jew here, so he demanded full recognition of the civil rights of the American Jew abroad. Citizenship, as he understood it, imposed duties on the recipient, but also an obligation on the State, and he was determined that the State should meet its obligations in the fullest sense. When, in 1857, the rights of American Jewish citizens were not respected in Switzerland, he said: "Slaves and cowards only will submit to such an outrage; we are men and must be treated as such." He visited President Buchanan to protest against this mistreatment of American Jews in Switzerland; he asked Lincoln in 1863 to withdraw an army order of General Grant expelling the Jews from the territory the general had occupied in Mississippi, Tennessee, and Kentucky; and he went to President Hayes seeking protection for the rights of American Jews in Russia. "If we had any political influence," he said, "there would be no American minister at St. Petersburg and no Russian minister in Washington." If he was one of the great Jews of the last century, it was not only because he was the organizer of American Jewish Reform and all its institutions, but also because he was great in courage.

Wise was unrelenting in his attacks on those who wished to Christianize the Constitution, insinuate their Christianity into Thanksgiving proclamations, introduce the Bible into the public schools, and turn Christian holydays into national ones. The timorous Jews were frightened by his frankness for he was no respecter of official persons, and had the courage to call even those in the highest position "imbeciles." When told to keep quiet—"It will do you no good," said a friend—he answered that his attacks in the *Israelite* had given courage to many a Jew who before this had denied his origin; that he had put the attacking clergy on the defensive by boldly refuting their dogmas; that the only way to handle demagogs and politicians who insulted the Jews was to attack them when they sought office. "They must realize that the Jew can defend himself."

In an editorial appearing August 23, 1872, in which he discusses the theme: "We are first Americans and then Israelites," he says: "It is a phrase and no more. . . . No honest man can or will sacrifice his convictions to any . . . human institution. . . . There is a law higher than all made by man. . . . If my government enact laws . . . contrary to conviction, I am an Israelite first and would treat my country as being in a state of rebellion against me. . . . I am a loyal citizen because it does not prevent me being an Israelite according to my conviction. . . . Therefore, first my God and then my country is as good a motto as any." The Americanization of Isaac Mayer Wise was now consummated.

BIBLIOGRAPHICAL NOTE

The material for this study was drawn from the memoirs and writings of I. M. Wise himself. In the *Asmonean* of March 17–24, 1854, he wrote of his life in Bohemia; in his *Reminiscences,* translated and edited by David Philipson (Cincinnati, 1901), he covered the period from his arrival in America in 1846 to 1857. The life of Wise since the Cincinnati days is illuminated in detail by editorials, occasional addresses, and autobiographical reflections which appeared in the *Israelite.*

11

BACKGROUND FOR THE HISTORY OF
THE AMERICAN JEW

Herder called the story of the Jew "the greatest poem of all time," and it is a fact that American Jewry may lay claim to a fabulous history. In 1649, when the Pilgrims still walked the land, there was one Jewish businessman in Boston. As late as 1880—that is, still within living memory—no more than 300,000 Jews called this country home; today there are about 6,000,000. Fifty years ago most Jews were immigrants and very few attended schools of higher learning; today a majority of Jewish youth is exposed to college, and five of America's eleven Nobel Prize winners, in the years 1959 to 1962, were Jews.

AMERICAN JEWRY BEFORE 1920

The Coming of the Immigrants. As far back as the medieval Crusades, and as late as 1648, European Jews, driven out of their native lands in Western and Central Europe, moved eastward into the Slavic realms. With the dawn of the modern age and the rise of an Atlantic civilization in the mid-seventeenth century, with the coming of mercantilism and the Industrial Revolution, with the beginnings of colonial empires in the New World, the Jews of Europe began to move westward. The farthest "frontier" fringe of Jewish settlement was first established in Dutch-ruled New Amsterdam in 1654. The first arrivals were Sephardim, or Spanish-Portuguese Jews, in quest, for the most part, of new economic opportunity. Some—but actually only a few—were religious émigrés. A few hundred Sephardim, at the most, came to these shores, and by 1720 they no longer constituted

---

This study appeared originally in Oscar I. Janowsky (ed.), *The American Jew: A Reappraisal* (Philadelphia, 1964), pp. 1–25.

a majority among American Jews. Intermingled with them ever since their very first day on American shores were Ashkenazim: German and East European Jews. Ashkenazim and Sephardim banded together to establish tiny Jewish communities in the tidewater towns of Newport, New York, Philadelphia, Charleston, Savannah, and, finally, Montreal, Canada.

By the 1820's the trickle of Germans had become a steady stream, crossing the mountains and flowing westward. Major Mordecai Manuel Noah could even dream then of a colony for Europe's poor and oppressed Jews—a haven at the western terminus of the Erie Canal, soon to become the most popular highway to the interior of the continent. By 1840 the newcomers had established little synagogues and communities in at least five towns of the transallegheny West; by 1849 they were among the Argonauts in California, and in the next generation they had spread out into the transmississippi plains and prairies. There was hardly a town of size in the whole country that did not shelter a Jewish shopkeeper or a modest congregation. By the 1850's and the 1860's, when the Central European immigrants were still coming in substantial numbers, East European Jews began to pour in, thrust from their native Russia by the hard times that had followed the breakdown of agrarian feudalism and the birth pangs of industrial capitalism. The Russian pogroms of the 1880's and the Czar's effort to crush the impending social revolution ultimately drove over 2,000,000 East European Jews to these shores. Today they and their descendants are settled mainly in two megalopolises: in the Atlantic "supercity" reaching from the Potomac Valley to the New Hampshire border, and in the Pacific colossus which strides from San Diego to the northern shores of San Francisco Bay.

Political Rights. The twenty-three Brazilian Jewish refugees who landed in New Amsterdam in the late summer of 1654 were denied even the most elementary economic and religious rights by Governor Stuyvesant and the Dutch West India Company. But these restrictions could not endure, for the Jews—because they were "population" and, even more, because they commanded economic skills—were needed in the "wilderness." By the time the Dutch flag was lowered over the Hudson a decade later, the Jews had wrested the right to settle, own land, and do business, but it was not until the 1690's, under English rule, that they were accorded the privilege of holding public religious services and selling at retail. It was not until the adoption of the Federal Constitution in 1788 that Jews were permitted to hold public offices of honor and responsibility. Still, federal rights, in those days of decentralized government, had little impact on the status of the Jews in the thirteen original states. It would take a century before New Hampshire Jewry finally achieved full enfranchisement—an event that would not come to pass until the centennial year of 1876, just a hundred years after the Declaration of Independence. By the twentieth century, however, as state-imposed disabilities gave way to federally-defended rights, nearly every office of public trust in America had had its Jewish holders. Oscar S. Straus, a former ambassador, served in the President's Cabinet as Secretary of Commerce and Labor in 1906, and a decade later Louis Dembitz Brandeis was appointed an associate justice of the United States Supreme Court.

The Right to Do Business. The United States was the first country in the modern Diaspora to enfranchise the Jew —a grant which, whatever else it secured to him, also enabled him to do business without let or hindrance. Lacking economic rights, the Jew would have been little attracted to America. During the Sephardic period, from the 1640's through the 1840's, most American Jews were petty shopkeepers, dealing in hard goods, soft goods, and wet goods: hardware, dry goods, and liquors—all under one roof. A handful were farmers, some were artisans, a few were wealthy merchants and merchant-shippers, fur entrepreneurs, land speculators, and candle manufacturers. By the fifth decade of the 1800's, the new immigrants crossing the mountains were largely storekeepers. Those who were successful became merchants on a large scale: department store owners, bankers, and early investors and executives in the railroad and insurance industries. Some, though not many of the native Jews, had turned to the professions of law, medicine, and engineering; one of the United States Army's outstanding ordnance experts in the antebellum period was a native-born North Carolinian engineer, Major Alfred Mordecai. No other business, however, attracted the successful businessman like garment manufacturing; by 1843 a Jew had written a brochure on the subject, and by the time the East European immigrants began to swarm ashore at Castle Garden, Jews of German background already dominated the industry.

The older generation of native and German Jews, frightened by the onrush of the new immigrants and perhaps unduly apprehensive about their own status, made every effort to disperse the "Russians" into the interior. But the humble East Europeans were often better economists than their would-be mentors. They gauged the economic trends more accurately than the millionaire Jews of Wall Street, for they knew by the 1890's that the last frontier had been reached, that there was no place for the rural peddler, and that the future lay with the city and the factory—with America's rapidly emergent industrialization. They insisted on remaining in the eastern metropolitan centers, entered into the clothing industry as laborers, and after thirty years of sweatshops and blundering efforts to improve themselves, created four "Jewish" labor unions whose social and economic policies are still among the most enlightened and exemplary of the organized crafts. Many of the Russian and Polish garment workers emerged from the sweatshops and factories to become highly successful apparel manufacturers.

Religion. Though most of the Jewish labor leaders and many of their followers were antireligious in the early days, this attitude toward religion was not characteristic of the American Jew. The first Sephardim who came here in the middle 1600's were devoted religionists and with little delay set about reconstituting the European-type religious community to which they were accustomed. Its central institution on these shores was the synagogue, and traditional loyalties, combined with the moral pressures exerted here, impelled newcomers to affiliate themselves. Despite the Germanic origins which prevailed among them, by the 1720's the immigrants of those early days were content to join—and, in some instances, even to establish—Spanish-Portuguese congregations, so that the Sephardic rite became typically American and was accepted by all Jews until the early 1800's.

The domination of the Orthodox Sephardim began to wane in the 1820's and 1830's, when the new, post-Napoleonic arrivals created their own Orthodox Ashkenazic conventicles. But Sephardic Orthodoxy began losing ground even among the older, well-established families, whose desire to integrate more closely with the relatively liberal American culture led some of them, as early as 1824, to reject Orthodoxy and the authority of the traditional Law. Thus Reform Judaism came to birth in Charleston, South Carolina, probably the largest and certainly the most cultured Jewish community in the United States at that time. By the 1840's, Reform, as an aspect of acculturation, was in full swing. The movement was particularly strong in "the West," the Ohio and Mississippi valleys, and it was there, in 1873, that the Reformers led the way in establishing the first real nationwide and enduring American Jewish institution, the Union of American Hebrew Congregations. Two years later, the Union created the Hebrew Union College in the Queen City of the West, Cincinnati. Yet, despite its early start and excellent organization and discipline, Reform was never to become a majority movement even in its palmiest days. Reacting indignantly to the sharp break with traditionalism that Reform formulated at the Pittsburgh Conference in 1885, the native-born Americanized Orthodox, mostly "Germans," abandoned the Union which they had supported, and a year later established the Jewish Theological Seminary Association. Thus was Conservative Judaism organized as a separate religious denomination in this country. Not an East European movement, even though the Russian and Polish immigrants had already organized dozens of their own synagogues a decade or two before that time, Conservatism represented an effort on the part of the well-Americanized Orthodox to maintain themselves in the community.

The Russian, Polish, Lithuanian, Galician, Roumanian, and Hungarian masses who poured in after the pogroms of the 1880's opened hundreds of new synagogues, fortified Orthodoxy and kashrut, and preserved the age-old Hebrew liturgy. Their vernacular, however, was Yiddish, and here, on these shores, they were soon to create a vigorous and appealing Yiddish literature. Because of their Messianic traditions and the oppression they had experienced under Russian rule, they were ardently ethnocentric and sympathetic to Jewish nationalism. Zionism, the new Messianism of the 1880's and 1890's, was generally as acceptable to them as it was distasteful to their Americanized predecessors.

Social Welfare. The immigrant East European shuls, and the Orthodox German and Sephardic synagogues which had preceded them, were not only places of prayer and worship, but hearths of education and centers of social welfare. The roots of present-day social philanthropy go back to the first American Spanish-Portuguese synagogues, which provided for the local and itinerant poor, advanced free loans, nursed the sick, buried the dead, pensioned the unfortunate, aided the old, and even collected money for the Jews of Palestine. Like the earlier Sephardim, the German immigrants of the nineteenth century were Europe-oriented, transplanting and practicing here their ancestral tradition of pious works. From the 1820's on, however, the Ashkenazic immigrants preferred to protect themselves and the later arrivals by creating their own mutual-aid and benevolent societies. Most of those new organizations divorced themselves from direct synagogal control, thus initiating the secularization of American Jewish charities. Even in the days before the Civil War, the existence of rival philanthropic organizations led to waste and inefficiency and brought about the beginnings of a federation movement, but it was not until the 1890's that federations became effective and began to include even the East European self-help societies. By World War I the federations were taken into the Community Chests, and thus received aid not from Jews alone, but from the urban community at large.

Jewish Education and Culture. The Sephardic synagogue-community, beginning with the seventeenth century, was concerned with education. In addition, there had undoubtedly been private Jewish teachers since the 1600's. By 1731 New York Jewry supported an all-day or parochial school whose curriculum was confined to Hebrew. Later, secular subjects were taught in Portuguese and in English, but English quickly became the sole language of instruction. The Central European pioneers of the nineteenth century continued the all-day school tradition—in German and in English—till about the time of the Civil War, when the public school system became firmly established. Ever since 1838, religion had been taught primarily in the synagogal "Sunday School," patterned after Protestant counterparts, and those congregational Sunday schools, plus an occasional afternoon Hebrew school, were to remain typical until the twentieth century. After 1910, the afternoon schools, under the influence of the new bureaus of Jewish education, were organized so as to effect a synthesis of Hebrew lore, American pedagogy, and Zionistic ethnicism. American Jewish education was consequently re-Judaized and improved, and this approach to the instruction of Jewish children was, by the 1930's, adopted even by the Reformers of the Union of American Hebrew Congregations.

The Jewish religion and the Hebrew language are, of course, central to Jewish culture, but few advances were made in those areas until the second quarter of the nineteenth century. The Sephardim, however, merely by maintaining their Jewish identity, had held the fort till the arrival of Central and East European Jews in larger numbers, and it is noteworthy that Gershom Mendes Seixas, American Jewry's first native-born clergyman, had a working knowledge of Hebrew. Still, it remained for a German immigrant, Isaac Leeser, the hazzan, or minister, at Philadelphia's Sephardic Mikveh Israel, to lay the groundwork for the American Jewish cultural system. From 1830 to 1868, Leeser furthered Sunday Schools and all-day schools, produced textbooks, prepared English translations of the traditional prayer books and the Hebrew Bible, created the first Jewish publication society, established a national Jewish monthly magazine, *The Occident*, helped organize the first union of congregations in the form of the Board of Delegates of American Israelites, and in 1867—a year before his death—even established a theological seminary, Maimonides College. It was Leeser's short-lived college that spurred on another immigrant, Bohemian-born Isaac M. Wise, of Cincinnati, to create the Hebrew Union College in 1875, and, a decade later, the memory of Leeser's efforts had its influence on the anti-Reform leaders, who in 1887 established the Jewish Theological Seminary in New York. These seminaries and the others that followed became, and still are, the nurseries of Jewish learning and scholarship on this continent. The crowning literary achievements of America's new Jewish learning at the turn of the century were the twelve-volume *Jewish Encyclopedia*, and *The Holy Scriptures*, as the Jewish Publication Society called its translation of the Hebrew Bible.

After two generations of lingering affection for their original German vernacular, the German-Jewish immigrants on these shores began to employ English almost exclusively. The first generation of East Europeans, equally devoted to their own mother tongue, nurtured a lively Yiddish literature, daily press, and theatre. Yiddish floated in a world of its own, giving emotional, intellectual, and spiritual sustenance to the millions of East European immigrants who yearned for the familiar culture of their old homeland. Yiddish proved to be a transitional culture on these shores, but it performed an effective service in enabling the newcomers to survive spiritually until they and their children could take deep root in American soil.

American Jewry until the 1920's constituted, by and large, an immigrant community and as such was concerned primarily with the struggle for existence rather than the acquisition of secular learning. The Sephardim and ante-bellum Germans, too, had rarely been distinguished for their general education and academic achievements, even though they had in their midst some notable lawyers, an occasional playwright, and a few fine physicians. It was, for the most part, not until after World War I that the children of the East Europeans began to make their mark in the world of literature and the fine arts.

THE EMERGENCE OF AN AMERICAN JEWISH COMMUNITY

In 1920, even though there were over 3,500,000 Jews in this country, one could not speak of a genuine American Jewish community. Such a community simply did not exist. Instead, there were *two* separate Jewish communities eyeing one another warily—the native, or "German," and the immigrant, or "Russian." No one national American Jewish community had developed as an organic structure; there was not even one organized *local* American Jewish community, for practically all Jewish institutions were still autonomous. The sources of conflict between the two large "communities" were many and varied. The East Europeans regarded their usually wealthier and more prestigious coreligionists of German origin with envy; the Germans looked down on the "newcomers" with disdain. The Orthodox and the Reformers distrusted each other, while both looked askance at the religious indifference of the Jewish labor union leaders. The five decades between 1880 and 1930 were filled with conflicts between the elite and the masses, between political conservatives and liberals, democrats and socialists. Immigrants and natives were arrayed against each other. The East Europeans, who wanted one central, all-embracing national American Jewish community—which, if only by sheer weight of numbers, they could hope to control—struggled against the Germans, who wanted decentralization and the right to go their own way—by which they hoped to undermine challenges to their traditional leadership.

Yet, though they were not conscious of it, the two hostile forces were wedded in a higher unity. Before 1820 the disciplined synagogue-community had claimed—indeed demanded—the loyalty of all Americans who called themselves Jews. Even after the 1820's—after the pull of American liberalism, permissiveness, and assimilation had drawn many away from the synagogue—Jews were still joined by a consensus: the consciousness of a common past, a common tradition, and a similar way of life. This sense of kinship remained very strong, and unfailingly obliged Jews to help one another here and abroad.

Since 1820, therefore, American Jewry has been held together, if not by the synagogue, then by sociocultural bonds and by the nourishing influences of a powerful subterranean current of religion and religious institutions. During the 1920's, ambivalence and hostility permitted only a tenuous unity, but a more closely integrated unity was to arise in the next decade. The quota laws, cutting American Jewry off from the intensely Jewish East European reservoir, made intraJewish assimilation here inevitable, so that Americanization could begin to move forward at a rapid pace even for the first-generation immigrants. The Jewish melting pot— intra-marriage—began to boil. The rise of Nazi anti-Semitism and its American imitators welded all Jews together, if only through resentment and shock and despair. Intense Jewish sympathies and loyalties were engendered by Zionism, which recommended itself increasingly as an effective defense against the burgeoning anti-Semitic threat. The new, ethnically motivated Jewish education, which had been taking shape since 1910, made children proud of their heritage, while the herculean efforts of Jews throughout Amer-

ica after World War II to salvage Europe's decimated Jewry
and strengthen the Palestinian community made American
Jews realize that, whatever their lineage, they were indeed
brothers. And when authority in the power structure was
finally shared with the wealthy sons and grandsons of East
European immigrants—as happened in the 1930's and the
1940's—unity became a practical possibility.

By the 1920's, then—antagonisms notwithstanding—an integrated, united, local American Jewish community was at
least in the process of becoming. The age of Jewish fusion
had begun. The "Spanish-Portuguese," the "German," the
"Russian" Jew was disappearing; soon there would be only
"American" Jews. A new "American" Jewish community
had begun to emerge.

INTEGRATION

Political Rights. The American Jew is both American
and Jew. As an American with roots going back to the seventeenth century, he insists on his rights. Ever since the 1650's
he has been compelled to fight for the achievement or main-
tenance of his economic, civil, and political liberties. The past
never lacked oppressions; prejudice was rarely less than
vocal. As early as 1793—only a decade after the Revolution
—Jonas Phillips, a Revolutionary veteran, was fined for refusing to be sworn on the Sabbath. Governors ignored Jewish sensibilities in Thanksgiving proclamations; Jewish children in the public schools were—and often enough still are—
compelled to submit to Christian religious indoctrination;
legislators imperiled the Jewish future through continual
efforts to "baptize" the Constitution, as Isaac M. Wise put it,
and make the United States a "Christian" nation; newspapers
slandered Jews *as Jews* well into the twentieth century.
Against many of these disabilities, the Jew has fought successfully and still continues to fight—for himself and for
other elements in American life—by sponsoring fair education, fair economic, and fair accommodation laws and prac-

tices. The new approach of today is really the old Jewish socialistic approach of half a century ago: protect all groups, and the American people as a whole, through effective social action procedures. Aroused by the waves of racism and anti-Semitism that threatened them in the 1920's and 1930's, American Jews in all large towns spontaneously began creating local defense agencies representing the entire range of what was still an inchoate Jewish community. These were the Jewish community relations committees, dedicated to the fight against anti-Semitism and to the furtherance of better relations with the preponderantly Gentile world in which Jews lived.

Economic Life. Though there is today no area of economic activity without its Jewish participants, it has never been easy for the Jew to fit into the "normal" occupational pattern—a fact due, in large part, to a past which compelled Jewish preoccupation with certain forms of commerce. Even today the considerable antagonism he often encounters in banking, insurance administration, transportation, utilities, and in many "heavy" industries helps maintain a Jewish preponderance in garment manufacturing, merchandising, trading, the service industries, and the professions. In the new consolidated community that he is in the process of creating, he has established his own vocational bureaus to offer special help to fellow-Jews and to advance their economic integration. In a world of commerce and rapidly proliferating automation, the American Jew seeks a white-collar job; in the smaller towns, he is frequently self-employed. His desire to conform, coupled with the overwhelming pull of the environment, and an almost obsessive passion for anonymity in business life, has led the Jew to adapt himself completely to the American social pattern in dress, language, demeanor, and even the name he bears. Moses has given way to Murray, and as soon as Murray becomes a Jewish stereotype, a new name beginning with "M" will be found.

General Culture. American Jews have made tremendous, almost fantastic strides in their absorption of general culture since 1914. In the professions, in music, in painting and sculpture, in the academic world, and particularly in the area of the sciences, Jews are often highly distinguished and, in numerous instances, preeminent—and this despite the fact that they constitute but a meager 3 percent of the American population. Though noticeable reinforcements in the sciences have come, especially since the 1930's, from the arrival of European Jewish refugees, some of them already Nobel Prize winners in Europe, native-born Jews who excel are not uncommon. Some of the best known of America's litterateurs are the children of Jewish immigrants; Jewish journalists and publicists are among the leaders of the general American press. With cultural and social integration has, of course, also come intermarriage—and, in some instances, complete assimilation and loss of Jewish identity. The intermarriage rate for the Jewish community as a whole is rapidly approaching the 10 percent mark.

JUDAIZATION AND COMMUNALITY

The Voluntary Suburban Ghetto. Politico-economic integration, cultural assimilation, and even a growing rate of intermarriage by no means pose a real threat to the survival of the contemporary American Jew, for there are many compensatory and countervailing forces and influences. Jewish cohesiveness, Jewish sympathies, the feeling of intra-Jewish kinship—these are stronger today than they have ever been. Ever since World War I, American Jews, as a whole, have been moving out to the suburbs, congregating together there to create voluntary physical and psychological havens, or "ghettoes," but in the best sense of the term. Motivated, on the one hand, by apprehensions and anti-Jewish social pressures, real or imaginary, and, on the other, by the pull of Jewish communality, Zionism, and an ethnocentric religious education, the Jews of today cluster together around their Jewish institutions. To promote their survival as Jews, they are fashioning a rather compact form of Jewish settlement—reminiscent, in some respects, of the medieval-type society—with a full complement of Jewish institutions, religious, educational, eleemosynary and social, all held together loosely by a Jewish community council. This development of an ethno-religious enclave has characterized the direction of Jewish life in America since the 1930's.

The Reacceptance of the Synagogue by Jews. Synagogue affiliation has again become de rigueur for American Jews—especially in the suburbs, where many today join synagogues for social, educational, and "folkist" reasons, if not out of a sense of piety. It is deemed un-American not to belong "to the church or synagogue of your choice," and the typical suburban Jew is in this, as in other respects, very much a conformist. But the new suburban world beyond the core city is the scene for other departures from past norms. The Orthodox in suburbia are fighting a gallant, but losing, struggle to retain their majority status in the Jewish group. Together with the Classical Reformers, who have outlived their integrationist day, they are fast giving way to the Neo-Reformers and Conservatives who, sharing an appetite for yiddishkeit, are slowly drawing closer to one another. Jewish religious loyalties, which are not only tolerated but encouraged by the American ethos, are further reflected in the decline of most of the bureaus of Jewish education as overall school entities, and by the growth and strengthening of congregational afternoon and weekend religious schools, whose curricula and instructional standards have been improved.

A new factor on the scene has been the reappearance of the colonial and mid-nineteenth-century parochial—full-day —schools. Reinstituted, in large part, by refugee Orthodox leaders after World War II, they have found rapid acceptance by the Conservatives, and even the Neo-Reformers are not immune to their appeal. Should the Catholics ever win their struggle to secure public money for their parochial schools, the Jewish all-day schools, fortified by similar governmental grants as well as by Jewish welfare fund money, are likely to flourish in larger numbers.

Social Welfare Trends. In the new Jewish suburban "community" slowly being pieced together by need and a subconscious romanticism, the most powerful component is the Jewish welfare fund. Through a united Jewish appeal, this common fund-raising effort has, since the 1920's, provided the money for overseas relief, for Israel, for national health, civic defense, and other needs, as well as for local requirements not covered by Community Chest contributions. Prosperity and government aid have combined to reduce the urgency of Jewish-provided financial relief for the sick, the aged, underprivileged children, and needy families. The inevitable coming of "socialized medicine" and increased government aid to health institutions will probably divert Jewish philanthropies to other forms of social amelioration in the Jewish community. The social welfare agencies of the coming generation are likely to concern themselves far more with strengthening and saving the Jewish family through psychological and psychiatric services and with developing viable, possibly even exemplary, forms of geriatric services.

Leisure. The new suburban spiritual and emotional refuge has already developed its own forms of leisure. The colonial Jews of Newport relaxed in a card-playing and eating club; the German immigrants of the nineteenth century created eating, drinking, and music clubs of their own, while their children established literary and social institutions which they called young men's Hebrew literary associations. Though submerged by the waves of immigration from Eastern Europe, the Hebrew literary associations reappeared almost immediately as settlement houses preaching Americanization. In the last generation the settlement houses have in turn disappeared, even in the core areas, but they have been resurrected in the suburbs as beautifully furnished Jewish community centers, deluxe playgrounds of middle-class youth. Supplemented in downtown urban areas by the older eating clubs, and in the more posh suburban pastures by elegant country clubs, the community center functions not only as a recreational institution, but, in many instances, as a

force for general American culture, especially in the fine arts
and in the drama. Its Jewish influences are, thus far at least,
negligible except in an associative sense.

Coordination in the Oncoming Community. There is no
lack of "togetherness" in contemporary American Jewish
life. The middle-class American Jews who live in the fluid,
wandering expanses of suburbia dwell together, often worship together, commonly receive their Jewish education together, and almost invariably swim and play golf together.
As much as the medieval Jew—and perhaps even more so—
the Jew of the oncoming twenty-first century has the assurance, vital for survival, that he can always live and enjoy
himself among Jews and that they will provide for him no
matter what happens. He is assured of prenatal care in a Jewish clinic and, though it may be cold comfort to him, he can
be reasonably confident that he will die in a Jewish hospital
or home for the aged and that a synagogue will annually re-
cite commemorative prayers for him long after his death!

Still, though this community and its institutions constitute
a growing, impending reality, "togetherness" is conspicuously
absent where coordinating agencies for religion, education,
defense, and social welfare are concerned. Here centrifugal-
ity is the usual—and wasteful—rule. To tie these various
communal agencies together, to avoid duplication and over-
lapping, to effect planning and direction—this remains one
of the challenges of the future. The challenge has not gone
unnoticed, for an overall council was created in some cities
as early as the 1930's. This marked the beginning of the
Jewish community council "movement," which as yet has
little influence in most towns. Once, however, the power
groups that dominate the Jewish welfare funds accept the
idea of a common council, see the advantages in working for
it, and surrender some of the prerogatives which are traditionally theirs by virtue of their larger gifts, there is no question that the community council will rise to power as a force
for purposeful planning in the Jewish community of the next

generation. This will come, because it is certain that a new federated Jewish community, more or less democratically motivated, is emerging on the American scene.

There are no gains without losses, of course, and there will be a loss in diversity of expression. Because it requires a medium of communication, this emergent federated community —or its Jewish welfare fund—will create, as in some localities it already has created, a local weekly magazine, impressive in format, rich in content, beautifully printed, and reaching every Jew who has ever contributed to a communal agency. Unfortunately, however, the need or hunger for communal peace is likely to preclude a vigorous editorial policy where dissent and controversy are concerned. The new successful community newspaper will not be—perhaps cannot be—an organ expressive of differences in opinion; its dedication to information, education, and harmony cannot but doom it to fashioning a community of bland conformists.

THE RISE OF A NATIONWIDE JEWISH COMMUNITY

History is not without some logic. People create the institutions they need in order to survive. That explains the development of local Diaspora Jewish communities ever since the Jews were exiled to Babylonia in the sixth pre-Christian century. But the local Jewish community, whether in present-day America or in ancient Babylonia, is not an island. It cannot live Jewishly by and for itself alone. To effectuate its purposes, to defend itself, and to move forward, it requires the spiritual, cultural, intellectual, and political support of a supralocal, or national, Jewish community. Just as municipal or state governments are federated into a state or a national entity, so the work of individual Jewish communities must be coordinated and planned, with smaller units organized into larger bodies, in order to further American Jewry as a whole.

The need for more effectual local and national organization has become especially compelling in the wake of the two global wars which spelled an all but total destruction for European Jewry. Before the Nazi holocaust, American Jewry was little more than a spiritual colony of Europe; but now the Jews of the United States have fallen heir to the mantle of world Jewish leadership—whether or not they are prepared for the task and whether or not they wish it—for America's Jews constitute the only sizable Diaspora Jewry still free and still surviving. *Noblesse oblige* has now been added to all the other reasons driving American Jewry to organize on a local, regional, and—above all—national level. For now, not only is such organization essential if the community is to function smoothly—and the community is a corporation of almost 6,000,000 units—but it is no less essential if the community is to fulfill the ineluctable obligation that history has imposed on it: to help all Jews everywhere in the world.

A nationwide Jewish community has been of very slow growth in the United States. This fact is no departure from the norms of Diaspora experience, for the Jews of the last 2,000 years never succeeded in forging a truly effective national organization. Problems of slow communication, governmental opposition, Jewish factionalism, and the objections of local Jewish vested interests have everywhere in the past inhibited such a development. Yet a national communal attitude has been evolving in America since the 1840's. A ritual murder accusation in faraway Damascus aroused and united American Jewry, at least emotionally, in 1840, and in answer to a nascent consciousness of larger common needs, continual, if unsuccessful, efforts were made to conjoin all of American Jewry throughout the 1840's and the 1850's. It was only in 1859 that American Jews came together in an embryonic nationwide organization—in response to the cause célèbre of Edgar Mortara, an Italian-Jewish child "legally" abducted by the Papal authorities in Bologna. The plight of a Jewish mother, bereaved of her son, shocked even Catholic monarchs. The Jews of the French Empire were sufficiently agitated to create the Alliance Israélite Universelle, while the indignant members of America's minuscule

Jewish community—numbering about 100,000—organized themselves into the Board of Delegates of American Israelites. Primarily a civic defense and overseas relief agency, the Board was never able to establish its authority and in 1878 was absorbed by the younger, more powerful Union of American Hebrew Congregations as the Union's Board of Delegates on Civil and Religious Rights.

The Union of the 1870's, made possible by the appearance of the telegraph and the railroad, still remains the closest approach American Jewry has ever made to a national representative body. At its inception, it set out to include and speak for all American Jews, whatever their religious preferences. It was not, initially, a "Reform" institution. Through its Board of Delegates, it reached beyond purely congregational concerns into the areas of defense and relief, and even attempted to settle the early East European Jewish immigrants in colonies on the western plains. But, as a national overall coordinating agency, the Union failed to command the support of even all the native-born in the community. It made no serious, sustained effort to cope with the problems of the East European immigrant masses; the latter in turn ignored the Union.

The failures of the Union and the aspiring B'nai B'rith—both of them essentially midwestern organizations—left a vacuum into which the financially powerful eastern Jewish bankers, merchants, and lawyers rushed. From their vantage point, particularly in New York City, the numerical hub of American Jewry, the eastern magnates assumed the role of self-appointed standard-bearers. For the most part devoted men who loved Jews and Judaism, they undertook to give the amorphous immigrant Jewish masses an effective leadership, and they won their spurs in the protest against Russian brutality after the Kishinev massacre of 1903. Three years later they organized the American Jewish Committee and offered American Jewry a vigorous, disciplined, and highly paternalistic leadership as well as a program of Americanization. Soon the American Jewish Committee, aided by the

Union of American Hebrew Congregations and the B'nai
B'rith, renewed the fight—ultimately successful in 1911—to
abrogate the Russo-American treaty of 1832, because the
Czarist regime had refused to honor the passports of American Jews.

In 1908, the Committee attempted, by itself, to organize
the immigrant Jews of New York City and other urban centers into kehillot, or overall local communities, which would
govern nearly every phase of the lives and activities of the
newcomers. This effort failed, but the idea of adapting the
European kehillah or *Gemeinde*—an authoritative, all-
inclusive community—to American forms of autonomous
living persisted. In later years, it would be resuscitated when
the "Russians" felt strong enough to rebel against the competent and well-meaning "Germans" who presumed to speak
for them.

The outbreak of World War I led to a temporary truce
between the competing groups within American Jewry.
Only a few months after the war began, the Orthodox, the
Jewish labor unionists, and the American Jewish Committee
buried their differences and banded together in an American
Jewish *Joint* Distribution Committee to help the Jews of
Eastern Europe, caught between the Russian and German-
Austrian armies. One of the most important developments in
the entire course of American Jewish history, this common
effort for relief united all the Jews in America and was,
within a generation, to create a national American Jewish
consensus.

One would think that, having worked together on various
problems—Czarist oppressions, immigrant aid, and the like—
since 1903, the two dissimilar communities, the "German"
and the "Russian," would by the time of World War I have
begun to merge. It was just then, however, that each body,
feeling sure of itself, made a determined effort to assume, or
to retain, hegemony in the emerging national American Jewish community. The test came in 1915, when the "immigrants" insisted on calling a democratically elected Jewish

Congress which would labor, at the war's conclusion, to secure minority rights for the oppressed Jews of Eastern Europe and to effect some form of Jewish autonomy in Palestine. The "natives" initially opposed the Congress, but overwhelmed by Jewish public opinion after a bitter struggle, they accepted their defeat gracefully and loyally joined in a temporary Congress uniting American Jewry. The Congress sent delegates to Versailles to lobby at the Paris peace conference in 1919. The following year, according to plan, the Congress disbanded, each group going its own way under the leadership either of the American Jewish Committee or of the newly formed permanent American Jewish Congress.

The "immigrants" soon found that, despite their numbers and the victory they had won during the war in forcing the "natives" to meet with them in a common congress, they could not dominate American Jewry. The Committee's defeat in 1916 had already alerted its supporters and followers to the fact that their hitherto undisputed leadership of American Jewry was a thing of the past. But the final decision—and compromise—came through historic forces over which neither party had any control. History decreed that, after the gates of immigration began closing in 1921, the two groups would find themselves cast into a common melting pot out of which one monochromatic American Jewish community would inevitably emerge.

Two rival American Jewries could not, in any case, maintain themselves in an age of expanding technology. The telephone, the intercity and interstate highway, the automobile, the airplane—these have become a guarantee and a promise of the ultimate creation of a merged and unified American Jewish community. Rapid transportation and instantaneous communication, annihilating time and space, have swept away the conditions which inhibited unification. Today, in the 1960's, it take less time for a California delegate to fly to a meeting in New York than it took his grandfather to travel by train from Baltimore or Boston. Today every Jew is his brother's neighbor. Physically and emotionally, American

Jews have become one entity. And this oneness is further advanced today by congeries of national agencies that for decades have been knitting all American Jews tightly together. The Jewish Telegraphic Agency, for instance, feeds news—the *same* news—to over a hundred American Jewish weeklies. The Synagogue Council of America—as persistent as it is as yet ineffective—attempts to express the common aims and needs of religious Jewry, Orthodox, Conservative, and Reform. The various rabbinical colleges—with their newly established branches in Los Angeles, now the second largest Jewish community in the United States—are nurseries of a common American Jewish culture, and their efforts are supplemented by the Jewish "secular" colleges that are now capturing the imagination of American Jewry. A Hebrew press persists, three Yiddish dailies still appear in New York City, and major organizations like the American Jewish Committee, the American Jewish Congress, the Zionist groups, and the B'nai B'rith publish magazines that appeal to Jews of culture, academic background, and philosophic training. Even the New York general press—*The Times* and *The Post*—supplements the Jewish newspapers by giving full coverage to Jewish news both here and abroad. Common news makes for community of sentiment.

The cultural stirrings in American Jewish life are evident in organizations like the Jewish Publication Society; the American Jewish Historical Society, and the American Jewish Archives, both of which collect and disseminate American Jewish historical materials; the Yivo Institute for Jewish Research, rich in Yiddish lore; the B'nai B'rith, with its Hillel Foundations and educational programs; the National Jewish Welfare Board, which sponsors national book and music programs; and the American Association for Jewish Education, which is making a valiant effort to raise the level of Jewish elementary education throughout the country. There is a widespread youth movement, without equal in Jewish communities elsewhere in the world. Through the B'nai B'rith and the Jewish community centers, but primarily through

the indefatigable efforts of the Jewish religious denomina-
tions, a knowledge of Jewish life and history, of the Hebrew
language and the religious heritage, is being assiduously culti-
vated, especially in summer camps, which are exerting a spiritual influence on the Jewish youth of this country.

Welding American Jewry together is inevitably a slow
and often painful process, for Jewish life abounds with
negative factors which are almost as important as—if not
more important than—positive factors in ensuring unity.
Outer pressures are and always have been no less crucial than
inner urges. In the 1940's the various local Jewish community relations committees that had emerged out of the fight
against Judeophobic prejudice joined together to represent
American Jewry in its struggle with anti-Semitism, religious
bigotry, and the reactionary forces intent on denying minority groups their constitutional rights to political, religious,
and civil liberty. This new nationwide self-defense group,
the National Community Relations Advisory Council, was
formed in 1944 by the Council of Jewish Federations and
Welfare Funds, which realized, from its successes with a
common Jewish welfare fund and a united Jewish appeal,
that only through union could American Jewry cope with
threats to its security. But it was not only the obvious need
to reduce duplication of effort and wasteful expenditure that
moved the Council of Jewish Federations and Welfare Funds
to press for a single, common national defense agency. It was
also the Council's consciousness of the fact that the American Jewish Conference, a new "Congress" called a year earlier, in 1943, could not and would not command the loyalty
of American Jewry. The Jewish masses, at least, hoped that
the American Jewish Conference, like the historic "Congress" of 1915–1920, would attempt to cement together all
Jews in this land, give them an effective and permanent national leadership, and work for a larger measure of opportunity in Palestine. But, as the Council of Jewish Federations
and Welfare Funds understood, the Conference could not
but founder on the question of sovereignty for Palestinian

Jewry and on the fears of some of the national agencies that their vested interests would suffer in a "national assembly" like the Conference.

Even the National Community Relations Advisory Council did not succeed in holding the various defense agencies together, and at the outset of the 1960's there were still three large bodies working separately toward the same goals and employing the same techniques of social action. Today the Council of Jewish Federations and Welfare Funds, its elite character notwithstanding, is the closest approach to a truly national agency uniting all Jews, for it embraces the federations, welfare funds, and community councils—whatever they call themselves—of practically every organized Jewish communal social agency in the United States. Ultimately the National Community Relations Advisory Council is again likely to include the American Jewish Committee and the Anti-Defamation League of B'nai B'rith, and again to give direction to a united defense effort. This drive toward cooperation, merger, and union, which is part of the centripetal tendency in nearly every phase of American life, will in the future bring about a common effort on the part of all national Jewish agencies, not merely those dedicated to the fight against disabilities. Eventually most American Jewish nationwide bodies will forge either a Congress of Community Councils or a Consultative Council of National Agencies in order to give intelligent guidance to the emerging national community, in the same way that the community council is attempting to coordinate the work of the local agencies.

TODAY AND TOMORROW

American Jewry and the Rise of a United World Jewry.
The creation of an overall national American Jewish "Congress" or "Council," whether composed of local delegates, of national societies and agencies, or of notable individuals, would not only give needed leadership to American Jewry, but would also provide help and guidance to World

Jewry. In this respect, the American Jew would be reflecting the aspirations of the United States government which, on a much larger scale, is attempting to influence all nations on all continents. The United States as a world power is reaching out everywhere to protect and further its international preeminence in commerce and politics. Hopeful that its politico-economic ideals of representative democracy in a modified capitalistic system will find acceptance among the old and new nations of the world, the American republic is determined to maintain the political hegemony which it has exercised for a generation since the fall of the British Empire.

Though American Jewry, in its relation to the Jews of the world, can have no political, industrial, or economic ambitions, it has resolved, since the Hitlerian destruction of European Jewry and the ensuing deterioration of Jewish life in Asian and African lands, to reach out and help its fellow-Jewries. This obligation is incumbent upon American Jewry by virtue of its inescapable tradition of assuming responsibility for its coreligionists, by virtue of the historic role of leadership thrust upon it, and by virtue, finally, of its sympathies and its wealth. In the last decade, consequently, the Zionists, the American Jewish Congress, the B'nai B'rith, and the American Jewish Committee have each created separate international committees and are working with their own overseas affiliates to salvage what they can of Old World life and to restore it to some semblance of its former stability. The economic arm of this effort at world rehabilitation for Jewry is the American Jewish Joint Distribution Committee; its prime agency in the new Republic of Israel is the Jewish Agency for Israel.

There are even individuals and groups working to integrate the efforts of American Jewish national agencies and the national agencies of all other Jews abroad into one worldwide organization dedicated to the religious and cultural survival of the Jewish people, and to the defense of their civic and political liberties in all lands. The sponsors of this proposed worldwide agency are particularly anxious to protect the State of Israel against the political enemies who have vowed its destruction. If such an overall Jewish international agency were ever to arise, it would probably be led by American Jews—at least as long as the United States continues to exercise hegemony in the world. The creation of such a world Jewish body, in which American Jewish personalities would play a leading part, becomes ever more feasible logistically in a generation soon to enjoy the use of supersonic passenger planes requiring but two and one-half hours to fly from New York to London.

The New Jew and the New Prospect. This generation is witnessing the rise and consolidation of the local community, the stirrings of an overall national advisory agency, and still vague but nonetheless promising *tentatives* to bring about an American-led international union of all Jews everywhere corresponding to the feeling of kinship that Jews bear one another. A new Jew is thus emerging here on American soil.

He is and will continue to be a completely acculturated American, indistinguishable in his physical appearance, language, and dress from his fellow-citizens. The typical young man—or woman—of the coming generation will be a college graduate, a white-collar worker, and, frequently, self-employed. Politically he will ally himself with the most liberal and democratic party, for he has found, even in this last half of the twentieth century, that eternal vigilance is still the price of liberty.

He will also have some conception of his historic relationship to the Jewish people of the past. It is a fact that even today the average Jewish religious school student, who has read one or two of the many textbooks on the subject, can boast a better and more systematic knowledge of Jewish origins and history than his parents and grandparents ever could —even though he is no Hebraist and is not likely to be one. And because he knows more, he is more sympathetic; with knowledge have come loyalty and devotion, not in parochial but in broad universal terms, to the ideals of his people and to the welfare of even the most distant of Jewries. This growing sense of kinship and the "style" of American life in general will bring the majority of Jews back into the synagogue. Some will come only to associate with their fellows. Others will seek education for their children and for themselves. Some will remain to pray, and in a world where science reaches out to embrace the infinite, they will reverently identify themselves once again with the spiritual ideals of their fathers.

What is actually in process in this generation, on the eve of a new century, is a blending of Americanism and Judaism. Like the historic mergers of Hellenism and Judaism, Arabic and Jewish culture, German methodology and Jewish lore, the new American Jewish synthesis will be expressed in the vernacular; like Philo's Greek commentaries, or Maimonides' Arabic *Guide*, or Zunz's German monographs, it will take a literary form. It will constitute, in effect, a fusion between the Jewish intellectual heritage and the various currents of thought prevalent in contemporary and future America. When, ultimately, books of enduring value begin to appear, works embodying the best in both cultures, books of such lasting worth that they will merit translation into other languages, including Hebrew, then we shall have witnessed the birth of another Golden Age in Jewish life. Barring a "historical accident," such a development is inevitable on this soil.

12

THE FUTURE OF AMERICAN JEWRY

Let there be no doubt about it: American Jewry is surviving and will survive.

Almost six million living Jews are irrefutable proof that we shall continue to grow, even though our gates are almost closed to immigrants. The character of our survival in the future is threatened by a residual social and economic discrimination on the one hand, and by an enveloping blanket of assimilation on the other. Both forces tend to draw Jews out of the Jewish community.

To meet the threat of discrimination, American Jewry has countered with an educational program aimed at enlightenment; and Jewish organizations are laboring to further the process of intergroup understanding.

Beyond the Jewish community, in many cities of the country, mayors' friendly relations committees meet to thresh out interracial and interreligious problems, and there have been notable successes. Moreover, rulings of the United States Supreme Court in the area of desegregation indicate that progress is being made even in the thorny field of anti-Negro discrimination. To the canker of injustice in employment, education, housing, and public accommodations, we have applied the cautery of remedial legislation. In addition, we are working hard to maintain an effective separation of Church and State. It is imperative that we do this, if we are to save the conscience of the Jewish child from the encroachments of those Protestant churches which seek to use the school

This address was originally delivered at The Dropsie College for Hebrew and Cognate Learning, in Philadelphia, on June 2, 1955, when that institution awarded Dr. Marcus an honorary degree. It appeared in the Centennial Edition of *American Israelite* (Cincinnati, Ohio), February 23, 1956, and is now reprinted with minor changes.

system as an instrumentality to strengthen Protestantism in its struggle with a militant Catholicism.

Assimilation is a threat to survival because it is an aspect of flight from prejudice, but by its very nature it also becomes a means of survival, as when it permits the individual to become so like his neighbor that he is no longer different.

Most humans living in a social environment welcome the chance to become one with their fellowmen. The process is unconscious, inevitable, and, on the whole, desirable. Similarity reduces the friction of daily contact to a mimimum: you do not dislike the like. We will survive, for we will be accepted because we are like others.

The Jew of today and of the oncoming tomorrow will be a native American living primarily in a half-dozen large cities. At least one of these cities will be in the West, for in the next century civilization, culture, and wealth will slowly shift from the Atlantic to the Pacific basin. Once the tremendous natural resources of Western and Southern Asia are exploited, culture and civilization and commerce will boom in that part of the world, and the American West will share in the ensuing prosperity.

Our children will begin to resemble their neighbors even in a physical sense, not only because of a common speech and common food, but by virtue of the results of intramarriage and intermarriage. In the common Jewish melting pot of intramarriage, the German, the Lithuanian, and the Galician Jew will have disappeared to emerge as an American Jew. The thousands of Gentile converts who annually marry into Judaism will all the more produce an American Jew who is ethnically and anthropologically not different from his next-door neighbor. Our grandchildren thus will look like their Gentile neighbors, will dress like them, and will eat the same food.

Fifty years hence, the percentage of those who will observe the dietary laws away from home will be minimal. Of course, kosher-style food will be consumed, with relish, in all large American cities by Jews and Gentiles. But this is not

Jewish tradition; it is but a delectable aspect of transculturation, a process whereby even immigrants impress their personality on their host group.

It will be increasingly difficult to distinguish a Jew by his name, even as it is today. It is symptomatic of this trend that, in 1953, the president of the Orthodox Rabbinical Council of America bore the good old Yankee name of Adams. Indeed, if our great-grandchildren cease to call themselves Irving and revert to the biblical name of Isaac, who will then even suspect that behind the name Isaac there stands a Jew?

When the twenty-first century rolls around, the typical Jew will be a culturally literate college graduate engaged in some form of nonmanual occupation. Already one out of every six gainfully employed American Jews has earned an academic degree. In time to come, he will be a white-collar worker, preferably self-employed; frequently a successful professional practitioner. In pursuit of his business, he will mix intimately with the Gentiles in association with whom he will be earning his livelihood.

American Jewry has been able to send over a thousand million dollars of their savings to aid their fellow-Jews in foreign lands; that money has been made through doing business with their non-Jewish fellow-citizens. The slightly more than 3 percent of Americans who are Jews do not live off each other.

At five o'clock, our Jew of tomorrow will leave his shop or office, pull out his politically liberal newspaper, and go home to suburbia.

When he descends from the train at six o'clock, he enters into a spiritual, cultural, and social world all his own, a world in which his evening relations with his Gentile neighbor are cordial, but limited. A new life, certainly a different life, begins for him in the home, in the synagogue, and in his town or country club. This specific Jewish world of his own we call the Jewish community.

The emerging American Jewish community is the unnatural child of philanthropy and anti-Semitism. Prejudice both here and abroad has compelled American Jewry to draw together to create the instrumentalities to save European Jewry, to rebuild Zion as a haven, and to erect barriers against the forces of discrimination on these shores. The natural desire of Jews to be with one another has added impetus to the fashioning of the present-day integrated Jewish community. In recent years, it has been hammered into shape by the Jewish Welfare Fund, the Community Relations Committee, and the Jewish Community Council.

Since World War II, common tasks have been creating a tightly interwoven Jewish community life. Jewish citywide social-welfare agencies are offering relief and medical and psychiatric services to the family, and especially to the aged and chronically ill. The unemployed turn to the Jewish Vocational Bureau; Jewish Centers hold out many opportunities for education and recreation.

In the suburban districts of tomorrow, with their wide-rolling acres, these centers are destined to become clubs for the middle class, and in the smaller towns of the next century, the country club will emerge as a community agency.

Jewish education tomorrow, as today, will continue to engage the attention of the congregations and the local bureaus. Even the denominational synagogues of the Reform, the Conservative, and the Orthodox will feel the impact of a growing, homogeneous community.

A new fusion type of religion may well be in the making. Even today there are various forms of religious amalgamation in the smaller cities. There is a Michigan town where the synagogue is sufficiently hospitable to include among its members the most Orthodox partisans and the most radical of Reformers. In another city, in Iowa, the rabbi has held Reform and Conservative services on alternate weekends.

Although there is much naïveté in some of these attempts, they are nevertheless symptomatic. Services will tend more closely to approximate one another; the typical American synagogue of the future will divide the liturgy between the Hebrew and the English; the organ, the family pew, and the vernacular sermon will be characteristic of nearly all houses of worship. But people will continue to fight about hats-off and hats-on.

Most Jews will be members of a religious society, for that is part of our American concept of respectability, and who are we to set ourselves up against our Christian neighbors?

By the year 2000 some communities will have introduced a form of overall taxation to include even membership in the synagogue.

The Yiddish newspaper will have ceased to be, but its place will be taken by an Anglo-Jewish one. And after supper, the learned Jew will be able to read an American daily Hebrew newspaper.

This new community will conceive of all Jewish life as a whole. It will find a place within its capacious arms for any person who states that he is a Jew. There will be room in this latitudinarian world of tomorrow for the Orthodox Hasid and for that board member of the Jewish hospital who is too broadminded to insist on putting a Hanukkah menorah in the lobby, but as a tolerant American is quite ready to prompt the nurses to sing carols around the Christmas tree in the lobby of the nonsectarian Jewish hospital.

This tight Jewish community will have come into being, not simply because we will have wanted it, but because of compulsive historic forces of kinship and rejection. This community, this commonalty, will come because it is already here. We can suffer it because as objects of history we have no choice, or else we can bend it to our purposes and become the subjects of history. I suggest that we make history.

Because this community, whether it be the local or the national, requires enlightened direction, there will be some who tell us to turn for guidance to the new Israel. Can we accept leadership from abroad? I doubt that the Israelis have enough to offer us today. The intellectual niveau of American culture is higher than that of present-day Israel; there are as many distinguished scholars in the field of the Science of Judaism here in the United States as there are in the new Jewish republic. Perhaps there are even more.

No people can live another people's life. The Israelis are developing their own national psyche. It is inevitable, by all the laws of history, that in an independent land they will differ from us nationally, culturally, and spiritually. The relations between the two should be amicable and helpful, and could be most productive of good if both Jewries were animated by a sense of deliberate spiritual rivalry, by a desire to attain goals that are common, not only to them, but to all Jewries.

That ultimate higher goal toward which we all strive is not the terrestrial, but the celestial Zion. And that Zion, as I interpret it, is our highest Jewish self in projection. What we seek is the fulfillment of the finest in ourselves and in our traditions. That goal is never reached in any land; it is the dream of a reality that lies beyond any horizon. We are conscious, and always will be, I trust, of our moral obligation to every segment of world Jewry, but because we have no sensible alternative, we believe in the primacy of American Jewish life for the American Jew.

We know who these American Jews will be. Though they will be molded within the confines of a partially secluded community, their prime characteristic will be diversity. They will be composed of differing groups, clustered around congregations, Jewish Welfare Funds, health, philanthropic, and civic defense agencies, cultural, social, and recreational clubs, centers, and lodges. Some will be Zionists of various shades; others Diaspora "nationalists," frowning upon both Israel and the synagogue, and yet denominating themselves Jews. Some will be secularists, and many more will be religionists.

All of them will have their leaders, and it is these leaders who are already of increasing importance in our lives. Many of them are professionals. They are the new managerial class, the civil servants who are to determine what we are to be in the future.

Some of them hold office because of their administrative skills and their capacity to raise funds. It is a striking commentary on our present-day life that at its climactic tercentennial meeting, American Jewry, after 300 years of distinguished achievement, was represented by men who up to that moment had shown little or no interest in the cultural and spiritual leadership of American Jewry.

Returning to the civil servants who head our local and national Jewish agencies, and to whom we have entrusted our future, I do not protest against them as a class, even as I would not protest against rabbis. But it is important that they be Jewishly literate. What a commentary on American life is the reflection that we have sent millions across the seas in this postwar period, but could not find the paltry sums necessary to keep alive the Training Bureau for Jewish Communal Service.

We must always be mindful that some of our national American Jewish agencies have tremendous influence. They represent us for better or for worse. Our spiritual and cultural fate is largely in their hands. And it is truly unfortunate that some of those leaders cannot guide us competently. It is not within some of them to give intelligent Jewish direction. Men without Jewish roots, extemporizing from job to job, from crisis to crisis, do not truly represent us.

It is not enough merely to survive; we must survive proudly as dignified and self-respecting Jews. It is imperative that our leaders be well-trained Jews. They must have a deep and sympathetic knowledge of Jewish life, literature, and history, even though their learning is derived from secondary sources.

If they are to understand the institutions which they lead, and would give them intelligent direction, they must know the rock whence they have been hewn. No great Jewish agency began in a vacuum; to understand it and lead it, one must be deeply rooted in the past which gave birth to that institution. Without historical perspective, no Jew who presumes to lead a segment of his people can know his place in the scheme of things. Still less can he comprehend his duty and the duty of his organization to the totality of Jewry.

Mere power is never an end in itself. If Jewry is to live meaningfully, its leaders must have an educational philosophy and a program to implement it. Otherwise, there will be no significant future for us. No people can rise higher than the spiritual level of its civil service. The prime criterion for every program must be the recognition that its goals are good for all Jews, not merely for a specific group. The common good must take precedence over the welfare of a particular group.

We shall survive as a Jewish community. But why should we survive? Is survival an end in itself? Surely it is not wrong to live, to maintain hallowed and beloved traditions. But I would like to believe that if we retain group identity within a larger context, then that separatism must be inspired by moral considerations. I would like to believe that, if I walk my own way, it is because I have a purpose, because I have something to give.

We have come upon sorry times. The long, liberal century that began in 1789 with the French Revolution died catastrophically at its height in 1919 when the Versailles Peace Treaty was signed. We are in the midst of a world of gathering clouds and impending tragedy. Christianity is on the decline; paganism, brutality, callous hard cruelty are in the ascendant. We are living in a world that seems increasingly indifferent to kindness, to love, to human decencies. It is this situation that rises to challenge the Jew to survive purposefully, to justify his separatism.

Let us survive to the end that we shall strive to create a universal society where men are tolerant of one another, where nationalism is not the highest good, and where world peace is not a hollow mockery, but a sacred and cherished ideal.

Surely the time has come for a new categorical imperative to teach nations to act toward one another according to the same spiritual standard that determines the relations of one moral individual to another. Is this not after all the sum total of all prophetic teaching? Is this not why we call ourselves Jews? If it is not to preserve these great truths, then why have we writhed in agony in the fiery crucible for over two thousand years?

The only salvation for all of us lies in a moral society. Let us work toward that end. When all is said and done: "The fear of God is the beginning of wisdom."

13

THE QUINTESSENTIAL AMERICAN JEW

Don't let anyone tell you otherwise, American Jewish history did not begin in late August or September, 1654, when Jacob Barsimson, of New Amsterdam, went down to the Battery to greet twenty-three incoming competitors and offer them a worried shalom alekhem. It began at the commencement exercises of Columbia College in the year 1800. It was then that young Sampson Simson read a Hebrew oration in which he touched on the mid-seventeenth-century origins of American Jewish life. Simson's address is the first evidence of a communal self-consciousness among American Jews. Ignorant of Hebrew, his admiring audience did not realize he was informing them that many of the New York Jews of his day stemmed from a widow and her four daughters. As a student of Jewish history, I can assure you that it is not important that we are the children of four women. What is truly significant is that she married them all off. This is American Jewry's first great achievement.

Simson's Hebrew oration had, of course, been written for him by the local "rabbi." Ninety-two years later, the Jews of this country established the American Jewish Historical Society. Their motivation was entirely apologetic. As a matter of fact, practically every work of Jewish history, even as late as the 1930's, was defensive in tone and spirit—written to convince America that Jews had helped Columbus discover her, had fought in her Revolution, and had contributed to her greatness. With rare exceptions, most of these works were of unscientific calibre. Yet it would be unfair to reproach their authors. A great many American Jews were still foreign-born. American historiography in general was just

Address delivered at the sixty-sixth annual meeting of the American Jewish Historical Society, Boston, Massachusetts, May 19, 1968. Published originally in *American Jewish Historical Quarterly*, LVIII, 15–22.

taking shape. The multivolume scientific works of James
Ford Rhodes, Edward Channing, and John Bach McMaster
did not appear till the turn of the present century.

It took two world wars to create an American Jewish historiography. After 1945, it was obvious that American
Jewry would exercise a protective hegemony over all the
Jews of the world. Within the short span of six years in the
decade of the 1940's, American Jewry became aware of itself: a course for credit in American Jewish history was initiated at a graduate school, the American Jewish Archives was
founded, the National Jewish Welfare Board established
History Week, *Commentary* magazine sponsored a national
conference on American Jewish history, and the American
Jewish Historical Society began issuing a quarterly. In antici-
pation of the tercentenary of Jewish settlement, the next
decade saw publication of seven works on American Jewish
history. Though the apologetic element was not absent,
they were on the whole acceptable. The magical year was
1954, and the culminating event of that great festival of history was the National Tercentenary Dinner. The guest
speaker was President Dwight D. Eisenhower. The menu an-
nounced a mysterious delicacy called "traditional stuffed
freshwater fish."

In a dramaturgic sense, this dinner on the night of October
20 at the Astor was the catastrophic climax of assimilation. In
Mr. Eisenhower's presence, the sponsors of the dinner were
ashamed to pronounce the ineffable name of that choice mor-
sel. Yet their gastro-ethnic compromise was of truly historic
significance, for call it what you will, it was still gefillte fish,
and when the elite of the Jewish establishment served it, who
can doubt the emergence of an integrated American Jewish
community? Today there are no Spanish or Portuguese
Jews, no German or Russian Jews; there are only American
Jews.

Fourteen years have passed since that dinner, and we are so
advanced in our historic studies that we can hypostatize or
incarnate the Jews of the past in the personalities of three

men. We can divide the last three hundred and some years
into intervals and pinpoint one man in each period as its quintessential personality. In reviewing their lives, we relive our
past and confront our future.

Historiographically, if not biologically, American Jewry's
great-grandfather was a colonial Jew. His beginnings were
anything but modest. On September 5, 1756, Hayyim the
son of Moses the Levite—we know him better as Hayman
Levy—was fined twenty shillings "for the indecent and abu-
sive language he gave the parnass president" after the latter
upbraided him for improper conduct in the synagogue yard.
Obviously, here was a young man in a hurry. He had arrived
on these shores from Europe during King George's War in
the 1740's. Levy was then some twenty years of age. He
married an American Jewish girl and probably started out as
a shopkeeper on a modest scale. By the time of the French
and Indian War in the 1750's, he was already a privateer and
a merchant of substance. Military supplies poured out of his
warehouse in New York for the soldiers on the northern
frontier. In his advertisements, he offered to ship all goods
free of transportation charges as far as Albany, and if the
items ordered were not in stock, he promised to dig them up
somewhere and waive his commission. Jews and Christians
alike admired and envied him for his enterprise and indefatigable energy. When the war ended, in 1763, the boom col-
lapsed and left him bankrupt. But his creditors rallied to his
rescue and put him back in business. Before that decade
passed, he had become one of America's noted fur trade entrepreneurs. The goods he sent to Schenectady, to Detroit,
and to Michilimackinac ultimately reached as far west as the
foothills of the Rockies. Iron, steel, paints, drygoods, scalp-
ing knives, Negro slaves—all were shipped north and west,
and if your heart bleeds for the primitive frontiersmen, save
your pity, for Levy also shipped them violins and playing
cards, oranges, pineapples, and pickled oysters.

Levy was a good Jew. He headed New York's relief drive
for the Jews of Hebron, Palestine, in 1763, found time to

father twelve children, and served as parnas of the congregation. The presidency was an onerous job, and even as he had reviled the parnas of yesterday, he now received his share of abuse. A zealous Whig patriot, he fled British-threatened New York and spent the war years in Philadelphia. There he helped establish a new congregation and became a large-scale contractor of garments for the American troops. When the war was over, he returned to New York, reassumed the presidency of the synagogue, and welcomed Governor George Clinton back with these words: "Though the society we belong to is but small when compared with other religious societies, yet we flatter ourselves that none has manifested a more zealous attachment to the sacred cause of America in the late war with Great Britain."

Although Hayman Levy was president of the Sephardic congregation Shearith Israel for six terms, he was himself no Spanish-Portuguese Jew. He was an Ashkenazi, a Central European. The fact is that Ashkenazim, mostly German-Austrians and East Europeans, already formed a majority of American Jews by the 1720's. They were to dominate the American Jewish scene into the early years of the present century. Among them was a sixteen-year-old Hungarian lad, Sigmund Shlesinger, who landed here in 1864.

This teen-ager started out in New York City as a horsecar conductor, but moved west after a year or so. He clerked in Leavenworth for a while and then followed the Kansas Pacific Railroad to the end of track. Wherever the construction gangs and the soldiers went, he followed. Shlesinger and a partner opened a cigar store at Hays City, Kansas; their whole stock amounted in value to about $5. Among their customers were General George A. Custer and Buffalo Bill. It was a tough town, and it took a tough marshal like Wild Bill Hickok to keep the lid on. Shlesinger never made a living out west; his was no rags-to-riches story. He clerked in a clothing store, tended bar in a tent saloon, waited on tables, shoveled on the railroad, sold groceries, baked bread, and brewed beer in a washboiler, but lived on hardtack and coffee. By the summer of 1868, he was hungry enough to join up with a company of fifty volunteer civilian scouts organized to chase the Indians who were harassing the Kansas-Colorado frontier. He was the fiftieth man recruited. He was no bargain with his narrow shoulders, sunken chest, and piping voice—but the government needed men and he needed a job. On the 17th of September, 1868, his detachment was attacked by 700 screaming Cheyennes and Sioux in eastern Colorado. Retreating to a sandy spit on the Arickaree Fork of the Republican River, the scouts dug themselves in with their bare hands and for four days and nights kept the relentless enemy at bay. By the time the beleaguered volunteers were rescued, nearly half of them had become casualties. The episode entered our history as the Battle of Beecher Island. Young Shlesinger kept a diary during his term of service. The laconic entries he made daily during the siege are fascinating: "Scalpt 3 Indians . . . killt a Coyote & eat him all up." He proved to be a gallant soldier, and his part in that frontier saga was commemorated in a poem:

> When the foe charged on the breastworks,
> With the madness of despair,
> And the bravest souls were tested,
> The little Jew was there.

Is this the quintessential Jew of nineteenth-century America? What was Jewish about him? What happened to him after the battle? By 1870, Shlesinger had settled down in Cleveland, married, and had begun raising a family. He opened a retail cigar store, then became a tobacco leaf wholesaler, and over the years achieved a considerable measure of success. Back in Hungary he had been exposed to Orthodoxy, but he abandoned it in this country, and evinced no interest in Judaism or in any of its institutions. Sometime after his marriage, however, his wife laid down the law to him. He sold his house in a Catholic ghetto, moved into a Jewish neighborhood, joined the temple, and began to take

an active part in Jewish affairs. Shlesinger served on the board
of his synagogue for sixteen years, was elected vice-presi-
dent, and interested himself in the conduct of the Sunday
School. He became president of a local B'nai B'rith lodge,
stood out as a stalwart in the Hebrew Relief Association, organized a free loan society, founded a Hungarian landsman-
shaft, and pioneered in putting together the Federation of
Jewish Charities. When he died in 1928, he was recognized as
one of the outstanding Jewish communal workers in Cleveland, the fifth largest Jewish settlement in the United States.

If Shlesinger was born in an east Hungarian village, then,
however Germanized he may have seemed, he was in reality
an East European Jew. At any rate, by the 1890's the East
European Jews were in the majority in this country. At the
very latest, they had begun coming here in the eighteenth
century. Haym Salomon, broker to the Office of Finance, to
the consul general of France, and to the treasurer of the
French army during the days of the Revolution, was a Polack, and Mordecai M. Mordecai, who operated a whiskey still
in Pittsburgh before the Revolution, was a Litvak. The "Russians," as the East Europeans were called, arrived in vast
numbers after the pogroms of the 1880's. I would like to describe the life of one of those "Russians" who landed at Castle Garden in 1889. He was a man whom I knew intimately,
whom I loved and revered, but for personal reasons I for-
bear to identify him except by his first name, Aaron. He em-
bodied within himself the quintessential history of the East
European Jews who had established a community of their
own in this land as early as 1852 and maintained it until the
day the immigration gates were closed in 1924.

When Aaron arrived here at the age of twenty-four, he
had already served the Czar for five years as a grenadier in
the Caucasus. There was no future for him in Russia. He had
no secular education and was master of no craft. He was a
dirt farmer, but the family had been driven off the soil, a
large leased estate, by the May Laws of 1882. He turned his
face westward, stopped in Hamburg long enough to trade his

Yiddish patronymic for something more German, and then moved on to New York. His only capital on arrival consisted of a few rubles and a watch which he had won in the army as an expert rifleman. He was tall and strong, so he went to work as a manual laborer. He got a job as a matzo baker and wheeled bricks in a brick factory, but he had no luck. He learned to run a sewing machine only to be discharged when he sewed two left sleeves on a jacket. He was eager to make something of himself, but clearly New York was not for him.

Aaron bought a basket of notions, started out on foot, successfully eluded all the constables who tried to stop him, and peddled his way without a license to Pittsburgh. There the erstwhile farmer got himself a decent job in a machine shop owned by one George Westinghouse, who made it his business to know the names of all his employees. Aaron married a Pittsburgh girl who had come from his home town in the province of Kovno, and they began to rear a family. When the panic of 1893 threw him out of his job, he turned to peddling again, ultimately making his headquarters in the Youghiogheny Valley in a village across the river from Connellsville, Pennsylvania. He made a good living peddling clothing among the Slavic miners and the coke-oven workers and was soon the proud owner of a wagon and a team. When his youngest son was born, he named the boy after his favorite horse—which was a compliment both to the horse and to the boy.

The year 1900 found him in the steel mill town of Homestead where he opened a clothing store and prospered. Every Christmas his landlord gave him a bottle of rye whiskey, and that lasted Aaron a whole year till the next bottle arrived. Driven by ambition, he moved to Pittsburgh and opened a small department store, but lost everything in the panic of 1907. Undiscouraged, he started over again, followed the Slavic millworkers to Wheeling, West Virginia, and there helped establish an Orthodox synagogue which he served as president. He was now clean-shaven, an American citizen, a subscriber to the local daily and to the New York Yiddish *Morning Journal.* Ever on the search for the fortune that always seemed to elude him, he moved south into the hill country, and by 1915, the second year of World War I, had established himself in a village in central West Virginia where the mines were working full time. He was the first and the last Jew to live in Farmington, a hamlet of about 800 people.

In this isolated spot, he achieved a measure of success and modest affluence. He helped establish an Orthodox synagogue in the neighboring community of Fairmont and tried to keep a kosher home. He had a cow, a horse, a stable full of chickens, and a vegetable and flower garden. He used an old straight razor to *shecht* his chickens, but when he was not looking, his boys used the wood axe to decapitate the squawking hens. In moments of leisure, he would call his sons about him, open up the family Bible, read a passage in Hebrew from the major prophets, and express his admiration for the social justice message of those great religious figures. Even so, he was no political or economic liberal. He had a complete and utter contempt for socialists, anarchists, and communists, and like most respectable middle-class businessmen he voted the straight Republican ticket religiously. As his daughter and three sons grew up, he realized there could be no future for them in that village where his oldest son attended the Methodist Episcopal Sunday School and played the violin in the church. He pulled up stakes, moved back to Pittsburgh, joined a right-wing Conservative congregation, and spent his declining days as an observant Jew. These are "the short and simple annals" of a Russo-Jewish American.

This backcountry merchant survived almost a decade after the passage of the Johnson Bill of 1924 which closed the doors to East European immigration and willy-nilly ushered in the age of the American Jew. What will the authentic new Jew of the next generation look like? I do not know. It may be, though I am by no means convinced of it, that he will be a city-dwelling college graduate associated with some form of retailing enterprise. Ironically, the Catholic and the Negro revolutions of these past ten years have opened almost every door to the Jews, but where these doors will lead no one knows.

There is no American melting pot. There *is* a Jewish melting pot out of which will emerge a quintessential type in the years to come. Today everything is being poured into the insatiable maw of that crucible which we call the American Jewish community: the young unwed Jewish girl who gives birth to a mulatto child; the children of fathers who founded Murder, Inc.; the New York taxicab driver who can solve all the problems of the universe—except the Long Island traffic —while he delivers you to the airport; the corporation lawyer who heads a world-wide electronic enterprise; the Jewish slum landlord who attends services with some regularity, is a devoted husband and father, and gives generously to the United Jewish Appeal; the Israeli émigré who has built a conglomerate mercantile empire; the clothing manufacturer; the haberdasher; the clerk; the manager of a chain store; the Polish immigrant who, arriving on these shores just a few months before the first quota law, has gone on to perfect a vaccine that will save the lives of millions of children yet to be born.

If we live long enough and wait long enough, this new Jew will emerge. This is inevitable, for we are all the objects of history. But we need not wait; the initiative lies with us. We can become the subjects of history. American Jewish social scientists of our generation have already developed a methodology enabling them to study and understand the world in which they live. They know the contours of the megalopolises that extend from San Diego to San Francisco and from Norfolk to Boston. They sense the relationship between the puny Jewish boardinghouse in the Catskills and the gargantuan kosher-style hotel on a Florida beach. They follow the flight of the Jewish industrialists to the South, the disappearance of the Jewish labor union, the struggle to storm the executive suite, the scramble of the Jew for politi-

cal office, the gallant resurgence of Orthodoxy, the turning
back to ceremonial of rationalistic Reform, and the eternal
persistence of anti-Semitism.

I would ask at this hour that we gird our loins and go out
in quest of the new Jew of tomorrow, that individual who
will somehow embody within himself the consensus of his
people. Let us with our sophisticated techniques hold up the
mirror to reality. Perspective is emancipation. To see where
we are moving is an invitation to shape our course. Not to
suffer history but to make history—this is the challenge that
confronts the new historian. Knowledge, meticulous, pain-
fully accurate, all-embracing knowledge, brings with it the
power to create, to mold, to survive. If it were my privilege
to dedicate this new building of the American Jewish Historical Society, I would dedicate it to this goal, the affirmation
of man's infinite capacity to make of himself what he will.
To this goal and this conviction, I would dedicate our new
building. I know and expect our Society will find no worthier goal and no worthier conviction.

INDEX